D1075052

DOCTOR IN ARABIA

DOCTOR IN ARABIA

By PAUL W. HARRISON, M.D.

ILLUSTRATED

THE JOHN DAY COMPANY
NEW YORK

PRINTED IN THE UNITED STATES OF AMERICA

Van Rees Press, New York

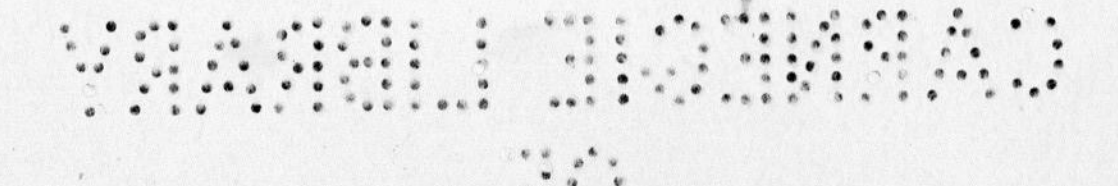

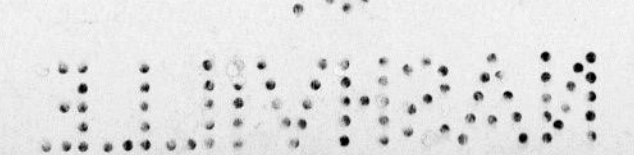

TO HER WHO MAKES
THE DESERTS OF ARABIA
THE VESTIBULE OF
PARADISE

CONTENTS

ILLUSTRATIONS

FACING PAGE

DOCTOR IN ARABIA

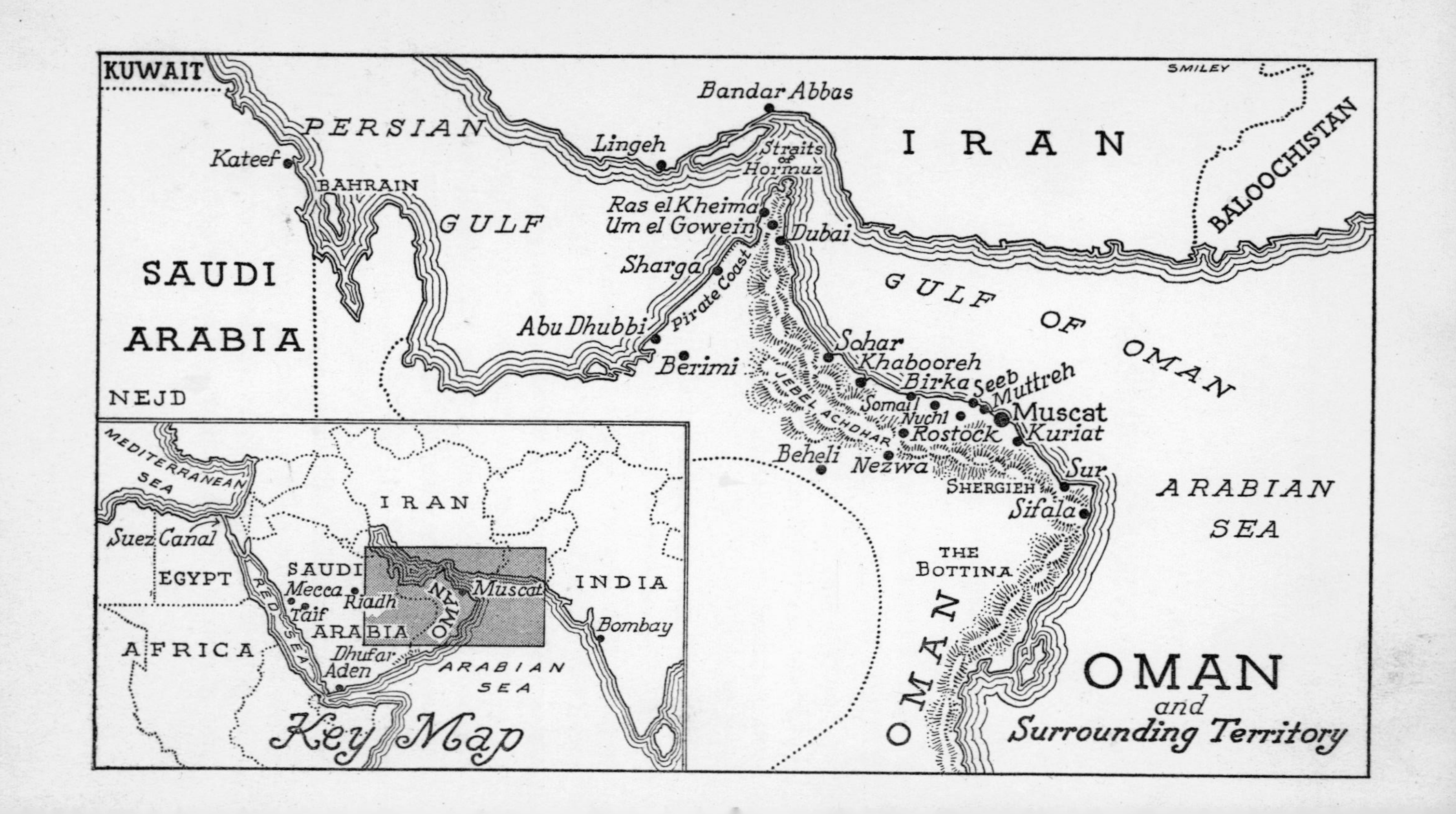
OMAN
and
Surrounding Territory
KUWAIT
SAUDI ARABIA
NEJD
PERSIAN GULF
Kateef
BAHRAIN
IRAN
BALOOCHISTAN
SMILEY
Bandar Abbas
Lingeh
Straits of Hormuz
Ras el Kheima
Um el Gowein
Dubai
Sharga
Pirate Coast
Abu Dhubbi
Berimi
GULF OF OMAN
Sohar
Khabooreh
Birka
Seeb
Muttreh
Muscat
Kuriat
Somail
Nuchl
Rostock
JEBEL ACHDHAR
Beheli
Nezwa
Sur
SHERGIEH
Sifala
THE BOTTINA
OMAN
ARABIAN SEA
Key Map
MEDITERRANEAN SEA
Suez Canal
EGYPT
AFRICA
RED SEA
SAUDI ARABIA
Mecca
Taif
Riadh
Dhufar
Aden
IRAN
OMAN
Muscat
INDIA
Bombay
ARABIAN SEA

I

INTRODUCING MUSCAT

WHERE ARE YOU going to locate?" That was the most frequent question of my last year in Johns Hopkins. I chose Arabia. Doctors there do not run six to the city block. They specialize in elbow room, in personal contact, too, rather than mass production, with the population counting four to the square mile, and in essentials instead of incidentals, with fees of five dollars per operation.

However, the real reason lay elsewhere. I wanted to pit the Christian way of life against the worst types of human trouble and sin. Wickedness and distress were knee deep in Baltimore, the beloved city of these meditations. Out in Arabia, they are up to a man's neck. It is a great thing to get into the construction gang for the Empire State Building, better anyway than putting one's life into a renovation plant for discarded furniture. At least it looks better at twenty-five.

There was another reason, of somewhat the same sort. I wanted to pit modern medicine against its hardest job. The novitiate is usually a very ardent worshiper at the shrine of Aesculapius. Sometimes the glory of that vision fades afterward. In the Hunterian Laboratory he has

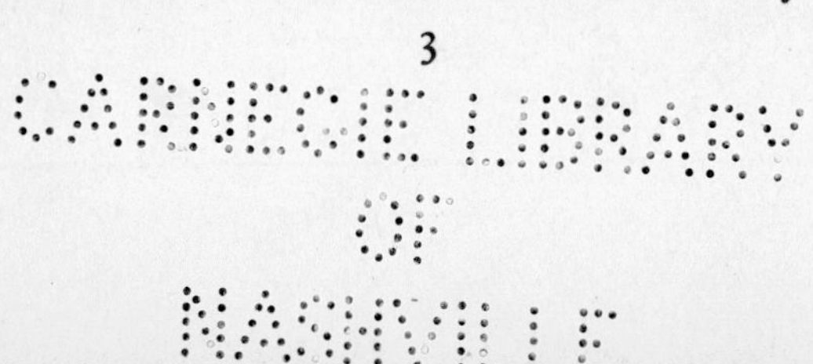

seen precise and simple surgery, lovely as a nude from the hand of Phidias. Dressed up for public exhibition, the beautiful goddess looks like a wrapped-up nun. Out in Arabia, surgery is not dressed up for public exhibition. Every nonessential is trimmed off, by simple poverty, and scientific medicine, the most splendid achievement of our modern times, is pitted against the whole range of human disease. We live only one life apiece. The battle of the giants is a good place to spend it.

So it happened that after finishing a delightful interneship in Boston, where a mixture of ink and ice water runs in men's veins, I found myself on my way to Bombay first of all, and from there to Arabia. There was quite a bit of ink there, but not much ice water. The mountains of human need were higher than I had expected.

A year after my arrival, when my tongue had been twisted around the beginning of the Arabic language, the mission sent me to work in Muscat.

Muscat is the first port of Arabia, on the Persian Gulf side. It is the capital of Oman, a tiny opera bouffe empire in the southeastern corner of the Arabian peninsula, an empire of bare rocks, three hundred miles long and a hundred wide. From the Jebel Achdhar range where the peaks run up to nine thousand feet and more, one can see the great jagged masses stretch as far as the eye can reach. Between the mountains run the *wadis*, which is the Arabic name for valley. They are strewn with great boulders, and are wild and desolate. Great volcanic upheavals must have marked the early history of this country, and there are enormous breaks in the strata where the hard black layers have been lifted bodily hundreds of feet into the air.

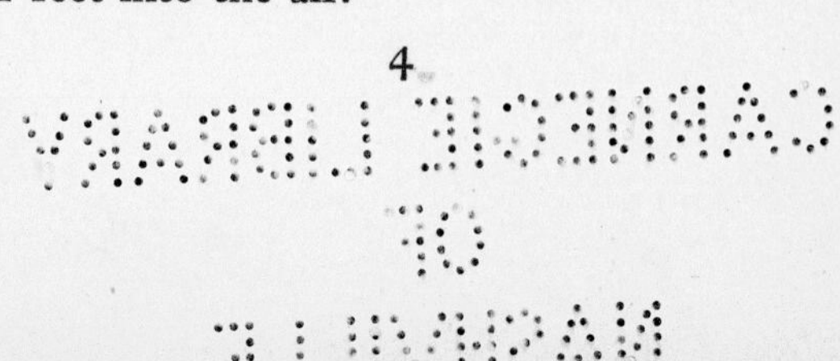

It is its utter isolation which makes the Arabs regard Oman as an empire in itself. Behind is the great desert which the Arabs call "the empty quarter," and which fills the whole of south central Arabia. When I stood on a high peak along its edge, the gray sand dunes were empty and dead as far as the eye could range. "Great distances and God," say the Arabs.

One of the resolute sheikhs of Oman crossed it thirty years ago, to make the Mecca pilgrimage. Half of the caravan carried water. As the water skins were emptied, the extra camels were killed. A little caravan of survivors came out alive on the other side, but it was looked on as a foolhardy and expensive exploit. Bertram Thomas has added this empty quarter to the list of inaccessible corners which the roving white man has penetrated. It was a hardy and expensive exploit for him too.

The rainfall is almost zero. On the coast it will average three inches a year. Inland no records have been kept, but the amount is less. Probably one inch a year is not far wrong. The airman in his plane and the visitor from the steamer see utterly bare, ragged rock masses. Such a landscape is certainly not beautiful, but there is a silent, austere grandeur about such naked and uncompromising reality. Silhouetted against the clear dark sky on a moonless night, the effect is quite overpowering.

But Muscat's worldwide reputation depends on its heat. There are many places further south where the wandering white man has lived. Muscat indeed is barely within the tropical zone, being placed quite accurately on the tropic of Cancer. But the bare rocky mountains accomplish two things. They shut out the breeze, and they soak in the heat, with the result that Muscat is reckoned as one of the three hottest places where white men live.

My first introduction to that heat was a memorable night when I lived further north and was passing through on my way to India. We sailed far in between the two headlands which enclose the harbor. The sun had disappeared two hours before, and the land was hundreds of feet away, across the water. The great rocks were furnaces, and the air shivered with their heat. At midnight the steamer beat a retreat, and once out in the open, we breathed real air again. I was to learn later that this extraordinary heat at night is Muscat's specialty. There is nearly always a little breeze during the day even in the summer, but after sundown it dies away, and the heat which the pitiless sun beats into the rocks during the day is released through the night. Occasionally a fierce half-hour hurricane blows down off the mountains on to the city. It is like the breath of a furnace. Colonel Trevor, the British Consul, told me that he had seen his instruments register 120° at midnight.

Along the edge of the water, in the shadow of the great mountains, nestle the little houses where men live. The day I landed I was much impressed, as the ship approached, by the whiteness and apparent cleanliness of the little city. Distance lends enchantment to the view. Once on shore I found that nothing was either white or clean. The streets are narrow and crooked, and the smells are unequaled in all Arabia.

The steamer crew went out to write the name of their ship in great white letters halfway up the side of a cliff. Several of the cliffs are covered with such names. It is considered very necessary for every steamer thus to leave her card at the front door of Oman. The names are dated, the faded ones being fifty years old and more, which is an interesting commentary on the transitoriness of the human embroidery with which we are fond of improving the face of nature.

Most of the Arabs move away from the city for three months during the summer. The hospital is closed, and the doctor in charge goes to India. Unfortunately the hot weather lasts longer than that three months' vacation, and for weeks each year I write letters at night stripped to the waist, with a little stream trickling from each elbow, as the typewriter plick-placks along. The elbow trickle is not much trouble for the two tiny lakes below can be taken care of. It is the dozens of tiny drops running down in front and behind that disturb the attention. They tickle.

One night I suddenly emerged from my preoccupation with a letter to realize that one of these drops was running back up again. This seemed to call for investigation, and I watched a small and very hard-pressed insect struggle against the current. He seemed to be having a bad time of it, so I rescued him and let him go. I felt sure that he was finding the climate of Muscat difficult.

That first season was a bad one. I worked nights getting our bathroom fixed up, and among other things I cast a cement mantel shelf in place. Digging the necessary hole in the wall was a laborious job, and one night I found myself working in a puddle of mud on the tiled floor. This surprised me extremely, for we had not got to the stage of using any water, nor had any leak developed in the pipes. Then I realized that the leak was in my own skin, a good many of them indeed. I could easily have made mud pies that night from my own mud. Muscat, and its suburb, Muttreh, two miles away, where our hospital is, are the worst places for human habitation that could be found along that entire coast. Why do people live there? We do not select the worst possible places to be government centers. We do not, but commerce does. Ten thousand people live in those cities, perhaps fifteen thousand. It is the largest town in all Oman.

The people are there because of the harbor, the only shelter for ocean-going steamers along the entire coast. Lord Curzon visited here once, and the Muscatees swelled with pride when he told them that they had the most picturesque harbor in the whole Near East. Two narrow rocky capes reach out like the fingers of destiny to draw the visitor in. The enclosed harbor opens to the north, and, when the wind comes from that quarter, the waves are gathered into the funnel with appalling results. The spray along the sea wall drenches the third-story windows.

The harbor is feared exceedingly by the steamers. Captain MacLean, one of my special friends, was once caught by a rising storm with his steamer well inside that dreaded funnel. Putting on all the steam that his engines could muster, he dragged his anchor bodily out into the open sea. I expressed astonishment that he should not have hauled the anchor up first, but he assured me that there had been no time for that.

In a storm, Muscat harbor is a bad place, but it is beautiful nevertheless. Sometimes it is as smooth as a sheet of glass, and the big fish swimming lazily through the cool water twenty feet below the surface can be watched by their perspiring human admirers. It is difficult not to be a small boy and wish for the magic wand that could make us all fish again, or at least for some of the magic ointment of Ali of the Sea, so we could go down there in the cool depths for a prolonged visit.

At night when the sea is quiet and the air hot, the phosphorescence is beautiful. I have seen the wake behind my boat shine with lovely bluish light for a hundred feet to the rear. Bright phosphorescent jewels dropped from the oars each time they were lifted, and six oar strokes on each side were shining and beautiful on the dark smooth surface. On such a night a flying fish often starts up at the boat's approach, and flies across the harbor for a long distance, trailing his tail in the water in a thin bright line. When a school of such fish is disturbed, the entire harbor is traced with an intricate hairline pattern of lovely phosphorescent blue. One night two of these little fish fell into our boat, which seemed a most pathetic ending to the beautiful exhibition they had given us, for they were carried home by the boatmen and eaten.

The picturesque nakedness of the Oman landscape is commented on by every visitor. It is a wilderness of bare, rocky mountains. I have never been able to get over my astonishment that far up on those naked rock masses, there are one or two tiny green trees, which stand as a perpetual proof that no possible earthly situation is completely hopeless. Off to the visitor's left as he faces the harbor is a peak which towers up four thousand feet high. Most of them are smaller, the hills immediately surrounding the steamer being under a thousand.

The austere strength of that picturesque land seems very forbidding.

The people are picturesque, too, as the new arrival promptly learns. The boatmen greet him first, in long narrow rowboats called hoories, three men in each. These redoubtable amphibians belong to the fishing fraternity, of whom there may be ten thousand or more scattered along the coast. They are reckless and cheerful seamen, and can swim as easily as they can walk. Even a wild northwest *shumal* in the Muscat harbor does not embarrass them.

A steamer entering the harbor will pass through a small fleet of these boats waiting for her to anchor. Treaties dictate that the steamer as it enters must render to the ruling Sultan a thunderous salute, which is noisily returned. The quarantine doctor boards the invader and declares her to be free from dangerous plagues and pestilences. The fleet of hoories then closes in like a swarm of flies on a dish of honey. No vast amount of business is to be expected, but dozens of the hoories struggle for a place of privilege next to the gangway, and absolute pandemonium reigns. Each boatman is anxious for a large share of whatever business there is, and the few passengers who are to go ashore congest the passage with huge, shapeless loads of bedding, furniture, and babies, all carried by these undefeatable boatmen.

If the passengers who are going ashore would only wait for half an hour, so that new arrivals could be gotten on board in peace, the confusion would be avoided; but the Omanee does not know anything about eliminating confusion. Indeed, I feel sure that he enjoys it, and certainly for those who love complete chaos this half hour must be pure joy. One or two of the boatmen are frequently pushed into the water, and sometimes even a passenger or one of his boxes; but tempers hold wonderfully, and a good time is had by all. Competing for a place at the steamer's gangway is Muscat's official game. It takes the place of football.

Once the steamer begins to recover from the onslaught of the boatmen, whose noisy energy at least serves to demonstrate that there is some vitality in the sunbaked place, a contingent full of dignity and poise arrives. These are the merchants of Muscat, a dozen or even twenty of them. They are saying good-by to one of their fraternity as he leaves for Bombay. The easy and natural dignity of these men is in vivid contrast to the violent activity of the boatmen who bring up their baggage. In a curious way the two seem completely harmonious because each is utterly natural. The boatmen act the way they feel, and so do the merchants.

Twenty-five years ago, the merchants of Muscat constituted a larger group than they do now, and their reputation extended from Singapore to Egypt. Only one is left of such stature as that, but though world movements have worked against them, their characteristics have not changed. They dress largely in white, and are immaculate. Their quiet dignity is outstanding. Most of these men have been in Bombay many times. Many of them have visited Europe. Practically every one of them listens at night to an Arabic broadcast of the world's news. My friend Abd un Nebi has four radios, and invites me in for the evening when American news needs an interpreter.

These merchants are the leading citizens of Muscat.

They are at ease if kings talk with them, and they are equally urbane and self-contained with beggars and coolies. For courteous consideration of a new point of view, they are unsurpassed, as also for their capacity to keep their own counsels and draw their own conclusions. They are sincere Moslems, but no supporters of Bin Saoud. Fifteen years ago when the forces of central Arabia took Taif away from the Shereef of Mecca, the enthusiastic advance guard got out of hand, and a number of the best citizens of that city were massacred. Sheikh Yusef ez Zawowee, the leading merchant of Muscat, was visiting in Taif when this happened, and he was killed along with the others. That sort of barbarity seems particularly atrocious in Muscat where even our religious leaders are courteous and dignified. The feverish nationalism which has swept over the world like a contagious insanity has found them immune. The recent tangle in Palestine has been discussed with little heat and no perspiration at all.

Complete independence these men will welcome when it comes, but the present supervision by Great Britain causes little resentment. Recently a new treaty has been concluded, and this adds substantially to the degree of independence actually enjoyed now. That is better, they think, than a futile and pointless struggle for what is impossible. In their courteous and dignified way, these men are realists. They know that schools and internal progress will have to come first.

A few years ago an Austrian scholar came with his wife to study the Arabs of this part of Arabia. He complained to me in astonishment that he had found only

Baloochees. He exaggerated the case, but it is true that the Baloochees are pushing the Arabs out. The boatmen are nearly all of them Baloochees and even some of the merchants. The immigrants learn Arabic and after a little time are indistinguishable from the older Arab families. New arrivals wear the picturesque costume of Baloochistan, but after a year or two they are completely melted in, and the boys in the hospital frequently have warm discussions over the nationality of some patient who has betrayed himself by his familiarity with Baloochee. Doubtless in the past the Arab race has absorbed many such streams of immigration.

Along with the group of dignified merchants, there will quite surely be a number of Africans, some of them slaves, and others slaves more or less recently freed. Slaves used to be imported from Africa in thousands. Muscat was one of the great slave centers of the world. One needs to read the works of Livingstone or Stanley to realize the dreadful extent and terrible effect of the slave raids which radiated out from Muscat in those days. That has all passed away. Slaves are no longer brought from Africa, but the city still has large numbers of slaves in it.

Not all are Africans. In former times children were stolen from Baloochistan, and brought over to Oman to be sold as slaves. One of our hospital staff was a slave for forty years, while an older brother of the others was stolen as a baby and is still a slave somewhere. This horrible traffic has not been completely stopped even yet. Only two years ago a shipload of such stolen children stopped for water in Dar Sait, five miles away from Muscat. One or two of the children escaped, but the rest were carried further. They have been sold long since to grow up as slaves somewhere in Oman.

On either side of the harbor is a castle built by the Portuguese in the 15th century. One is dedicated to St. Joseph, and one to Mary, which must have given those individuals a restless night or two in their graves, considering the type of military adventurers who put them up, and the purposes of avarice and cruelty and lust which they served.

Smaller watch towers guard every *wadi* which could give entry to an attacking force, and are to be seen scattered over the peaks in every direction. I have never been anywhere in Oman where these watch towers are lacking. The largest fortification of them all is fifteen miles back from the coast, guarding Rostock, which was once the capital of Oman. It is a tremendous affair, and, when I visited it, we measured a brass cannon which was over fifteen feet in length. Local tradition credits this fort to the Portuguese also, and we found that the brass cannon which attracted our attention had a Portuguese inscription.

The energy of the Portuguese in the day of their military and naval greatness must have been almost unbelievable, and many colorful traditions of their ferocity and determination persist among the Omanees. No victims of false modesty, they, nor of any other sort of conscience. Ten years ago it cost the Sultan a good many thousand rupees to build the two-mile road which connects the towns of Muscat and Muttreh, but if local tales are to be believed, it did not cost Albuquerque a cent to build anything. When five thousand laborers were wanted for a government enterprise, they were

An air photograph showing the environs of the hospital at Muttreh (the larger of the two buildings in the lower center of the picture).

The Muscat waterfront. On the rocky bluff at the right can be seen two of the formidable castles built by the Portuguese in the 15th century.

summoned and they came. The work continued without pity till the job was finished or the men died. If they died they were replaced, and the job was finished anyway.

They were a pious army and accompanied by priests with lots of prayers. Fortunately these were for their own use only, and they made no effort to convert the natives. It is very remarkable that no trace of hostility to missionaries has been left as a legacy from those days of conquest and blood and pillage. Probably that is because after a hundred years of military occupation they were driven out. Local tradition has it that the commander made one of the local girls his wife, and on a Christmas day, when they were drunk to the last man, she opened the doors of the fortress and let the Arabs in. The opportunity thus offered was utilized so thoroughly that the Portuguese have never been seen since. Unfortunately this last is not quite true. A few Portuguese have been in Muscat for years, as wine merchants, teaching the people to drink, a form of conquest which does more harm, I am afraid, than the bloody and picturesque exploits of their ancestors.

The Portuguese were tremendous castle builders, but like the Turks three hundred years later, they left behind no permanent trace, political, social, or economic. The more ancient history of Oman is of greater significance, though it lacked all glamorous military coloring.

A colony of protesting puritans from the corrupt courts of the Caliph in Damascus, invaded Oman about eight hundred years before the days of the Portuguese. These immigrants came in different waves, and apparently in comparatively small numbers. They were of the

Khawarij, a party bitterly opposed to the transfer of the caliphate from Medina to Damascus, and they supported Ali in his wars against Damascus. Later they deserted his standard, and became typical individualistic Irishmen, against all the different varieties of government then in vogue.

They were puritans of the first order, and detected lots of abuses in the Caliphate courts of those days. As usually happens to puritans, they came to be hated most viciously by the powers that be, and were hunted like wild animals for their rigorous views and individualistic political convictions.

They were partisans of Ali, and supported him up to the time of his defeat at the hands of the Damascus governor. So read the historical treatises, and doubtless so it was; but it is difficult to believe, for the religious tenets which they brought with them came to dominate the whole of Oman, and have persisted to this day. The fact that they were partisans of Ali in the early days, must mean that at that time the Shiahee position was quite undefined, for the teachings of the Abadhees, as the Khawarij came to be called in Oman, are the farthest possible removed from Shiism. They are, indeed, a purified and simplified Sunnism.

The immigrants were probably only a few hundred, and they must have formed a small colony. Without doubt they found the country inhabited and cultivated, much as it is today. However, they were soon ruling it from one end to the other, and their faith displaced all other varieties. Coming as proscribed heretics, they have remained a minority and somewhat despised community in the world brotherhood of Islam. One of their leaders explained to me that in Mecca he had to place himself in one of the four great orthodox divisions of the Sunnis, when he made the great pilgrimage.

Minority communities tend to be tolerant, and Oman is no exception. In courtesy and hospitality to strangers, they are unsurpassed. Struggling through the heavy sand of Dubai to call on a friend perhaps five miles away, I stopped at a fisherman's hut to beg a drink of water. It was midsummer, and in midsummer on the Pirate Coast, pedestrians need drinks of water pretty frequently. So far as manners were concerned it was a member of the royal family who received me, courteously spread a mat in the shade for me to sit on, and brought dates, buttermilk, and fresh water to refresh me in that stifling heat. A loincloth was the wrinkled old fisherman's only covering, sincere hospitality his only crown, but he was one of this world's born kings.

Religious convictions are deep and strong in Oman. They observe some of the rules of the straitest sect of the Wahabees. Tobacco is forbidden, as also music and dancing. On our recent visit to Sifala it was impossible to take with us a portable gramophone, which otherwise might have enlivened the evenings of the boys so far from home. We even left our crokinole board behind, for games are likely to become hilarious, and hilarity is frowned upon, in that sunbaked wilderness. "It is our intention," said one of the religious leaders in Nejd when I discussed these things with him, "to make religion difficult."

Also running true to form, these Arabs have been incorrigible individualists, and even their religious interests have never been able to unite them for any long period into a stable state. Their history has been a weary repetition of intrigue and assassination, revolt and riot, and wars great and small. When we were guests of Seyyid Hamid in Sohar, he showed us the room in the royal castle where his own granduncle had been killed, and buried where he fell. A son or brother was the assassin, which indeed is the case usually. The atmosphere of the whole community is that of restless distrust. It is no accident that the costume of an ordinary man must include a rifle and cartridge belt, and a formidable curved dagger. In Sohar on this same visit, I asked the head of the customshouse to send some message to a friend. He summoned one of his servants, and the note was entrusted to him. "But I can hardly go now, I left my rifle at home." The director puzzled a moment. Evidently it was out of the question for a man to appear without this part of his costume. We do not attend dress dinners in our shirt sleeves. "Well, take mine then." So the messenger carried the accoutrements of his master, and was able to appear in public and carry the note. But the rifle is more than a particular sort of necktie. On the least provocation its owner's hand is against every man, and every man's hand against him.

II

FIRST EXPERIENCES

Muscat I found to be an interesting and paradoxical place. The whole of Oman is a wilderness of bare rocky mountains and seemed the embodiment of utter poverty. Later in that year I stood on the top of Jebel Achdhar, the highest of the Oman ranges, and for forty miles the eye ranged over a vast waste of mountains and valleys, like monstrous waves of some dreadful rocky sea. Scattered through this sterile and desolate wilderness are tiny oases where water for irrigation is available, but they are few and small. From one oasis to the next our caravan traveled for twenty and thirty miles, with the very stones themselves turned almost black by the sun's heat, and the bleaching bones of dead camels our only milestones.

But in spite of a rainfall of only three inches along the coast, and perhaps one inch inland, Muscat was a hive of activity, and everybody had plenty of money. It was a curious activity, and it centered in the Government house where the British consul lived. No matter when I dropped in on some sort of errand, the place was swarming with impressive uniforms and suppressed energy. The air was electric with politics. Germany was working for a port in the Persian Gulf and had a strong consulate and commercial establishment in Lingeh. Russia was aiming at Bandar Abbas, and the whole of northern Persia was reckoned as under her protection. France maintained an establishment in Muscat, and from the big consulate on the Muscat waterfront, Great Britain held them all off.

But that was not the real Muscat, as I soon learned. Nor was it the never-ending duel between the great powers which gave the place its curious feverish prosperity. Under the surface there was another contest, and it was a more serious affair. The harbor always had in it a few small gunboats, up to half a dozen or even more. They came and went. They had no part in the international diplomatic game, but their officers bustled in and out of the consulate, and sometimes their faces were very grave.

There was another feature in the situation. The harbor was full of great sailing boats which brought nothing in and took nothing out. We used to watch them from the hospital verandah. Nobody ever put any cargo on board such a ship, yet each morning it was obviously sunk in the water six inches lower than at the previous sunset. Once they were adequately ballasted in this mysterious way, they hoisted their sails and were off. Almost always they left at night, and a little later there would follow one of the gunboats from the mosquito fleet, as we called it.

It took me some time to realize the size of this contraband traffic. In the warehouses of that little city a million rifles were for sale, and endless quantities of ammunition. These were brought into Muscat on the regular steamers in broad daylight, for treaties had been signed by the Sultan with the French as well as with the British, and they did not allow the importation of arms to be prohibited.

Both French and German arms were available in Muscat in those days, but the ironical feature of the situation was that the greater part came from England. It was then that I learned the meaning of the initials, B.S.A.* All of these goods were destined for the Northwest frontier of India where the wild tribesmen would pay three or four hundred rupees for a rifle which we could buy for fifteen.

It was not possible to prevent the rifles coming in, but the mosquito fleet worked with great efficiency to keep them from getting across to the near-by Makran coast. Not one in ten were actually delivered to the rebellious frontiersmen, but the small percent which did filter through made lots of trouble. One day there was a little visible activity aboard one of the gigantic dhows. They had bought a large square water tank, which after some time had to have its top completed on board. Such a succession of events is a little unusual, and it did not escape the eyes of the spies who were everywhere. It was not in evidence when the ship sailed out to sea, nor did the gunboat which overhauled them waste any time searching through the usual cargo. A grappling iron was run under the dhow, and it brought up the water tank, which was fastened to the keel below with a big chain. It was broken open and found packed with rifles to the top. The rifles were dropped into the deep sea where

* Birmingham Small Arms Company of Birmingham, England.

no diver could hope to recover them, and so the fruits of several months' hard work disappeared. But the boatmen were good sports; they would try again. The gunboat crews enjoyed the game, too, and a good time was had by all.

It was a profitable sort of wickedness, and it brought lots of trade to the city. It certainly brought trade to the hospital. Into my consulting room would stride tremendous black-bearded giants, who obviously were not born within a thousand miles of Muscat. Usually however they did not stride, but rather crept, for we saw them only when malaria had them in its grip. Muscat, then as now, swarmed with mosquitoes, and no stranger long escaped an attack of fever. Malaria and dignity do not go together, and some of these limp monsters were pathetic figures. They repented of their sins till our quinine cleared their systems of the vicious fever. Then they went back with more energy than ever. It was no part of our work to ask them what they were doing in Muscat.

Over this remarkable mixture of energy and wickedness, prosperity and fever, the Sultan in his palace presided. He diligently fostered the arms traffic, while the British consul worked day and night to throttle it. Developing the traffic made the Sultan rich, and suppressing it gave the consul a good salary. The traffic itself made Muscat prosperous, but it marked the Northwest frontier of India with a dreadful long row of graves, where the finest officers that England ever sent out were buried, and with them the best soldiers of all North India.

The Sultan was a good showman, and the soul of hospitality. He did not care for missionaries, but occasionally I had to go there to present my official salutations. The palace was set in the midst of some really fine gardens, and he kept a lion in a cage to give the place an air of regal magnificence. For many years he kept in addition a tame ostrich, which had the run of the town, and being royally connected was free from all interference. This tremendous bird could reach down over almost any wall in the city and pick up whatever took his fancy. The poor of the city anathematized him, for an ostrich's appetite is enormous, and extremely comprehensive.

My appointment was not a permanent one. Dr. Thoms had opened medical work in Muttreh two years before, and, when he went home on a year's furlough, I took his place till he came back. Nothing could have been finer than the co-operation that Mr. and Mrs. Barny, the evangelistic missionaries of the station, gave the medical work, but it is no simple matter to get work of this sort under way, and the three of us together did not accomplish a great deal. Medical work has to earn its own reputation and make its own way, and the best friends in the world cannot help it very much.

The purpose of missionaries is to change people. We want them to become Christians, but in Arabia that is an extremely slow process. If we had some dazzling inducement to offer, doubtless a good number would be ready to enroll themselves under any name we might choose, but that is not the kind of Christians that we want. Mohammedan countries have all of them been slow, hard fields, and the supremely important equipment is patience. The medical missionary is sent out because he is supposed to be an extra legible illustration of what the Christian faith is. There is truth in the idea; for, while the evangelistic missionary, I am afraid, is often a better example of what a Christian ought to be, the work of the doctor is more easily understood, and vastly better appreciated.

I had not realized till I arrived in Muttreh what a terrifying appointment this was. The very place where the patients were housed contradicted the Christian faith. In a new station like Muttreh, whatever quarters can be rented form the hospital. Living quarters were upstairs. In-patients lived below. Houses in Arabia are about as badly adapted for hospital patients, as can be imagined. A small central courtyard is surrounded by a number of small rooms. They have no light nor air except through the little square door which is the sole entry into that particular burrow. The floors are of mud, and there was not the faintest suggestion of bathroom facilities. For that purpose the patients used the sea beach which was close by.

Our hospital had formerly been the home of an Indian doctor who lived in Muttreh for many years. It was unique in possessing a very heavy iron fence which enclosed a tiny yard of clear sand immediately in front of the house. Impressive iron lampposts stood at each corner, and added much to the effect. Just what purpose this tremendous fence was intended to serve, I could never find out, but it served us excellently as a bit of advertising, and as an identifying address. Our house was "The father of the iron."

That iron fence was not the only remarkable feature of the medical situation as I found it. The people wanted medical attention and they wanted lots of it. Moreover they wanted it free. They agreed with Sweitzer that our work is really an acted prayer, and no one ever heard of a doctor who charged for his prayers. Now this of course is a beautiful religious concept, and the selfless doctor working himself ascetically thin for the good of grateful but indigent patients is a first-class idea. However, in a missionary hospital the situation is more like that of the colored church, whose pastor explained to his congregation, that while salvation is free, there is considerable freight on it.

The medical missionary is a gift to the community, and his time and services cost the people nothing. But most missionary societies expect their hospitals to become self-supporting after a reasonably brief period of subsidization. "Self-supporting" here means simply that the hospital collects in fees money sufficient to pay its running expenses. Medicines, notably those for the treatment of venereal disease, and those needed in surgical work, are expensive things. There is a good deal of freight to be paid on this brand of salvation.

Ruthless elimination of the weak and unfit has produced some remarkable types in Arabia. The bushes and even the smaller plants are covered with spines. The goats have been trained almost to gnaw their living from the bare rocks. The people have been trained, too, and by the same hard conditions. They meet the new medical arrival with a sublime determination to gnaw off from him the last grain of benefit that is extractable.

Every medical missionary working in Arabia knows something of this, but not all of it, for Muttreh is unique. The richest man in the city used to come on foot to the free clinic of the municipal doctor, and unblushingly demand free treatment, like all the rest of the poor in spirit, who want the blessings of western medicine. We had to behave like undiluted pagans to extract a microscopic fee from the head of one of the imported mercantile communities, a man whose business transactions dealt in lacs * of rupees.

I found it necessary to case-harden my external spiritual surface to a degree quite distressing. Iron such as is found in the teeth of these people cannot be met with altruistic putty, that is not if a hospital is to be kept floating. This perpetual contest between sharp teeth and case-hardened armor plate is not too bad a game except when I remember that I was sent out primarily to serve as a legible edition of the Christian faith. The terrifying contradiction there, I have not been able to resolve to this day.

* A lac of rupees is a hundred thousand, i.e. about $30,000.

III

INLAND OMAN

No one in this world or the next knows quite so much as the recent medical graduate. Like all the others, I had come from the best medical school in the world. I made a painful discovery. However much I knew, it was evident that I was no salesman. My predecessor had been having clinics of a hundred and fifty a day. Mine were about twenty-five. Moreover half of these might better have stayed at home, being anxious principally to strive for more children, when they already had more than enough.

So I decided that the time was ripe for a long tour into the inland country. Our mission is a great believer in tours. All of our stations are on the coast because port cities were all that were open in the early days. But our objective is the inland country, and it is by means of tours that we get acquainted. The hope is that eventually we can have our mission stations and hospitals placed in the midst of the people that we are out here to reach.

There were said to be a million people living in that wilderness of mountains which we call Oman. I wonder who is responsible for that estimate? Not one of the towns has ever been counted, to say nothing of the wandering tribes in between. I doubt if the population of Oman exceeds half that number. But even half a million people ought to furnish, I thought, a more respectable amount of work than I was finding in Muttreh.

In most parts of Arabia it is not possible to plan for trips such as this one, without a long preliminary effort to get permission and make arrangements. Oman is a more friendly and courteous country, and in those days under the Sultan, that was very conspicuously true. The inheritance of a minority status among their Mohammedan confreres has had a marked effect, and we knew that there was nothing to anticipate except courteous hospitality. Wayside mosques are found everywhere and the traveler uses them as shelter in a storm, and for sleeping quarters at night. We shared such quarters with other travelers and with lively little local goats.

That trip introduced me to the donkey and the camel. We traveled by day and slept at night, for it was a winter trip. They were long days. Before the sun was up we rolled out, and after some coffee and dates we started the day's trek. Twenty-five miles is about as far as the day will bring such a caravan, and the sleep that follows is of the deep semicomatose variety. The donkey is a far more fatiguing carrier than the camel, but he is also a good deal faster.

We made an impressive show, about half a dozen of us all told, each on his donkey, with various miscellaneous boxes for medicines, and bright red quilts folded up to act as saddles. We had surgical instruments with us, and tooth forceps, and were ready for any emergency. Food we bought as we went along, living largely on Arab bread and dates, and a chicken at night, purchased from the villages we went through, doubtless at a large advance over its usual price.

The trip was a great success, at least from the standpoint of numbers. The inland towns and the Bedouin tribes believe that Johns Hopkins is a good medical school. At least they accepted with hospitality and enthusiasm this recent product of its laboratories and wards. We certainly had no lack of patients. One day I tried to see two hundred, a thing which is absurd of course. We were able, though, to do real work on the trip in spite of the unwieldy numbers. A large number of malaria cases were given quinine, and all sorts of dirty ulcers were dressed. This was one of the most satisfactory parts of our work, for we could teach the patients to care for themselves.

One of the sheikhs whom we visited asked me with sudden and rather startling abruptness, "Can you pull teeth?" I assured him that I thought I could. "Very well. Pull one from the mouth of this slave, and if your work looks competent, I will have you pull mine." I was appalled at this incredible brutality, and had my mouth almost open to refuse indignantly to do any such thing. However, I decided to look into the slave's mouth. Perhaps he did have one which needed pulling. He did, to my enormous relief. It was pulled with great success, and thereupon the sheikh opened his own mouth without a word, and I pulled a huge molar for him too. We gave a good deal of attention to teeth on that trip, and pulled eighty-six in one day, which seemed a rather dreadful contribution to human comfort.

The Bedouins live largely on milk, and have teeth

which are splendidly formed and equally well preserved. In the towns, on the contrary, we found the teeth in shocking condition. Without doubt a deficient diet is primarily responsible, but dirt and neglect contribute. Some of these teeth have been so loosened by pyorrhea that they can be picked out with the fingers, but some are nailed in and clinched. The people differ in their reactions too. Some run away at the mere sight of the tooth forceps. The Bedouins are of a tougher fiber. I remember one in Kuwait who endured without the flicker of an eyelash, a struggle with an enormous molar, which lasted fifteen minutes.

The day before we visited Beheli, one of the larger inland towns, we earned no end of reputation, by removing a lipoma the size of a tennis ball from the side of a man's head out in the open air under a tree. I have done many operations much more difficult than that, without getting any credit for it at all. But the fates were all in my favor that morning. The audience was small but select, and evidently it included a good advertising agent, though who he was, I never learned. The fame of this great performance spread far and wide, and I was welcomed into the city with a salvo of musketry like a visiting ruler.

A week or two later I made another home run. We were visiting a town of some size in the throes of a severe cholera epidemic. Quarantine regulations have eliminated cholera from Oman now. It is many years since it has been seen. In the days when this tour was undertaken, it was a fairly common epidemic, and a cholera epidemic is a dreadful thing. From where we were housed, the groans of the dying and the suffering of the patients with severe cramps were in our ears constantly.

The sheikh demanded some advice. "How is such a plague to be handled?" I told him very nonchalantly that I knew how to stop it, but telling him would do no good for my instructions would be disregarded. This whetted him up to a very imperative pitch. What I ordered would be carried out if it took long rows of gallows to do it. "Very well," I would tell him, even though I knew it would do no good. This incredible frigidity on my part, I had learned by experience. Pushing an Arab is an extremely futile amusement. Letting him push you will sometimes produce great quantities of results.

I explained in detail. The disease is due to tiny wriggly worms, too small for the eye to see. My magical microscope however could show them. They come from the discharges of patients already sick, and by means of water or food gain access to the intestinal tract of a second patient and make him sick. All that is needed to stop the appearance of fresh cases is to drink nothing but boiled water, eat nothing but cooked food, and see that both are protected from flies until they are consumed.

Soldiers carried the word around, and the order was edged with lurid threats. Anyone caught drinking unboiled water was to be shot at sunrise. The epidemic stopped as if cut off with an ax. Not another fresh case developed. It was a real home run so far as that town was concerned, and the neighboring towns as well.

In those days the Sultan in Muscat ruled over the entire province of Oman. We carried letters from him to the governors of the different districts and were invariably received with the utmost cordiality. The hospitality of these inland governors was appalling. A huge platter five feet across was piled with rice to a height of three feet, and a whole boiled sheep very decently interred in the white mountain. His boiled legs, amputated at the knee, could be seen sticking out, two on each side. Sitting down before a meal such as this, the utmost that I could do was to excavate a tiny hole on one side. The Arab camelmen sitting down with us had appetites that were unbelievable. Pounds and pounds of cooked mutton, they ate, with incredible masses of boiled rice. Each left a hole in his side of the mountain that was gigantic, compared with the tiny burrow that my side showed. I used to fear exceedingly that the following day would see them in acute equatorial distress, but I did them an injustice. Their intestinal tract was equal to all the demands made on it.

The inland country we found almost as prosperous as Muscat itself, and partly on the same account. The sheikhs were all engaged in the arms traffic. They carried the rifles across country and put them on board dhows at one of the ports of the so-called Pirate Coast. I am afraid that a good many of the rifles sent across in this way did reach their destination, for it was difficult to intercept such shipments.

In those days the oases of inland Oman were largely made up of plantations owned and operated by Arabs of birth and breeding. These men lived on their plantations, and the work was done for them by large numbers of slaves. Men have never raised any crop of significance in Oman except dates, and a date plantation does not require a very great amount of labor. The number of slaves was large, and, so far as we could see, no one was expected to work very much. In the Bottina district, which lies along the coast, irrigating the gardens is an exceedingly laborious process, for the water has to be raised from wells that are twenty to thirty feet deep. But even there the slaves were so numerous that the working hours for each man were very moderate.

In the morning everybody gathered in the big reception hall to meet any stranger who might have spent the night as a guest of the plantation. The old chief was in the seat of honor at one end of the long room. At the other the official coffee maker browned a suitable number of green coffee berries in a long-handled pan over the fire. These were pounded to powder in a resounding brass mortar. The slave who was responsible for this important task put lots of energy and rhythm into it, and, inasmuch as his mortar was a very effective inverted bell, it served to summon the whole plantation. It took half an hour to make the coffee, and was reckoned as one of the most important tasks of the day.

The maker of this bitter beverage, ostentatiously poured a cup for himself and drank it in full view of everyone, before serving anyone else. This, of course, demonstrated that no poison had been put in. It is a very effective guarantee, for it would not have been easy to introduce anything into the pot after that first cup had been poured out and drunk.

When the coffee was nearly ready, a second slave passed around a tremendous platter of pancakes a foot and a half in diameter, and the thickness of blotting paper, with butter and sugar in between, like layer cake.

That ration of bread with butter and sugar, left the fingers a little sticky, but for delicious taste I will pit it against any breakfast in Paris or New York. Coffee followed the sugared bread, and the *mejlis* buzzed with an extremely active exchange of gossip, during the whole time. We usually spent an hour at breakfast. Like other visitors we carried in our pockets a dozen or more letters directed to various individuals of the plantation, and these were now distributed. Every scrap of news was listened to and discussed, and the education of the community in current events was attended to with scrupulous care.

That trip was my first introduction to slavery, and it added a great deal to my education. No one could miss the gracious features of this courteous and hospitable life. It was a slave economy, but the slaves were obviously contented, and extremely well fed. Some of them needed treatment for obesity. If there was discontent in their minds, not one of them told me about it. At one of the places where we were entertained, the master of the plantation was absent, and the entire place was administered in his absence by his chief slave. The courteous and dignified hospitality which we enjoyed at his hand, I do not expect ever to forget. We found that one of the local governors was a slave and from all reports he made a most excellent governor and gave universal satisfaction. Most of the slaves were menials of course, but they seemed contented, and many of them would come in evenings to listen to simple readings like the parables. My own Arabic was very limited then, and they were a sympathetic and noncritical audience.

The patriarchs who owned the plantations were men

of fine courtesy and intelligence, and their long white beards and dignified manners remain a delightful memory. Their knowledge was limited, but they did not always know it. A pint cup filled with date stones was usually close at hand in the *mejlis*, and I watched while the cost of a list of purchases was calculated by counting out on the floor the required number for each item, and then counting the whole lot. The method was cumbersome, but evidently it gave satisfaction.

One of these interesting old chiefs asked whether America was a cold country. I told him that it was cold in winter. "How cold?" That is not the easiest question in the world to answer in a country where the winters are barely cool, and thermometers are unknown. However, after a moment's thought, I told him that in my country it gets so cold in the winter, that water becomes hard like a brick. My host felt much hurt at being made the butt of a rude joke like that. To reckon his intelligence so feeble that he would accept a transparent falsehood, was a grievous insult. He turned the conversation into other lines, and the matter was not referred to again.

We found a second reason for the prosperity of the country. Oman dates were being exported to America where they commanded double the price of others. I must admit that I did not then, nor have I since, shared this high opinion of the Oman date, and unfortunately for Oman, America eventually came to agree with me. America now buys scarcely a box of these dates, but then twenty-eight thousand boxes of sixty pounds each were sent in a single year. The local price went up to nearly or quite twenty rupees a box. Even more than the arms traffic, this was the foundation of the inland's country's prosperity in its plantation days.

We passed on beyond the mountain districts where our friends had offered us such wonderful hospitality, and came to the edge of the great "empty desert" where even the Bedouins can scarcely live. On the edge of that desolate country Arab hospitality could scarcely keep us decently alive. We found there more flies than we had seen anywhere else, which quite astonished us in such an utterly dry country.

One day we sat down before a very modest little mountain of rice, in which were embedded fragments of mummified salt fish. Determination can put anything into the human mouth, but it takes a good deal of hunger to slide a meal of that sort down into the stomach. I am sure that the psychic messages that my gastric glands received that afternoon reduced my gastric juice by nine-tenths.

However I must say that if I did not find Arab hospitality attractive that day, the flies did. I have never seen them at mealtime in such numbers. They settled down in clouds, and the surface of the rice was simply black. Nor could they be brushed off. The rice remained black, and the handful which the right hand carries to the mouth was only kept free from these satanic insects by the constant hard work of the left in shooing them off. Even so one of the boys ate a fly, at least he insisted that he did, and we all believed him. I have no doubt that each of us ate several, but this I did not stress, for in that country it is supposed to be a dangerous accident to eat a fly, and the emotional reaction to this conviction of sin on the part of my Arab friend cost him his entire enormous meal.

We had a good time on that trip. It lasted almost four months. I learned a great deal about the needs of the country, and came back with plans for a chain of small hospitals stretching across Oman. We sold a thousand copies of the Gospels, and we dreamed a great dream of a developing Christian community in that hospitable and courteous country. The dream did not come true.

I was transferred to another station, and Dr. Thoms on his return lived only a few months. He was killed in an accident.

IV

OMAN'S BACK DOOR

MEDICAL WORK IN Muttreh was given up after Dr. Thoms's death. It was twenty years before the mission could send a doctor to Oman again and take up where Dr. Thoms had left off. In the meantime the situation changed. Great Britain and France composed their differences, and the deadly trade which had been laying the golden eggs did not survive for twenty-four hours. The million rifles that filled the warehouses were bought by the British government and done away with. Ammunition shared the same fate. The place was swept clean, like a small boy washing from his slate a very bad picture. Not another rifle was allowed entrance. The mosquito fleet found work elsewhere. The arms traffic was gone.

The Sultan was compensated by the Indian government, which meant most likely that they made good his loss in customs charges on these goods. That was a mere fraction of his profits from the trade. He was bitterly opposed to the new enactment, of course, but he had no choice in the matter. Everybody had been making money by the sale of rifles, and, when this source of income was suddenly wiped out, Oman rose as one man in rebellion, to cast out this ruler who had betrayed them. Nothing was left of the old kingdom, except a narrow strip of coast where a few gunboats of the old mosquito fleet were able to enforce submission. Every European, missionaries included, was credited with this destruction of the country's wealth. Inland Oman was closed.

The Mission had developed a strong hospital in Bahrain. The reputation of its surgical work spread over the whole Persian Gulf. Oman has a back door as well as a front one, and that back door was in Bahrain's sphere of influence. The Mission entered on a long ten-year effort to enter Oman through the Pirate Coast.

The Pirate Coast is the first hundred miles of Arabian littoral encountered after entering the Straits of Hormuz. A number of small lagoons run inland from the sea for a few miles, offering shelter where sailing boats can hide from their enemies and from storms. Each lagoon has a town attached. No pirates are there now, or rather no piracy is practiced now, for the war vessels of the unconquerable British have made such activities impossible; but in the days of the East India Company, brigands from this section were a notorious scourge, and had to be suppressed more than once by naval expeditions.

There are a full half-dozen towns scattered along this hundred miles of coast. Dubai, which has the best lagoon, is the largest. Its population cannot be less than thirty thousand. In the glamorous days of the buccaneers an astonishing number of great cannon were sold to these robber barons, and they lie about now as picturesque landscape decorations. At Um el Gowein, eighteen of these impressive giants stand in a row in front of a dilapidated castle, to teach the wayfaring man what becomes of marauders.

Since the British gunboats have made piracy impossible, and more recently have taken away the munificent profits and gambler's fascination of the arms traffic, the Pirate Coast has turned to pearl diving. In the days when I first made their acquaintance, the industry was at the peak of its development. There must have been a thousand boats engaged in the work, half of them from Dubai. They averaged, I imagine, about twenty-five divers to a boat.

The pearling reefs stretch along the western shores of the Persian Gulf for three or four hundred miles. In those days Kuwait was the center of the pearl trade in the north, and Dubai in the south. The Bahrain Islands were the largest center of all, and there buyers came each season from Paris and London to make their purchases. Dubai never reached the size or importance of Kuwait and Bahrain, because in Dubai the industry was carried on largely by means of slaves, and in spite of all impressions to the contrary, a slave is the most unprofitable labor machine that has ever been devised.

The foreign contacts and travel connected with the pearl trade did a great deal to civilize Kuwait and Bahrain, but no such effect was felt in Dubai. Twenty years before my first visit, one of the mosquito fleet from Muscat, in its effort to stop the dreadful stream of rifles flowing across the narrow straits, landed a force of marines in Dubai, and searched the house of one of its leading men for rifles. The information upon which they acted was correct enough, but the rifles had been spirited away and none were found. The officer commanding made one mistake. He searched the women's quarters, and that perhaps without allowing them sufficient time to escape.

When the soldiers came out, they found themselves facing an infuriated crowd, armed to the teeth. The attack of the Arabs was so furious that only a cannonade from the gunboat saved the landing party from annihilation. As it was they left a number of dead behind, and doubtless a far larger number of dead Arabs. Discipline and great courage made the best of a very bad situation, and the marines retreated in good order to their ship. It was twenty years before any white man, official, doctor, or what not, was allowed in the place.

It was the missionary who reopened the city. The uncle of the sheikh of Abu Dhubbi had a paralytic stroke, and I was sent for. The trip was a great success. I doubt if there were ten people left untreated in that tiny town. Liniments for aching bones, and Epsom salts for constipation, were in great demand. Dietetic habits were such that at least one dose of Epsom salts was good for nearly everybody.

When we finished in Abu Dhubbi, we went across the bay perhaps thirty miles to carry greetings from Hamadan, the ruler of Abu Dhubbi, to Saeed, the ruler of Dubai. "It is a good thing," said the sheikh after cordially passing around the coffee, "that you did not try to come into this town on a steamer." But the ice was melting, and I had a very pleasant visit of a few days, and went on to complete a medical trip of a few weeks in Um el Gowein. The sheikh there was so pleased with me and my work, that he gave me a tremendous gold watch. It must have weighed a pound, and, when a suitable lever was pulled, the hours, quarters, and minutes were struck, each with a different musical note. We finished up by staying a few days in Sharga.

The purpose of the trip was to open the Pirate Coast, and we certainly seemed to have succeeded. The local ruler gave a tremendous feast in my honor. Apparently every important man on the whole Pirate Coast was there. When we were filled up like automobile tires at thirty-five pounds, the spokesman of the evening rose and made a little speech. To what department of the British government, he wanted to know, should they send a petition asking that I be placed permanently somewhere along this coast. The petition was to carry every signature that counted in that whole district.

I think that was the highest peak which my popularity ever reached. I was much moved, I assured them, by such an expression, and at the end of so short an acquaintance. The petition need not be sent to the British Government, for I had no connection with it. The American Mission would be glad to receive the petition, but it would be three years at least before they could comply with the request, for we were dreadfully short-handed. In the meantime I would try to make them a yearly visit.

But popularity is a broken reed. When I got back to Bahrain, I sent in an unrequested and, I am afraid, an undesired, report to Bushire headquarters, on the state of the slaves along the Pirate Coast. Such reports always leak out. As the Arabs might say, if such a letter is locked in a safe and sunk in the sea, it will still be reported back promptly to the people it tells about. It was sent back to the country where I had been so popular, and the door of the Pirate Coast was locked in my face. It was three years before I could get permission for the briefest sort of visit.

I was afraid that would happen, and I tried hard to persuade myself that I might better keep still. But who is to come forward and break a lance for the slaves in that district, if not the missionary, even if the Mission program is set back for three years and nothing is accomplished? I had seen a good deal of slavery in the plantations back of Muscat, and it is a pleasure to testify to the good treatment that those slaves received, and their evident contentment with their lot. But on the Pirate Coast the situation was very different. Thousands of slaves were there, and with them dozens and hundreds of diving boats were manned. "And the dark places of the earth are full of the habitations of cruelty." While I was in Abu Dhubbi three slaves tried to get away to Bahrain. They stole a boat, hoisted their sail, and made a run for it. Fortune refused to smile on their desperate effort, and they were captured. They were beaten so severely that one of them died.

During the trip through the hinterland slaves often came in after the day's work was done, to talk and listen. I knew very little Arabic then, but they were lenient judges. If any of them were dissatisfied, not a word of the sort was poured into my ears. On the Pirate Coast, after the others had gone to bed, the daily letter had been written, and it was time to think of a nap, sleep was often still far away. I can see them now sitting silently next my chair, till I woke with a start to their presence. I knew what they wanted to say before they began.

The Baloochee slaves were the most pathetic. They rebelled bitterly against their bonds. All the slaves were miserably treated, but the Africans were more patient. Their souls were manacled along with their bodies, but still they could sing. The next world will have to have in it something for the African slaves that I saw on the Pirate Coast, or God's own justice will be stultified. One of these slaves was his master's secretary, for he could read and write, whereas his owner could do neither. Could I help them run away? I told them that when the time came for us to start, if they would swim out to the boat where I was a passenger, I would gladly pay their fare to Bahrain, and do my best to get the captain to accept them as passengers. That was all I could do. It was not enough. Not one of them even tried to come with me. I gave them what encouragement I could, and assured them that the British Government would establish a consulate on that coast within a few years, and their freedom come with it. It was a false hope. The slaves are there still.

But in spite of what I had reported about the slaves, the Pirate Coast knew me now, and my reputation grew in my absence better perhaps, than it would have in my presence. The man most concerned to keep me at a safe distance died. He developed a tremendous crop of boils, and passed on too precipitately for it to do me any good. He sent an urgent request for me to come, but a wire from his son overtook the letter to say that it would be no use. However one of the merchants of Sharga decided that he had carried his big troublesome hernia long enough. Would I come down for a thousand rupees and mend it?

I would. A thousand rupees is a pretty good fee, and, even though it is the price of stopping the hospital for a month, I always feel myself a real surgeon when someone offers me as much as that. Moreover that money reinforced very substantially the finances of the Kuwait hospital, where I was working at the moment. It was a very active surgical trip, and we had lots of weather, as a traveler said once. Our supply of rubber gloves ran out, and we did twenty-three hernias barehanded. I had been working out a technique whereby simple operations like hernias can be done almost without touching the patient except with sterile instruments. We thought that we were going to register a perfect score, but we did not. The last one of the twenty-three developed a tiny stitch abscess. Somebody is always taking the joy out of life.

We had some more joy taken out of life before we were finished. The Pirate Coast is full of strictures. In Bahrain, gonorrhea is treated with various medicated drinks, and sometimes, like the American cold, with contempt. But along the Pirate Coast the local practitioners apply various salves and goos internally, at the end of crooked sticks and wires, and a tremendous crop of strictures results. One afternoon I had five stricture cases sitting in a row, waiting for attention. They were given spinal anesthesia, one after the other, a sort of wholesale surgical invoice, and internal urethrotomies put the plumbing in order for the entire group. I gained lots of reputation on that trip.

On a later trip I gained a lot of notoriety, which is

not the same thing, and it was one of that row of patients who was responsible. This particular individual had his plumbing put in order as described above, and he felt very much obliged. His I.Q. was distinctly not high, but he was a very popular barber, and his loquacious friendship carried our name far and wide. He came back for inspection and dilatation if necessary, as I had asked him to do. It had been two years since his operation. We passed sounds and congratulated him on the fact that he needed no treatment at all. His good result was proving surprisingly permanent.

Twenty-four hours later his wife came to report that he had fever. This I assured her was not uncommon. It would not be serious. That was ten in the morning. At four in the afternoon, I went to see him. He was comatose, with a temperature which registered 110 on my clinical thermometer. He died perhaps ten minutes later. That thermometer was sent to the Bureau of Standards in Washington. It was found to register a few tenths of a degree too high at that temperature. His fever therefore had stood between 109 and 110.

This shocking result was bad enough. It was made worse by a chloroform death. A boy of ten who needed to have his hernia repaired, stopped breathing at the first whiff of the anesthetic. Artificial breathing started him again, but he stopped a second time. We started him once more, but like a drowning man the third time down was the last, and without another smell of chloroform, without even the scratch of a knife, he was carried out to be buried. We did not do much more on that trip. I was glad to return to headquarters and rest some nerve back into my surgical soul.

A trip to the Pirate Coast was always a colorful affair. One of the last ones was especially good. A messenger came from the sheikh of Dubai. "Saeed wants you to come and treat his wife." "Yes," I said, "where is the letter?" It appeared that the sheikh did not feel free to send a letter. Would I please accept a verbal message and come. This is an unheard of way of doing business in Arabia, and I doubted if the necessary permission from the British would be forthcoming. I was more doubtful still about the Dubai end.

However, I did get the permission, and with the messenger as a passport we started. I was traveling third class, or deck as we call it in the Persian Gulf. We all slept together under the awning, and got along without the amenities of a cabin. We changed steamers at Lingch, and the weather changed too, "rough and stormy." The chief officer looked me up. "The captain wants to see you." So I went up to where he sat in state, and he kept me waiting quite a while. Finally I was ushered in. "No," he said with fine emphasis, "I do not want to see you." I itched to assure him that the sentiment was heartily reciprocated, but did not. I talk too much anyway. "All that I want you for is to tell you that you cannot travel deck on this ship." White prestige, it appeared, was being undermined. I only wish I could believe that I was accomplishing half the good that this emissary of white prestige thought I was.

I assured him that I had traveled deck on many ships, that the Bombay office sold me such tickets. It did no good. Silence might have served my purposes better, but I doubt it, for the man's convictions on the matter seemed very definite. So I paid twenty-three good hospital rupees into the ship's treasury and was registered as a second-class passenger. Then I went down and had a good time visiting with my Arab friends.

It appeared that the authorities were still not satisfied. The chief looked me up again. "The captain is sorry that the only second-class cabin available has natives in two of its berths. He has opened a vacant first-class cabin for you." I told the chief officer to assure the captain, who was so concerned about my lily white soul, that I had not been down to look at my second-class cabin yet, but, if two Persians were in it, that was perfectly satisfactory to me. I was staying on deck, thank you, because the air was better there and the company extremely congenial. This, the chief officer and the captain seemed to find as difficult to believe as my inland patriarch had the story of water which became hard like a brick; but I had a good time that night, and we exchanged lots of fine stories.

As luck would have it, I came back from that tour on the same steamer. This time, however, one of the engineers was having a very bad time with dysentery, and his colleagues thought he was going to die. A little morphia and emetin performed a first-class miracle, and the crew's gratitude reached even to the redoubtable captain, who did not send for me this time, even though I was again ruining white prestige. We parted good friends when the trip was over.

On this trip we had with us the loudest-mouthed agitator I ever met. He hailed from North Africa somewhere, but the government had passed him on to Baghdad, and after a time they decided that they too could get along without him, so he had been living in Bahrain.

But he found the cloven British hoof there, so he was moving on to the free air of Dubai. He was quite sure that no undesirable alien like myself would be allowed to contaminate the sacred soil of free Arabia. But, when we arrived, the authorities of Dubai welcomed my contaminating foot quite cordially, while the agitating reformer was refused permission even to land. He mourned the incorrigible refusal of foolish barbarians to be led in the right path.

The captain and the reformer were each of them unique in their way, but the most remarkable experience of that trip was meeting Nasr bin Luta in Ajman. One of the world's rare noblemen, he must have been eighty at the time, and some of the responsibilities of buying and selling pearls he had already placed on the shoulders of his son. He was very wealthy, though not of the financial stature of one or two giants in Dubai. He brought me to Ajman to remove a stone from his bladder. The operation was a success, and in twenty days he was as good as new.

But he was not thinking of himself only. He insisted that I devote my time to the needy community, and to make that possible he built a date-stick hospital with twenty-foot verandas, the most comfortable quarters in the heat which I ever saw. We had from thirty to fifty patients in that hospital. He provided beds for those who needed them, and blankets as well. These latter were to act as mattresses. No one wanted anything to cover up with. Every morning and evening he sent slaves with great vessels of milk and supplies of bread and other things as well, so each could have just the diet which the doctor recommended. "I am anxious that

God give me a good result," said this earnest old man, "and I am going to help the others too, as much as I can."

I have seen many gentlemen in Arabia, but never another quite like Nasr bin Luta. I used to sit and discuss business ethics with him. The pearl business was beginning to collapse under the pressure of Japanese competition. Prices were down. This man had about thirty boats out, for which he was responsible. The owner of such a pearl boat buys its catch. "Yes," he said, in answer to a question, "I am taking the catch at a hundred and twenty-five rupees a *choe*. The price in Dubai is a hundred, but men cannot live at that figure. Indeed," he added, "it is as much as they can do to live at a hundred and twenty-five." I asked him how he could carry a loss as heavy as that, for after all he would have to sell eventually, and the Bombay price was a hundred.

"No," replied the old man, "I do not think that I shall lose. God never yet has let me lose. I have not always made very much, and I am not really very rich. Maybe I will lose this year, but I am responsible for the men, and they have got to be taken care of. And anyway," he added meditatively, "God wants the men to be taken care of, and I do not believe that he will let me lose." Nor did he. The market recovered a little and the benevolent old merchant went under the wire with a small profit. It was men of this sort that Paul had in mind when he told of "those that by patient continuance in well-doing, seek for glory and honor and incorruption," and I am sure he was right when he said that God gives men of that sort eternal life.

We did lots of work in that date-stick hospital. The deep verandas were full of patients. The heat was the worst I have ever experienced in Arabia. All along that coast ocean steamers have to stand several miles out from land, and that shallow sea was turned so sickeningly warm that no one cared to bathe in it. It was above blood heat. We all of us lived and worked stripped to the waist. Operating was the most difficult. One afternoon as I worked in the little operating room, with the sun beating on the roof just above my head, and the air as utterly steamy as a laundry wash room, I finally found myself racing with the growing blackness of the world, as I put the last stitches in the skin incision of a hernia. With my last grain of consciousness I dove through the door, before the whole universe blackened out. I knew that the air outside was at least a little better than our steamy oven. It would be more correct to say that I dove at the door. My head struck the top lintel, with force enough to crack one's skull. It was just what I needed, and I did not faint clear away but sat on the sand outside recovering.

One night at nine o'clock, there was a disturbance. Some animal was there moaning, trying to get in. We found a man crawling on his hands and knees, stark naked. Two days before he had started toward us with a strangulated hernia. The pain was very severe and one piece of clothing after another fell off. He had no idea where. The pain became worse and worse until his mind was almost unhinged, and a few hundred yards from the hospital he fell from the donkey and completed the journey on his hands and knees. He was half unconscious from the dreadful pain, but he kept going till he reached our door.

Our hospital was next to the sea, so I delegated half

a dozen able-bodied men who were staying with patients as their friends to carry this new arrival down to the sea bodily and dip him in a few times to wash off the sand. The operation room was prepared, and, when they brought him back nice and clean, we were ready for him. With a few c.c. of spinal anesthetic and half an hour's work, we put to bed an exhausted, but comfortable and happy patient. His clothes were brought in a piece at a time by honest travelers who had seen them in the road, and he went home two weeks later, a great believer in medical missions.

Not every strangulated hernia is in such desperate shape as this one, but they always present a very grave problem. They are the most frequent serious emergency that we see in Oman. Apparently the possibility of strangulation hangs over every hernia though it must be admitted that only a few actually go on to this disastrous termination.

Just what causes a hernia to strangulate is a puzzling question. The intestine which is out of bounds slides peacefully in and out of its burrow for years until one day it slides out and finds sliding back impossible. That does not sound very dangerous. Its rented quarters outside the abdominal cavity have been satisfactory enough, up to this time. Any ordinary Oman hernia expects to remain down throughout the day. In the natural course of events it does not come back home into the abdominal cavity till night.

But as a matter of fact, the inability of the intestine to slide back where it belongs is very serious. It cannot slide back because the neck of the sac has become tightly filled and sliding is impossible. Even very slight irritation to the delicate peritoneal surfaces causes swelling; and, when the pressure in the neck of the sac is so great that smooth sliding is not possible, it is only a very short time until it becomes so great that the circulation of the blood is interfered with. The flow of blood through the veins is stopped first. The intestines and their supporting membranes swell further, and soon all circulation is impossible and the death of the intestine imminent. Sometimes this gangrene of the intestine, as we call it, takes place within a few hours, or indeed in far less time than that. Sometimes enough blood trickles through to keep the tissues alive for some hours or even for several days. But the end of the process is the death of the imprisoned intestine, and it usually comes on rapidly.

The pain caused by a strangulated hernia is dreadful, but it is a good sign. Within the abdomen, pain is caused by distension and hardly by anything else. A dead segment of intestine causes no pain, no matter how distended it is. That is why the surgeon is so alarmed when a strangulated hernia comes in complaining of no pain. I remember once two strangulated hernias were brought into the Kuwait hospital within an hour of each other. One complained of the most dreadful pain. The other was quite comfortable. The acutely suffering patient was readily relieved, and his intestines were still viable. The intestines of the second patient were almost gangrenous, and he did not get well.

Strangulated hernias run their course to a fatal termination at different rates of speed, but in each case, time is the deciding factor, and if the obstruction can be relieved before the intestine dies, the patient recovers merrily, just as in an ordinary hernia. Once gangrene of the intestine has set in, the situation is very different. The dead intestine must be removed, the patient carried through his profound toxemia, and eventually the continuity of the intestine re-established. In the best hands the mortality is very forbidding. A quarter of the patients will be lost. And the patient with a strangulated hernia who is treated by faith instead of works just simply dies, and that is all there is to it.

Moreover it has to be the right sort of works. In Muttreh when a strangulated hernia appears on the horizon, every other activity in the hospital stops, no matter whether it is the middle of the day or the middle of the night. A piece of bread halfway to the mouth does not get there, and a word halfway written is not finished. The clinic patients have to wait an extra hour, even if they include the ruling sheikh of the city. All hands report to the operating room, and we hope to be operating on such a patient within fifteen minutes of his arrival, day or night.

We have been very fortunate in our results in these cases. They usually are brought in suffering very great pain, which in this case is a most welcome sign. In case after case it has been an undiluted joy to watch the intestine released from the constricting band, recover its color and turn from the dark dusky purple which means a stagnant circulation to the natural salmon pink which seems to the surgeon at that moment the loveliest color in the world. Sometimes if there has been a delay of hours in having the strangulation relieved, that heavenly pink color is long in coming. Then we wrap the coils in towels wrung out of warm saline solution. After ten minutes perhaps, the color gradually returns, and something deep down in the surgeon's soul turns a lively pink along with the slippery and interesting intestines he is working with.

Intestines which wait ten minutes to turn pink are very close to gangrene, and the patient is likely to have a bad time after the operation is over. The intestines are like a sensitive joint, and when stiff and sore from severe trauma, they forget how to perform their normal function of gently pushing along the gas and other intestinal contents. Then the patient has a bad pain, for his intestines become much distended, and he blows up like a balloon. The surgeon has heart failure. However, the intestine always picks up its job eventually, and I have never seen one of these post-strangulation intestinal paralyses result fatally.

If only the patient would come in without delay, these cases would almost never be lost. The pain is so severe that one would expect them to knock at the hospital door very promptly indeed, but there are always friends to suggest a poultice or an incantation, anything to avoid the necessary operation. Many operations are optional affairs. Even appendicitis will get well more often than not if it is left alone, but death is the only outcome for the neglected strangulated hernia.

In the early days of the Muttreh work we had a strangulated hernia to treat, which illustrated about all that there is left to say on this subject. One of the Indian merchants of the city sent a hurry call just as darkness fell. His hernia had strangulated. Unfortunately he had less pain than usual, though he had enough to satisfy most appetites. When I saw him, the strangulation was already twelve hours old.

I am afraid that I was too emphatic. I urged of course that he let nothing prevent the operation being done at once. He said yes to get rid of me, and, after making arrangements for his immediate transfer, I went to the hospital, where everything was gotten ready without a moment's delay. However, the carriers came without the patient, and with a note explaining that one of his friends had suggested some local applications known only to Indians. These would infallibly cure the condition without recourse to the knife. This caused me acute distress, which was interpreted as pure disappointment at missing the chance of performing another operation. I went back to the patient's house and explained again that I feared for the outcome if he waited any longer; but the more I argued the surer he was that operation was unnecessary and dangerous.

He waited two days, while he used his infallible poultices, and then at nine P.M. they brought him in. He had a very poor imitation of a pulse. His pain had long since stopped. That was a bad night. The governor of the city was dining with us, and the meal was brought to an abrupt close by the arrival of the patient. It was raining, a thing which happens in Muttreh only about once a year, or even less often than that sometimes; but, when it does happen, we can get a good deal of rain in a short time. Every roof in the city leaked, so far as I was able to learn. Certainly our roof leaked. By careful search we found a place in the operating room where the table could be placed and the operation proceed without being drenched by dirty water from the ceiling. I had to stand however with a neat little stream running down my back. Asepsis is not ruined by a stream of cold water running down the back of the surgeon's neck, but it diverts the attention, nor may he wave his gloved and more or less sterile hands around in the air promiscuously, lest they meet an unexpected deluge somewhere in the dimly lit environment.

However, if that happened, it did no great harm. None of the descending streams of water were a tenth part as dirty as the mass we opened into. Gangrenous spots opposite the mesentery were scattered over the entire imprisoned coil of intestine. There must have been half a dozen to ten of them. The foul intestinal contents had leaked out into the surrounding tissues, and what we had to deal with was a gigantic abscess cavity full of pus and feces, and gas bubbles. It was widely drained and nothing more. The semi-gangrenous perforated loop was surrounded by a big wet dressing. One rubber tube was put through the uppermost hole and pointed upward. A second was put through the lowest hole and pointed downward. These drained into big bottles. The patient was given glucose solution intravenously, lots of it. He took away from the operating room a much better pulse than he brought to it. Having put him safely to bed, we went upstairs to visit with the patient governor.

The patient declined to die that night. His intestine stood by him. It recovered, and, without help from its medical friends, healed its little holes shut. Four days later the patient was having normal bowel movements, which may stand as proof for those who need it that the human intestine is a first-class fighter. It does not ask for a fair chance. Given a quarter of a chance, it can do anything. But the abscess had burrowed far down into the pelvis, and in spite of extreme measures we could not get it drained adequately; so within ten days the man was dead. With sulphanilamide we could probably have saved him, but that was long before that useful drug was discovered. If only he had not delayed quite so long!

The only other strangulated hernia that we ever lost in Muttreh, we lost for just the same reason. He came in with only twelve hours' delay, but in his case twelve hours was more than enough. His hernia was enormous, larger than an adult head. It was the largest hernia that I have ever seen strangulate. It slid in and out through an enormous opening, and hung down two-thirds of the distance to his knees. He had been in for inspection several times, and we had urged operation. What we had in mind, however, was the disability such a gigantic hernia causes. Wherever such a man sits, there is a watermelon in his lap, and it is so big that his condition cannot be hid. No exertion is possible. The man is a real cripple.

I know of no statistics on the point, but the impression is that large hernias do not strangulate. Narrow-necked hernias would certainly seem to offer a greater opportunity for constriction and strangulation than those with a wide opening, through which, as in this case, it would seem that any imaginable mass of intestines ought to slide back and forth in peace.

But in Oman there seems to be no type of hernia which may not strangulate on occasion. Moreover when these large hernias do get tied up, the patient is in extreme jeopardy. The hernia of my Indian friend was a small affair, not larger than a goose egg, and I was surprised to find that it could contain a coil of intestine nearly six inches long. His general condition stood up for days. But when my Arab friend of the lap watermelon was brought in after only twelve hours of distress, he was already in extremis. His pulse was barely countable, and glucose brought only the most fleeting and insignificant improvement. We opened the enormous hernia and were met by such a mass of utterly dead purple intestines as I have never seen before or since. There were about eight feet of them, swollen and distended to double their normal size. The sickening odor of complete gangrene filled the operating room. We snipped them out like a dead thing, put a tube in, above and below, and were barely able to get the patient back to his bed before he died. When a man with a hernia of that size finds that he cannot get his intestines back into place within the abdomen, the fastest taxi and the nearest hospital will not get him on the operating table a minute too soon, nor will the whole faculty of Hopkins and Ann Arbor be able to save him, if he delays.

It is not fair though to close the subject of strangulated hernia on this note. Last year we had a nice case, one of Muttreh's handsomest future citizens, and, granted he inherits his parents' good qualities, one of the most promising. His mother had in her eyes the dreadful fear that only mothers' eyes can show. The four months' baby was a fighter. He had a different look in his eye. There was a pain down there, a little to the right of his middle, where it did not belong and he was mad. When I told the mother that he must be operated on right away, that I regarded the prospects as good, for his pain was still severe and intermittent, the fear in her eyes lightened a little. The father carried him in and helped keep him quiet till operating started. A little of that mother's fear and dread went down into my own soul, I who had dared to give a good prognosis on the work of my own hands, with a baby like that in the balance and his mother my judge.

But the light in her eyes was justified and not the cold fear in my heart. We found a tiny knuckle of gut caught and pinched most dreadfully in the smallest hernial opening I have ever seen. But that intestine belonged to a Baloochee. The world will hear from the Baloochee yet! Even the line of actual constriction recovered its color within a few seconds after the pressure was taken off. We gave him just enough chloroform to reduce his active protests to manageable proportions. Within a few minutes of the placing of his last stitch, he went back to resume his interrupted breakfast. A Baloochee baby so far as I have been able to observe, is always glad to resume his interrupted breakfast at any minute of the day or night.

I lost my big fat watch on one of these trips. The sheikh of Berimi came in for treatment, and his eyes were big and round as he looked at it. I gave it to him, just like that. There was guile in this extreme generosity. I planned to visit his city the following year, and I intended to ask him for a house and a good-sized piece of land for a branch hospital. He probably knew that I intended to ask for something when I gave him the watch. But when the time for the trip came, I was called elsewhere, and I have never seen Berimi. The sheikh has died long since, so the watch is a total loss. Gambling is a poor way to serve the Lord.

The effort of ten years was successful. We doctors did open the Pirate Coast, and through that door it would have been possible to enter Oman. But when the Mission at long last had a doctor available for the field, they voted to reopen the hospital in Muttreh. They felt, and time has shown them to be correct, that Oman could be entered from either side, and Muttreh, being more central, is the better location.

◇◇◇

V

REOPENING MUSCAT

THE MISSION FINALLY secured some additional doctors. The new arrivals were sent where work had been longer established. The task of reopening Muscat fell to me.

Some vigorous discussion preceded the decision to reopen the Muttreh hospital. Principles of fundamental importance were involved. Mission finance was on the downgrade, and there was much feeling against taking on new responsibilities. When the available dish of bones is inadequate for four dogs, why attempt to distribute it among five? That seems an unanswerable argument, but it is a dangerous line of thought even for its proponents. The dish of bones is not adequate for four dogs, is indeed entirely inadequate for one. The first step toward carrying out such an idea would be the closing of all our Arabian hospitals, and the accumulation of financial backing till at least a quarter of a million a year is available for one hospital. In a pinched and niggardly way an apology for a hospital might be thought of perhaps for a hundred thousand, but certainly not for less than that. The best is none too good, and on the Mission field we want the best.

It is well to look squarely in the eye this idea that the missionary ideal is a hospital which will furnish to all who need medical relief the best that scientific medicine has to offer, with American millionaires paying the bill. It takes an incredible amount of money to furnish the best that medical science has to offer. However, I am not sure that such a program would be impossible. Probably there are some places where it could be put across, if it were brought forward with the right propaganda pressure behind it. American millionaires are a very generous tribe.

The real reason why such an idea is incompetent, irrelevant, and immaterial is not that it is visionary and perhaps impossible. For the development of the emerging Christian Church, in the mission lands, as well as for the whole indigenous community which we serve, it is about as helpful as rat poison. Any city putting up such a hospital could have a hundred in its visible church within a week. The church invisible in that city would be invisible even to God. Every undesirable character in town would be anxious to attach himself to this golden chariot, and it is almost equally true that everyone attached to it would be an undesirable character. Henry Ford has had lots of good ideas besides planetary transmission and the V-8 engine. His insistence that unearned charity is dangerous and bad, is illustrated on the mission field every day.

It is not necessary either for a hospital to spend a hundred thousand dollars a year for the evil effects of unearned charity to manifest themselves. A vastly smaller budget than that can have bad effects. Every missionary in Arabia, and no doubt those from other places as well, can tell no end of painful tales about men who were anxious to become Christians, granted only that a good income were forthcoming, without the trouble of a competitive struggle for it.

Muttreh had to follow the opposite course. It was not very pleasant in prospect. An Irishman fell on hard days, and reported to his friend that starvation was staring him in the face. "That," said his comforter, "must be very disagreeable for both of you." We had the same experience and like him found it very unpleasant. We did not have vision enough at that moment to see that missionary hospitals like medieval monks, must add to fraternity and chastity the virtue of poverty. We added it, though, because we had to. One of our colleagues sacrificed part of his appropriation and handed it over to us; but a couple of years later diminishing returns at the home office took even that away from us, and our vow of poverty became complete.

The hospital, therefore, was self-supporting practically from the start. This self-support is not complete. The salary of the medical missionary comes from America. Various missionary societies help us out with boxes of medical and surgical supplies, which are worth their weight in gold. The hospital building was a gift from home, and irregular gifts from time to time have made possible a steady improvement in equipment, and also some outside work among the date gardeners and fishing villages.

But the running expenses of the hospital are met by fees collected from the patients. We do not charge everybody a little. We are socialists. When a rich man comes to the clinic, he has to pay for the four men who

Dr. and Mrs. Harrison, pictured at Northfield, Massachusetts, during a trip back to the United States.

The hospital at Muttreh, which is run on an annual budget of $1800 and where the patients sleep on the floor and live generally under the conditions that prevail in their homes. Dr. Harrison and the hospital staff frequently work on the veranda, where their figures and those of patients are faintly discernible in this picture.

preceded him, and for the five who follow him. It works out that fees from operations and outcalls carry almost the whole burden. It works out, too, that it is one thing to charge fees, and very much another thing to collect them. Our first assistant spends a large part of his time and energy collecting the hospital bills. The hospital is pitted against all the other shops of the city in this struggle for existence. We have service to sell. It is good service, and it is sold for a low price, but we have to sell it. Moreover we have to sell it against the competition of every purveyor of goods in the place, for the potential purchasers have very little money and getting our share of that little is a rough-and-tumble scramble. No one gains any impression in this hospital, that upon opening a magic spigot, a stream of gold sovereigns starts running.

This struggle to get the hospital fees collected costs lots of time and effort. At first we wasted considerable mental energy regretting this. We have learned better. The effect on the patients is good. They appreciate what the doctor does for them, if they pay for it. So does the community as a whole. This hospital, which is compelled to collect fees and be self-supporting is looked on with real affection as a local institution which is a credit to the city.

Self-support has had the best results of all on the hospital staff. Selling our services against the open competition of the market place is a very healthy thing. Several of the hospital staff are earnest Christians. This strenuous effort to collect fees and keep out of bankruptcy, has made them members of the community, standing on the same footing as all their neighbors.

Nothing has been more difficult than this matter of maintaining community relationships on the part of those who have become Christians. The hospital group has had no trouble. With much tribulation they enter into the Kingdom of Heaven, and with much hard work they stay there.

Hospital finance has been made much more difficult by the fact that the old prosperity is gone. America buys no more Oman dates, and Baluchistan buys no more rifles. The great war, with its tremendous stimulus to trade and commerce, was finished long since, and its effects deflated. The fall in prices has been ruinous. A package of dates which sold for four rupees twenty-five years ago, sells for three-quarters of one rupee now. The volume of exports has dropped and dropped, and for years the balance of trade has been against us. The total unfavorable balance of ten years runs between two and three million rupees. Where such a sum came from no one can say. Undoubtedly it was hidden away somewhere as accumulated capital.

Japanese goods have come in like a flood. They are cheap and, price considered, of very good quality. Since the world began no such colors have been available, and at such prices. The chief decorator of the Harrison home decided that the dining room would look well in orange curtains. Look well it certainly did, a real night-club effect. The gorgeous satiny curtains cost her about twenty-five cents a pair. The Queen of Sheba never dressed in such colors as the poor Baloochee women wear every day, scarlets, greens, oranges, and pinks, in such riotous confusion as the tame, conventional taste of the West knows nothing about.

But the cloth industry which reached considerable proportions once has been destroyed. They did not succeed in clothing either the men or the women a tenth as brilliantly as the Japanese mills have done; but with brilliant clothes has come greater poverty, for the dispossessed weavers have nothing to do and nowhere to go except to the date gardens, where starvation conditions prevail. Only a handful of weavers remain, and one of these explained to me recently in Birka, that their busy seasons were two, the spring and fall, when visitors come and go from Zanzibar. Many Oman Arabs live in Zanzibar, and they return occasionally to visit their old home. They still buy the locally woven cloth, but almost no one else does.

To make the burden still heavier new and higher taxes have been imposed. The government must have more money. A new school building is going up in Muscat, and there are plans for free government dispensaries. Roads must be built, and roads are expensive. Taxes are a new thing in Oman. Customs duties we have always had with us, and in the old days they brought a large revenue. Now the customs receipts sink lower and lower, and they are to be reinforced by taxes, in spite of the hopelessly low prices and growing poverty. "Sahib," said a dignified old Arab to me, "last year I paid ten rupees, tax. That has always been the figure. This year I was forced to pay sixty." And the result is that the garden owners move away to Zanzibar or India or somewhere else, where handicaps are fewer.

Making the hospital self-supporting, even in the partial sense that we mean here, is a very difficult task. Meerook, one of our Muttreh friends, has been working for ten to twelve cents a day for months, and though an unusually good workman he is employed not much more than half the time. We have never succeeded in getting our income above forty-five hundred rupees a year, which is about eighteen hundred dollars. Sometimes we look back covetously to the days in Bahrain when a fee of a thousand rupees occasionally came our way. That was really the price for a month's service on the part of the entire hospital staff, but it is a fine memory, anyway. The highest fee that we have ever received in Muttreh is about thirty-five dollars. Indeed it is months and years since we have gone above fifty rupees which is less than twenty.

Some patients come in who are too poor to pay anything. Recently a woman found her way in from Kuriat, fifty miles away. Her foot required amputation. She not only had nothing to pay, but the hospital had to feed her during her stay to prevent her perishing from simple starvation. Cases of that sort are not uncommon, but most of the patients pay a little. Their fees, however small they look to us, seem heavy to them. A month's wages amounts to only three dollars, or ten rupees, even when work is steady and a month's wages is a considerable fee.

Fees as small as these have implications that are many and serious. The average operation fee we will estimate above the truth at ten rupees. Very well, what can we give a man for ten rupees? Can we mend his hernia? We can. The operation requires five cents' worth of soap, fifteen cents' worth of spinal anesthetic, a nickel's worth of silk, ten cents' worth of kerosene to steam the dry goods and bake the instruments. We will allow twenty-five cents for the gauze which is used up. The hospital staff costs eight rupees a day, and our patient stays in fifteen days. He is one of twenty other in-patients, so the cost of his hospital care is six rupees. Thus we have spent on him eight rupees. Before he is through he will probably need a rupee's worth of medicine, quinine if nothing else. Even if his fee is only ten rupees which in a very rough way is a month's wages, we still have made a rupee on him.

We have made a rupee on him under certain circumstances. In the first place, if he feeds himself. In the second place, if his friends take care of him, if he brings his own bedding and cooking utensils, and lives there in his room, just as he did at home, expecting from us nothing beyond the mere operation, and the actual surgical care of the operative wound.

But what a disgraceful way to run a hospital! On the contrary it is the best way. America would do well to imitate us. The psychological atmosphere of the patient's everyday life comes with him into the hospital. We know nothing about hospital smells, nor do we expect the patient to spend his day alone, looking at cold white walls, and a square monotonous ceiling. Home does not look like that, though a morgue certainly does. The patient brings with him his usual home sights, and his usual home smells. These seem pretty bad to us sometimes, and occasionally something has to be corrected, but we do not lie awake nights trying to improve the patient's taste in this regard. The psychological environment that mother used to make is sedulously preserved, dirt and all. The result is that the patient feels natural and happy, and that means that he is not afraid, and that means that he gets well.

It is a mistake to call these institutions hospitals. The Presbyterian Hospital in New York or the Massachusetts General in Boston are very impressive affairs, educational institutions almost as much as institutions for treating the sick. The investigations which they carry on are the foundation of medical progress. With them in mind, who will say that Muttreh has a hospital? What we have is really a nursing home, as the English call it. It is a home where people who have been operated on are nursed back to health.

The nursing sister in charge of some home in London may rise in protest, but our nursing homes are of a different sort. There is no radio in every room, no bed either, for that matter, nor anything else, till the patient arrives. Then, as the Indian would say, "There is too plenty." In this room twelve by twelve feet, one corner is filled by a sack of charcoal or a bundle of firewood. Bedding in various stages of decrepitude is spread over the floor. Wives, at least one, and usually several babies enliven the landscape. Pots and pans, and above all a coffee pot are never lacking. Food materials are brought from the bazaar. Cooking is done on the spot.

These relatives, female and otherwise, do the nursing. They do it well. Not even in the Massachusetts General will you find such an atmosphere of cheerful optimism as in this primitive place, where the patient lies on the floor, taken care of by his wife, and other relatives, from his baby to his grandmother, sleep in the same room. Even the baby is sure that the patient will get well, so he does, and a good time is had by all.

The partitions separating the rooms do not reach to the ceiling. Ventilation is better that way. Also everybody can hear what everybody else says, and the talk fest of the early evening is tremendous. Frequently one of the patients has a gramophone, and if the community votes for it, the night is filled with music and the cares that infest the day steal away, though no one could claim that they do it silently. One of our recent patients was related to the leader of a local band of musicians, and during his convalescence we had music almost every night. We had to enact a ten o'clock curfew rule, so that the other patients could get some sleep.

Morning is a fine time, too. Every room makes coffee, and some of them tea. There is bread from the bazaar, and dates. Hospitality is exchanged back and forth, and the nurses and patients gather in little animated circles, for the exchange of all the gossip of the place, past, present, and future. If any one is so incredibly poor that he has no coffee, he is fed by his neighbors. Indeed this feeding of the poor and unfortunate by those who are better off, is a very frequent feature of hospital life. The hospital was built with this hospitable association of the patients in mind. That is the advantage of the long row of individual rooms, with a veranda in front. Inside the rooms the introverts can have as much privacy as they want, and on the veranda the extroverts can have as much publicity as they want. The vote goes to the extroverts, always.

But it is shocking to treat sick patients that way. The floor is hard and unsympathetic. How can people get well that way? The Muttreh patients do not think so. Only last night a sheikh from Baluchistan begged to be released from the punishment of a bed we had given him. He found its soft and tepid support very irritating. Might he please be allowed to lie on the floor. This enormous boon was granted at once. His bedding, with him in it, was hoisted by the four corners and deposited on the hard and satisfactory cement floor, where he has been happy ever since. We have beds, nearly a dozen of them, but they are largely unused.

The rooms have cement floors, and cement walls for a few feet up from the bottom. This darkens the room somewhat, and is not what we intended at first. White walls look cleaner, and are more cheerful. But the Arab has been taught by his mother that it is bad manners to spit on the floor. My mother taught me the same thing in Scribner. But the Arab uses his education badly. He must not spit on the floor where he might step in it, so he spits on the wall where he can look at it.

The Mission has a classical tradition on this point. It is not an Oman story but it might just as well have been. A patient was taken into the Bahrain hospital late one evening. Suffering from nothing more serious than a chronic cough, he was put into the corner of a large ward and left till morning for further investigation. That was a considerable error, for, as he demonstrated, a chronic cough can be a serious disease, serious at least in its effects on the hospital. This particular ward had just been redecorated and was very nice and white. That is to say it was nice and white till he was put there. His prowess as an expectorator was unusual, and by morning the decorative scheme of the room had been changed for ten feet in both directions. When the doctor in charge put his head into the door to wish his new patient a cheerful "Good morning," he hastily withdrew and walked clear around the block before trusting himself to discuss the elementary principles of hygiene with his new guest.

After their operations, the patients stay inside their rooms for a few days. Later they spend most of their time on the verandas. We have lots of veranda space, and a cement floor is a cool place to sleep. It is clean, too, or at least more or less so. So each patient can entertain as many of his friends as care to visit him, and they can stay as long as they wish. Most of our patients, I think, leave us hoping that they can come back for another stay in this interesting and hospitable place.

The hospital accommodation which our patients receive looks extremely primitive to us, but it does not look that way to them. They are very well satisfied indeed, and are not offended by being asked for a fee, but quite the reverse. Their self-respect is preserved. Each pays for what he gets, and gets what he pays for. There are three grades of hospital rooms, rated at five rupees, ten rupees, and twenty-five rupees. Veranda space is available for nothing, for those who desire it. These figures cover the patient's entire stay, however long it may be. The operation fee is separate, and is usually five to ten rupees.

In this way we have managed to import the straightforward attitudes of the market place into the hospital. The patient regards the doctor as the purveyor of a first-class article at a reasonable price. The shady and slippery outlook of the begging bowl fraternity is gone, and no one supposes that the doctor is a religious adept of a special sort, begging from some and giving to others, and capable of doing great magic when persuaded by a sufficient reward.

We feel, too, in this little primitive place, that we have at least come to grips with the most baffling problem of modern medicine, i.e. the problem of bringing scientific medicine within the reach of ordinary men. We wrestle with a giant considerably taller than any with which American doctors are acquainted, but the difference is not so great as might be supposed. In America hospital charges and medical fees have been allowed to run far ahead of the capacity of the people to pay, even if they do get five dollars a day, instead of ten cents. It is increasingly evident that some form of insurance must care for these charges. Out in Arabia I imagine that the final answer will be state medicine.

We realize in Muttreh better than most men at home do, that a medical discovery is incomplete until it has been brought within financial reach of the people who need it. A tract against dancing for a man whose two legs have been amputated is about as useful as neosalvarsan at two dollars a dose in Arabia at the present moment.

We have not brought the resources of modern medicine within the reach of men who earn ten cents a day, but we have made a start. Hernias, an occasional appendectomy, gastro-enterostomies, a rare cholecystectomy, urethrotomies, and prostatectomies, we can keep inside our ten-rupee fee. Orthopedic work we cannot. Unfortunately it has not been possible to get patients to stay long enough to attempt any orthopedics worth the name, irrespective of fees.

In medicine we are only getting started. Eighty grains of quinine for a case of malaria, as practice runs now, costs about ten cents. A single intravenous injection of five grains as the course starts seems to give us our best results. Salvarsan for syphilis is an unsolved problem, but by reducing its cost to the naked price of the drug, ten rupees will carry the patient quite a little way into his required course of treatment. Bismuth we use with the salvarsan, and plan to carry on such treatment for a long period, if and when we can get patients to persist in their treatment. It would be almost better if these remedies were less rapidly effective in clearing up the visible signs of the disease. It is almost impossible to carry treatment even to the point of a ten-rupee expenditure nowadays. Who is going to spend time and money in curing sores some more, when they have already been cured and are quite gone?

VI
THE STAFF

THE MEDICAL MISSIONARY comes out from America under the impression that he is the whole circus. Eventually some side shows are to be organized. He discovers on arrival that he is the side show. His main job is to develop a creditable circus.

A building must be provided. Even if the arriving doctor were as wise as he supposes, which he is not, he can do very little with his bare hands. The supporters of medical missionary work are a generous group. They have housed every one of our doctors in a small hospital. It takes a good deal of trouble to build a hospital. Somebody has to give a lot of money for the purpose, and somebody else has to give time and thought to its construction. In our mission the doctors never build their own hospitals. Their medical training seems to have atrophied their business and engineering capacity, if indeed they ever had any. The clergymen are more versatile. They teach our schools and they build our hospitals. The Muttreh hospital cost fifteen thousand dollars, and was two years in building. The clergyman who put it up mixed brains with cement and the combination proved a great success.

But the institution which goes by the name of the Knox Memorial Hospital is not a building. It is a group of men. Its most important member is a woman, an angel rather, temporarily sent down here to put a little sweetness and light into one of the world's darkest corners. Every member of the group sits at her feet in complete devotion, and tries to put into his work some of the spirit which she puts into him.

Barring the missionary element it is a local staff. Except for the head compounder, who can manage a little English, its members cannot read nor write. They wear long Muscat gowns and embroidered Muscat caps and they talk Muscat talk, which means that Persian and Baloochee, Arabic and Hindustani, are all readily at hand in wholesale quantities. Limited retail deliveries of other tongues are available on demand. All the local diseases and depravities are well understood. Like the Oxford Group we share with our patients.

For this remarkable group we thank a man long since dead. Years ago he married a wife in Baloochistan, and while they had African blood in them, and Persian as well, to all intents and purposes they were Baloochees. They had three little boys and were waiting for a fourth. Great Britain and Persia between them have tamed Baloochistan very considerably during the past twenty-five years, but in those days Baloochee savagery had almost no limits. A neighboring tribe raided the district where El Mas lived and carried off his biggest baby to be sold as a slave. The boy has never been seen since and unless death has released him, he is a slave now. Stealing men of one's own kind and selling them as slaves is a thing unheard of among the Arabs.

The father was a resolute man, and with his wife and remaining children he made his way to Dubai, then as now the southern center of the pearl diving world, and, because of the thousands of slaves held there, a center of cruelty and oppression. The ruling sheikh was hopelessly weak and every man did what was right in his own eyes. That is to say, the owners and captains of the diving ships did. The working divers did as they were told. But business was good and there was a great demand for divers, so the new arrival was promptly taken on to one of the diving boats. His legs were rather small and short, but above the waist he was enormously strong, and as a rope-pulling assistant he fitted immediately into the routine of the boat.

In that city of hard and wicked men, the hardest and wickedest was the captain of this particular boat. A man of tremendous size and strength and a pitiless bully, he had worked his way up by virtue of naked strength and was reckoned as one of the leading citizens of the place. After a few days one of the divers failed to perform some routine duty in a satisfactory manner. He was killed in cold blood before all the men and his body thrown overboard for the sharks to eat. A thrill of horror went through the crew, but not a word of protest was spoken. After all, in the East as in the West the captain of a ship at sea is a czar.

A few days later, one of the men woke in the morning prostrate with malaria. Burning with fever, he lay helpless on the deck, as the men prepared for the day's work. "What is the matter with you?" It was the captain speaking. "Get up and go to work." "Captain, your pardon. This terrible fever. I can work by noon, I think." But the captain was in a red fury and cursed the sick man for a lazy dog. A large basket lay near by. It had had dates in it. Into this empty basket the captain jammed the unfortunate diver and crowded the cover down into place. The whole he threw overboard to the sharks. Again a thrill of horror shivered through the company, but no word passed between them and the work of the day went forward without comment or remark.

A pearl boat is entirely decked over. A small hatch leads down to the hold where supplies are kept. That night in the inky darkness men softly talked. "What are we to do?" "No one is safe on this ship." "Any one of us may be the next." "Yes, but after all, he is the captain." El Mas, the new recruit from Baloochistan, was a man of few words, but it was his corner of the blackness that spoke next. "On me is the holding of him firm and tight. On you the tying of him with ropes. In the morning when he washes for prayers." So the next morning when the captain washed his hands for prayers, for he was a pious Mohammedan, he was suddenly embraced from behind in a grip that ten men could scarcely have broken. Men with ropes were upon him on the instant. They tied him to the big mast, and the ropes sank into his hard body half out of sight.

The mutineers were in charge now and they turned the ship toward Bandar Abbas. Four days it took to reach port, and no drop of water was given to the unhappy captain, tied in the sun all day long. But it takes a good deal to kill a man of that sort; and, when port was reached, the crew scattered and he was released, still living and fiercely planning revenge for his maltreatment.

I asked Mohammed, who was telling us the story, why the unspeakable captain was not killed outright. "Well," said Mohammed, "they certainly wanted him to die, and four days in the sun like that with no water would kill most people. But no one wanted to have the death on his own individual head. That would make him a murderer, and murder is wrong." This kind of truncated ethics is almost universal in the Orient. Walook, our sweeper, recoils in horror from the crime of drowning superfluous kittens. Condemning them to slow starvation is a commendable act.

Bandar Abbas is a city of Persia and El Mas would have been safe there, but his wife and babies were still in Dubai. He found a boat which was bound for that place and went to get them. On arrival he found the furious captain already there, and the authorities looking for him. There was barely time to see his wife and babies, all alive and well and to speak the necessary word to his friends, before he was arrested and marched off to prison. He knew that he would not be instantly killed, for a public execution the following morning, would serve the ends of justice better, that is, the ends of Dubai justice. Dubai knows only one unpardonable sin—and that is mutiny on the high seas.

The prison where he was to be confined, El Mas knew very well. It stood next to the sea. His prison room was on the second story. "On me," he had said to his friends in the scant minutes before he was arrested, "is getting up into the window when the tide is high at midnight, and jumping into the sea with all my irons on me. On you the fishing of me out of the deep water promptly, for the irons will be heavy."

And so that night as midnight approached, a boat floated to rest under the high window, and, when there was a dull splash, as of a heavy object falling from a considerable height, four men slipped silently over its sides, with ropes between their teeth. The ropes they tied to heavy weights which they found down there, and El Mas was hauled to the surface. Then they rowed furiously till they had put him on board a sailing boat, one of the fastest in the entire city; and, because the wind was favorable, it was only two days until El Mas and all his family were safe in Bahrain. Bahrain is also a city of divers, but the British flag floats over it and, although there has been plenty of oppression and injustice there, too, conditions have never approached those prevailing in Dubai.

El Mas lived in Bahrain for many years. He was a leading spirit among the divers and one of that community's most respected citizens. A perforated duodenal ulcer caused his death. He did not know much about hospitals and when the doctor urged operation he refused to have anything to do with such an idea. Twenty-four hours later, he did consent, but it was too late. The three little boys whom he brought to Bahrain have remained an indivisible unit ever since. Their wives quarrel often enough, but the boys themselves, never. Nothing has ever split them apart. Kumbar, the youngest, is still a happy and irrepressible boy. Mohammed, the oldest of the three, has been the clan leader ever since their father's death.

Mobarrek, the second in point of age, comes first on

the hospital staff. He was known to Bahrain as a naughty small boy who led his comrades in various escapades. Bahrain has a number of delightful date gardens, and, when the fresh dates are in season, the rich and the great spend their evenings in the gardens enjoying the shade and eating the dates. The poor and the ragged spend parts of some afternoons there, too, that is if they are young and daring, and can run fast enough when discovered. It is well for the gardener to have reinforcements available before he decides to drive such trespassers off, for the youngsters coalesce readily into a belligerent and reckless group, each with a first-class stone in his hand; and one man can hardly handle such a group, even if all the laws regarding property are in his favor.

Adventures of this sort were abandoned in due time, and the impish youngster explored other avenues of excitement. His father was very much of a puritan and tobacco was strictly forbidden. That, of course, made the prospect more fascinating, and one of the relics of his past, which Mobarrek has never succeeded in shaking off, is a devotion to the water pipe, by means of which the Oriental wafts himself to Paradise. Opium, fortunately, he never learned to use, in spite of the fact that its use is very common throughout the Persian Gulf.

At an early age the Mission school gathered into its fold this attractive exponent of juvenile self-expression. No end of cerebral elbow grease was expended on him. Doubtless he gained real benefit, for ever since his loyalty to the missionaries has been quite limitless, but his letters he has never learned, to say nothing of the whole art of reading. It is difficult for a lively little Baloochee boy to keep his mind on the meaningless characters in a book, when the whole fascinating world beckons to him through the window.

From school he graduated to the profession of house boy. There he learned more, though perhaps never enough to give the Mem Sahib much rest or confidence as to what surprising scrapes he might get into next. Mortality among the dishes was high when he washed them, but dishes in the Orient do not compete with Methuselah in any case, and on the whole he was a good boy, with lots of energy and real courtesy and respect, especially toward the Mission ladies. One summer he was taken to Kashmir in India, and there he saw ice and wrapped himself in a heavy woolen coat for the first time in his life.

Kashmir was a strange place full of remarkable things like mountains and ice glaciers and caverns that were deep and mysterious. Effreets and other creatures of a dark imagination live in such strange places. One morning, bringing two eggs from the kitchen tent and leaving them on the breakfast table, he went back for the bread, only to find on his return that one of the eggs was gone. He went back and brought another egg, and then the bread was gone. No marauder would be about at that hour, and he speculated on effreets and jinn. What he feared most of all was that his Sahib, whose good opinion he greatly prized, would conclude that he had eaten the missing articles. The evidence seemed very conclusive.

But the Sahib had traveled before. "No," he said, "there he is"; and he pointed to a crow watching with insolent nonchalance from a safe distance. "Keep the door at the far end of the tent shut when you are setting the table and you will have no trouble." The crow is too wise a bandit to come into a tent and steal unless he can see a way out at the other end. He is a believer in straight line production.

From being house boy Mobarrek came into the hospital. There he was a great success. He is one of those fortunate individuals who are born with fingers that can do delicate things. Salvarsan brought in the era of intravenous medication. This really fine bit of technique Mobarrek picked up without a slip, and up to date he has had no sore arms to repent of. Therein he differs from some of his colleagues. Ali Kumbar of Bahrain is another real genius of surgical delicacy, but he could not quite believe his Sahib when warned that carelessness with salvarsan is repented of in sack cloth and ashes. Some people will learn only from experience, and it was not long before Ali did a good deal of repenting. It was a large and extremely talkative Bedouin whose arm swelled up to twice its size, and who had no sleep for several nights. When salvarsan is injected into the tissues about a vein, it hurts. Fomentations several times a day were required, and aspirin at night. For a month Ali was unable to get his self-esteem up to anything like a normal level, with this protesting Bedouin dogging his footsteps all day long.

Because of his desire to do his job well, Mobarrek learned enough English to be a first-class compounder. He takes the blood specimens from our malaria patients and stains them. He does most of our minor surgery. He adjusts the fees and collects them. What makes him unique is that in all this he is just as much a member of the local community as before. Of all the assistants we have trained, it is he who suffers from no thirst to be like the sahibs. As a result he occupies a place of great influence among the younger element of the city. He is one of the best hockey players in Muscat. Because he is an open and earnest Christian, he is unwilling to play on Sunday, but even that did not disturb his position among them, nor jeopardize his membership in the leading hockey club of the place. He has organized a tennis club and developed a surprising skill among the members. Altogether we would scarcely know how to run the hospital without him.

Mohammed is the chief of the department of mechanical transport, and of all the engines in the hospital as well. On him is the responsibility for the water supply of the entire institution, which is not an easy assignment in this dry country. But Mohammed did not begin life as an engineer. He began it as the son of a pearl diver, and, as might be expected, it was not long until he was a pearl diver himself. Pearl diving is not an attractive occupation. Five months of extreme overwork in the summer are followed by seven months of enforced idleness in the winter. In those days, however, the rewards for the work were good. The competition of cultured pearls from Japan had not yet ruined the market, and three to five hundred rupees was not uncommon as the result of a season's work. On that, a very comfortable life of loafing was possible for the rest of the year.

The oldest baby having been stolen, Mohammed as next in line grew up to be his father's right-hand man in everything. He did not steal dates from the gardens. He helped spank the young ones who did. As he grew older, he accompanied his father on some of his diving trips, making himself useful to the cook and helping to serve coffee.

When he was old enough to be accepted by the captain, he enlisted as a rope puller. Every diver has such an assistant, so that he can get back to the surface quickly after his dive is over. He can stay under water only a little more than two minutes, and it is important to spend as small a part as possible of this tiny bit of his time going down and coming up; when the water is from 50 to 70 feet deep, this matter is very important indeed. So the diver is carried down rapidly by a heavy stone, and, when he feels his breath getting short, he jerks the rope as a signal and his assistant pulls him up with great speed. When the proceeds of the season are divided, the rope-pulling assistant gets only two-thirds of a diver's share.

But Mohammed's career as a pearl diver did not last long. When his first season was about half over, the Gulf was swept by a tremendous hurricane. Nothing like that fearful night had been seen in the Persian Gulf for fifty years. It struck with no warning when the men were sound asleep. Of the thirty men on board Mohammed's boat only one slept with him on the deck that night, for the sky looked threatening and all the others went below. After their exhausting day, divers sleep the sleep of the dead, almost. That night the twenty-eight men down below did indeed sleep the sleep of the dead.

Scores of the diving boats were anchored together

in the lee of a convenient reef. At about nine or ten o'clock the storm came. Boats with free space around them were turned over in a matter of seconds. Those closer to one another were driven crashing together to utter destruction. Mohammed's boat went over. Every man below decks was drowned like a trapped rat. Mohammed woke to find himself floundering in the water in a black pandemonium of crashing timbers and drowning men, with the gale howling through the wreckage like a demon, and the waves being whipped up into small mountains. A broken spar floated near him and he seized it. He was its fourth passenger as it was blown free from the wild confusion out into the empty waste of stormy waters.

They floated through the dark night, but the storm had long since blown itself out, and it was a peaceful ocean world that they saw, when morning came. Only two of the spar's passengers were left. A round slippery piece of wood is not easy to hold on to hour after hour. As the day wore on his companion looked him in the face, said Good-by and slipped off and down into "the mercy of God" as the Arabs say.

And on the shores in Bahrain that morning, in the pale dawn, wild-eyed, choking women watched sail boats and launches push off from the shore on their hunt for such survivors as might still be floating or clinging to broken ships still unsubmerged. They searched everywhere. The sea was a sheet of glass, and an object could be seen a long distance. Dozens and scores of divers were picked up, for pearl divers are not easy men to drown, and they knew that rescue parties would be on their way to the diving reefs long before the sun was up.

But the ocean is a big place, and the storm had driven some of the wreckage long distances. Mohammed saw the day wear away to noon, and then hour after hour almost to sundown, and the horizon contained nothing that offered any hope of rescue. He knew that once the sun went down his last hope went down with it, for through a second night he could not possibly last, and in the darkness all search by the rescuers would be useless. But as long as there was light, there was hope, so he determined not to surrender and slip till the world became dark. When that time came and it was not an hour away now, he knew that he would exchange the darkness of the world above for the deeper darkness of the world below.

And then, as he mustered the little strength that remained and kept his arms wrapped round that slippery mast, there was a voice from behind: "I am afraid that one's dead." "Dead men slip off," replied a companion in the launch; so one of them swam over to the derelict and shook him. "Are you alive?" There was no strength to reply, not even enough to move his head, but Mohammed found himself able to open and shut his eyes as his rescuer looked at him. The man shouted in delight, "Come over and haul him in, he is alive, he can wink."

So they hauled Mohammed in and deposited him gently on deck next to a fire and gave him some hot tea, and very soon as he said afterward, "I was a son of Adam again."

"No," said Mohammed, after we had persuaded him to tell us about it, "pearl diving is not a very good way to earn a living. A good season used to afford a fair sum of money, but I never went back after that experience. There are other ways of finding your daily bread besides diving for pearls."

But the other ways were precarious and uncertain, and ten years ago Mohammed was glad to come onto the hospital staff. He began as a sweeper like all of his successors, but he was soon promoted. He is the hospital philosopher. A snake to him is not a venomous reptile, but a beautiful streamline mechanism, which he studies with interest and admiration. The sahibs from the West with their bright red tempers Mohammed finds extremely interesting phenomena. Such tempers develop well in the bright red climate of Muscat, and material for study is abundant. Mohammed is a very competent automobile mechanic, and there is a doctorate in philosophy under every motorcar hood, if only the philosopher's mind is there to find it.

Mohammed has also taken a postgraduate course in psychology by marrying two wives. The comfortable illusion so popular in some quarters, that such a harem is a harmonious love nest, Mohammed entertained before he tried it. At least he says he did. Since that day his most vivid dreams have been unable to reach any such dizzy imaginative height. But No. 1 he really loves, and No. 2 has produced for him a fine son, his only child. So Mohammed, as a gentleman, has loyally kept them both. He has come to feel that women have lots of human nature in them. Men, he is sure, cannot get along without women and women cannot live without quarreling.

Kumbar is the youngest of the trio; the youngest,

the most irresponsible, and the most popular. His period of free play was shorter than that of Mobarrek, but he lost very little, even from a small boy's standpoint, for, as general errand boy with one master after another, he found life a variegated and gorgeous affair. His first job was with the interpreter for the British consul. This interpreter filled an impressive place in the life of Bahrain. His fine team of horses were Kumbar's special care, and he could mount and dismount at full speed, like a circus acrobat. This interpreter exercised his wickedness, and there was plenty of it, on the public. His servants thought everything of him. However, his depredations on the public were unusual even for the Orient, and he was hastily excused from further connection with His Britannic Majesty's representative, and was also ordered to leave the town hastily, i.e. the following morning, and never came back. Forty thousand rupees were left for some time in the care of the small errand boy, who carried the responsibility very well indeed. The retreating munshi was anxious to take his loyal little servant with him to Baghdad, but Kumbar's father said "No."

So he took service with the ruling sheikh of Bahrain, and made himself extremely popular there. But this sheikh, too, was gently but firmly helped into retirement, for extremely adequate reasons, and his son ruled in his stead. So Kumbar's job disappeared again. He had been such a favorite that his salary was continued for some months, and he found a place eventually with one of the lesser sheikhs. Here his popularity was very nearly his undoing, for he and his companions got into a very nasty scrape with a milk girl. Kumbar spent some months in jail as a result of this misadventure. By this time his brothers were working in the hospital, and they asked if we could make a place for him. They were careful to explain their brother's immaculate innocence, but it was evident that they wanted him where they could supervise his self-expression. So the staff was expanded, and Kumbar's medical career began.

He too began as a sweeper. Keeping the hospital clean is a hopeless task at the best, but the sweeper does the best he can, and no matter what the offense, like a customer in a chain store, the patient is always right. Kumbar had no difficulty about that. He and the world have always been good friends, and they are still. He gets into more fights than all the rest of the staff put together, but that seems to be part of the popular man's equipment everywhere. On our long medical tours he is incomparable. I doubt if the sentiment of fear has ever darkened his soul, and no matter how belligerent a Bedouin may be, he is always Kumbar's friend. But the sea is a different thing, and when the waves become visible to the naked eye Kumbar crumples into a helpless heap. He has prepared for death many times on these trips. Mohammed, who worked as a pearl diver, looks on this feeble surrender as astonishing.

Kumbar is an outdoor man. From Monday to Thursday he travels on a donkey from date garden to date garden to pull aching teeth and distribute quinine to those who shake with fever. He pulled fifty teeth on one of these trips, and those asking for quinine run into hundreds. Ulcers he washes clean, and shows the owners how to keep them clean. Hernias and hemorrhoids, abdominal tumors and fractures, he reports to headquarters, and arranges for them to come in for operative treatment.

We worked for some time with this staff of three men, but the work increased and we needed an addition. The boys produced Noobie as a candidate. Noobie was taken into this family group almost as a brother, partly because, like their own elder brother, nearly his whole life had been spent as a slave.

Noobie is proof for those who need it that the human spirit has a strength which cannot be broken, and a beauty which cannot be effaced. He was stolen as a baby in Baloochistan, and sold to Arab Bedouins in Oman. His earliest memory is that of rebellion against strange masters, and through the years his spirit never acquiesced. This is a common reaction when Baloochees are carried away into slavery. The African settles into such a life with less protest. He was forty years old before any opportunity to escape presented itself, or rather it was forty years before Noobie succeeded in getting away. He "ate many blows," as the Arabs say, and wore many manacles. He had various matrimonial experiences too, but even that did not quiet or tame his spirit.

But one day while he was suffering for his sins and wearing the usual heavy jewelry with which unsuccessful efforts to escape are rewarded, a stray camel passed close by at dusk. Noobie called the camel, and it came over to where he was. Mounting, irons and all, he raced it savagely through the night for fifty miles and left it dying behind him at early dawn, while he painfully hobbled, shackles and all, to Muttreh eight miles away. It was a long, tedious struggle, but Providence was with him. No Arab keen to keep the slaves where they belong met him, and finally he arrived at the Delectable City. Around such a fugitive, the poor of Muttreh will rally instantly. A friendly blacksmith removed his ankle bracelets, with the big ball and chain attached. He went over to Muscat, and the British consul gave him his freedom.

Slavery is a dreadful thing, and one would hardly suppose that out of it could come anything except a brutalized spirit and a ruined personality. But the nobility of the human spirit is unconquerable, and Noobie brought out of this academy of suffering a sweetness of spirit and a sympathy for those in trouble which are unique.

He began as a sweeper and at that work he was excellent, but when Kumbar was lent to another doctor for a long tour, we put Noobie in charge of the ulcer room. The effect was astonishing. We did not know that Muttreh had in it such an appalling number of ulcers. Seventy-five will come most mornings—on occasion a hundred. From his hard slave days he had learned patience and gentleness. He is the friend of every ulcer in the city. Some of them are dreadful affairs, with odors that are clinging and persistent, and visitors with an unvulcanized esthetic sense retreat hastily into the outside air.

Noobie is a polygamist. At least he used to be, tandem polygamy that is, for a slave would hardly be allowed two wives at once. He is almost so still, even if he is one of the deepest and most sincere Christians that we have. But every now and again a visitor turns up to visit Noobie in his glory as a free man. He has a wife who dates from his free days, and a very good wife she is too, and the two think the world of each other. But these visitors, women from the dark twilight land of slavery where Noobie used to live, greet him with deep and undisguised affection, for he was their husband once. He certainly is a good husband now. No doubt he was then, too.

Walook is the most recent addition to the Muttreh staff. He worked many years as a boatman, one of the city's best. In the old days no road connected Muscat and Muttreh, nor did the ancient, free, and accepted Fords of the Persian Gulf offer in Muttreh their last full measure of devotion before ending on the scrap pile. In those days a notable fraternity of boatmen carried passengers in canoe-shaped row boats from Muttreh to Muscat, and from both cities to steamers in the harbor. These little boats manned by three oarsmen, and carrying up to half a dozen passengers, traveled on occasion for twenty-five and fifty miles along the coast.

Walook had a great reputation among these intrepid amphibians. He was one of the few who sometimes carried passengers all the way to Sur, which is a hundred miles away. Day and night they would row, and, hoisting a tiny sail to take advantage of any favorable breeze, they would land their passengers long before a sail boat could arrive. But when an unexpected storm came up the story was very different, and once or twice hostile Bedouins on shore very nearly ended the earthly career of this daring sailor and his passengers with him.

The Muscat harbor is a funnel-shaped affair between high cliffs, and the large end of the funnel faces out so that the *shumal* wind is gathered into it in a very terrifying way. The captains of the British India steamers fear this harbor exceedingly. On a bad day they have to haul up passengers in big baskets with the winch, just like other cargo. Ten years ago we embarked on the steamer in a heavy storm and that was an experience not easily forgotten. The little boats point their noses almost straight up in the air when a huge wave strikes them. On the far side, they seem to be pointed vertically downward. There is a certain fine idealism in being pointed at the stars, but aiming straight at the ocean's bottom is a coldly realistic thing, which sends a shiver up even a hard-boiled back.

A few years ago an enormous Indian banker, embarking in such a storm, actually tipped Walook's boat over backward with his weight when its nose was pointed at the North Star. He could not swim a stroke and the boatmen had their hands full. However, they eventually rescued him. It takes a good deal to defeat three Muttreh boatmen.

Later a road was cut through the mountains, and the motor taxis came; so the boatmen have almost disappeared. Walook looked here, there and everywhere for something to do, and, when we promoted Noobie to be Curator of Ulcers for the province of Oman, Walook came on as sweeper. For pure anxiety to do all that he can for the institution, and complete indifference to the clock, personal comfort, and such trifles as fever, headache, and hunger, we have never seen his equal. It is a new job for him, and he can find more ways of making a mistake than anyone in my long experience. But Walook is a jewel, and already we would be lost without him. He is more than capable of following up each patient in the hospital, and keeping the place clean, no matter what they do. Lately, however, thousands of crows have settled in our vicinity, and the hospital roof is a favorite place for them to congregate. The sanitary habits of crows are extremely imperfect, and so far Walook has been rather defeated by them. But we are meditating dark meditations on the subject of crows, and one of these days the mortality among them is going to be high.

◇◇

VII

FAMILY HEALTH

THE HOME IS the foundation of society, but in Mohammedan countries that foundation has not been well and truly laid. To be reckoned a real family physician is the greatest compliment that can be paid to a doctor anywhere, and where the family is broken by divorce and polygamy, the need for the family physician is greater than ever.

Instincts are powerfully developed in Oman, the acquisitive instinct along with the others. A bright little girl of eleven was a great favorite with us all. Her mother too seemed unusually intelligent and advanced. Even the Baloochee community was shocked at the news that this mother had accepted a sum of five hundred rupees from one of the leading young merchants of the place, and that this little girl was to become his second wife. He already had several children by his first, and she was much opposed to the new match.

The indignation shown by the community over this event was the only encouraging feature of it. The mother had to listen to a good many hard words from her critical neighbors, and I imagine that the young man was criticized by his friends, too. At least he was criticized by the friends of his first wife. However, it did no good; the marriage took place according to schedule, and it was only a year till the tiny wife had a baby. She aged rapidly and was drawn and withered before ever she reached the age of twenty.

Interest in sex is open and frank, and thus are avoided many of the psychological twists which come from our excessive concealment of everything connected with it. But Arabia is a man's world, and he has turned over to the women the whole burden of keeping family life at least clean enough so that society will not fall to pieces. I asked a youngster in inland Oman how many of his companions were waiting till marriage for their first sex experience. He looked at me with much surprise. "Why, none of them, of course."

Their sisters wait. The first misstep means death, and only too often the merest suspicion brings down the last final penalty on the head of a completely innocent girl. Three years ago, I had the Kuwait hospital in charge for the summer. On a day of those days a girl was brought into the hospital an hour and a half before she died. Eighteen hours earlier her brother had been informed that she was in a neighbor's house. He concluded that this meant adultery at least in the near future, and so he sent for her, seized her, cut her throat from ear to ear, and stabbed her fearfully with his large curved knife. Her chest was opened for inches on each side. The knife missed the carotids and jugulars, but the trachea was cut clean across. The girl lived through the following night, and in the morning an older woman, her mother perhaps, brought her in.

She was entirely conscious, but of course unable to

talk. Lying still she was in no respiratory distress, but she saw death before her, and her dark eyes full of fear followed me about the room with a last flickering hope in them, that was terrible. Through the great hole in either side of her chest, her heart could be watched as it beat steadily along. The lungs were collapsed against the posterior wall of the chest. It seemed incredible that she could live at all, but lying quietly her respiratory needs were minimal, and she showed no dyspnea. The diaphragm moved up and down, doubtless at a somewhat accelerated rate, but in the preoccupation of the moment, it was not counted. Mud of some medicinal sort had been plastered over the edges of the chest wounds to stop the bleeding, and was scattered thickly over the lungs and diaphragm. She died in about an hour and a half, eighteen to twenty hours from the time that the wounds were inflicted.

I was much shaken by the experience, but the next day I was quite unable to discover among the immaculate males of that city of self-righteous hypocrisy anyone who disapproved of this vindication of female chastity. My somewhat heated suggestion that the brother pick on someone his own size, and kill the man first next time was looked on as a dangerous lapse from sanity, like preaching bolshevism at a formal dinner on Park Avenue.

This principle of a double standard is carried to dreadful lengths all over Arabia. Every doctor is occasionally approached by some mother in distress, asking that her girl's life be saved by the performance of an abortion. In life's last extremity, women stand together. A Bedouin mother looked me straight in the eye. "Sahib," she said, "it was not her fault. She did not consent. But she is only a little girl, and he is a full-grown man." There was a pause then. "Her brother will kill her." But I told her, "No, abortions are a forbidden way of escape. It would be murder." I can see her yet, that magnificent Bedouin mother, as she dropped her veil back over her face, and led the doomed girl away. We do not forget mistakes of that sort.

For I do not expect to say no to the next child whose mother looks me in the eye, and begs me to rescue her. We sacrifice the baby for the mother without hesitation when the tubercle bacillus is the lethal agent. Why should we hesitate when the murderer is to be her own brother? "Is it lawful (in the hospital) to do good or to do evil, to save a life or to kill?"

A wonderful Indian nurse lived in Bahrain for many years. She worked for a time in the Mission hospital, but she was born a Brahmin; when she was born again to be an outstanding Christian, she brought some of her Brahminism along, and taking orders from unsympathetic sahibs was irksome to her free spirit. So she set up an independent medical unit of her own. Cases that were beyond her, she sent to the hospital, but no end of obstetrical work she handled herself. In fearless courage she was equaled by few men, and her standing offer was known through the whole community. A girl in trouble could come to her and tongues would not wag. She could leave her baby behind, and go back to face the world as she was before.

Sundri rescued a good many girls that way. Certainly it is much better than abortion, when the girl can get away to such a home and keep her brothers ignorant of what has happened. Unfortunately that is usually impossible.

But women are born to a hard life even if no dreadful catastrophes such as these overtake them. Their fathers first, and their brothers and husbands afterward, they must serve and obey absolutely. They bear the babies and care for the children. They carry the water and fuel, and cook the food. They eat the food too, but only after the men are through. All the heaviest burdens of poverty are theirs.

The greatest heroism of the world is unrecognized and unsung. It is in the family circle that it is found. I am sure that this world has in it few things so heroic as the overflowing joy that the family physician sees every day in Oman, as the women carry on the race. One would suppose that women in Muttreh would be anything but happy. The world starves them with a poverty that is bitter and crushing. Their husbands beat them when they are angry, and divorce them when fascinated by a new pretty face. In that land of poverty the husband gets little enough, but his wife gets less. Babies are fat and pretty for their first two years. Their mothers are gaunt and old before they are thirty.

Nevertheless weddings are contagiously and effervescently happy affairs. Our neighbors just to the rear are utterly poor. One night there was a wedding. It was hot and sweaty, one of Muscat's worst. Up to midnight and beyond, I heard the women as they brought the bride to her bridegroom. It takes several hours to do this in correct Arabian style, so the little procession passed slowly up and down the different streets, in an irregular journey to the house. The women were singing out to the world their childlike exhilaration over the happy event. I lay sweating through the hot night, trying to sleep but waking repeatedly to hear this group of women singing songs of pure joy as they took the bride to her new home. I knew just how poor these people were, and I marveled that the women could find anything to be happy over. The modest little girl of perhaps thirteen or fourteen looked out on a road that might well have made the most stoical weep in fear and apprehension: hunger always, beatings whenever her husband was angry, babies as often as nature could be forced into producing them, fever and dirt and heat. Who could sing on such a night?

But they did sing. One of the women was a superb soprano. She led the rest and the music came through the hot air of that dreadful night sparkling and fragrant like a breath from Heaven. I lay wondering at the utter heroism of women who refuse to surrender the loveliness of life, and their happiness over it, even when that incomparable jewel from God is buried in fifty feet of mud. And the voices sang of the happiness and love and joy which God has put into the world, and they rejoiced with the spontaneity of children over it all.

I went to sleep a number of times and woke up again to listen to the music. Some time past midnight I woke to realize that something had happened. The group was closer now, indeed almost under our window. There was a new note in the singing. They were no longer scattered happy children, but a compact choir still led by their soprano. Pure joy and happiness was now set to the most attractive music of the evening, but there was a militant note in it, as if those singing were consciously holding up by their resolute happiness some comrade who needed support. The verve and spirit and contagion of their joy gave me a thrill as I listened, and I added my own prayer to theirs for whatever comrade it was who needed help.

A thunderous musket discharge gave the explanation. In Muttreh, when the bride has been delivered into the arms of her husband, the party of friends which has brought her, remains outside and waits till a cloth with a trifling blood stain is brought for inspection. A musket is fired to announce that the marriage has been consummated, and the girl's untouched virtue vindicated.

It is a rough and painful initiation into the world's great sisterhood of mothers, which a girl of thirteen has to go through on her wedding night, for the husbands are older than that, and gentleness is not what custom demands. It is a hard initiation into a harder life that is to follow, and there are few things in this world so superb as the devotion of such women to the beauty and loveliness of life, a resolute devotion which refuses to be blinded to the essential fragrance of life's high experiences, even when cruelty and sin are mixed with them.

And for the gallery where the world hangs its pictures of really grand and significant heroisms, Oman will present this one. A hot breathless night, and a group of mothers whose faces are lined with poverty, and premature age, and hunger and sickness and trouble; those women sending the joy and happiness of their souls through the cracks of a semi-transparent date-stick hut, to hold up with their courage and faith and joy the hard-pressed little bride, so that she might not lose the beauty and the joy of the experience, in the pain and hardship of it. And if God is a God of beauty as He is a God of Righteousness, He is not going to forget those who show devotion like that to the beauty He has put into men's souls.

Women have to carry the burdens when a new home is set up. They carry them afterward too. The best of such families seem never free from the menace of divorce. On our trips to Seeb and Birka we used to visit a most attractive member of the customs staff. His home was an oasis in the surrounding desert of poverty, ignorance, and dirt. We were entertained there a number of times, for he was a real friend.

Abdur Rahman had two wives, and the harmony and evident regard between them seemed to contradict all that we of the West are accustomed to assert regarding the disadvantages of polygamy. One of the wives had a baby girl, and she was just as pretty and sweet as such little girls can be.

But some whim struck Abdur Rahman and he decided on a new matrimonial deal. He divorced both of his wives and sent them off, and now he has two new ones. His two divorced wives are still young and extremely attractive. They will probably both find new husbands without great difficulty. But homes such as we know, homes that the whole structure of our civilization is built on, are not possible in Arabia. No matter how attractive a wife may be, no matter how faithful she has proved, no matter how many fine sons she has given to her husband, the menace of divorce hangs over her always.

Sometimes there is a very beautiful spirit of love and regard between two partner wives, in spite of it all. In Sifala, a pathetic case of extreme trichiasis came in for operation carefully led and encouraged by a second woman who was her partner wife. Such a spirit is far from universal, but it is not rare. Every missionary in Oman can tell of a number of instances. The burdens of even a polygamous family, the women carry far better than the men. It is the never-absent possibility of divorce which is the more serious thing.

In contrast it is a pleasure to tell of the beautiful things a family physician sees. A Bedouin family came in for operation while we were on a tour to Birka. Among the Bedouins as among no other class in Arabia, family life sometimes attains to the beauty and stability that we know in the West. Without question it is the extreme poverty of this class which creates a general attitude that makes such a development possible. Polygamy is impossible when people are so poor as that. But family life of the sort that I saw in Birka is the loveliest thing in the world, no matter what its foundation. There were no children in the family, to the great disappointment of all. An ovarian cyst the size of a child's head was the trouble, and it was one of those which have the habit of twisting on its pedicle, and causing frequent and severe pain. It was an easy condition to relieve, and I hope that they had lots of children afterward, though of course there was no assurance that they would. But the case remains a gem in my memory for nowhere East or West have I seen anything more lovely than the affection and loyalty between that Bedouin and his wife. Even in the days of the operation and the convalescence after it, when weariness and impatience are almost inevitable, I heard not the smallest word between them which carried anything in the way of emotional freight, except pure devotion and regard. It saves the doctor's soul to meet such a family occasionally. He is convinced over again, and he needs it, of the possibilities of family life in Arabia, once the men and women have a fair chance.

Matrimony in the mixed ocean of Muttreh society is a troubled sea at the best. Even our tiny Christian community is beginning to realize its complexities. Sheero is a very good Christian, the Sunny Jim of the congregation. He lacked a wife, which seemed to him a serious deficiency. We all agreed to that, but no way of mending the situation was in sight. But Sheero has been accustomed to do what seems right in his own eyes, all through his past twenty-five years. What Baloochee indeed, anywhere, walks in any other path? So Sheero collected money from his friends after the custom of Oman, and went back to Baloochistan where he came from, and there he presented such an impressive appearance that he had no difficulty in marrying a wife. Indeed from what we heard, it appeared that he had married into the local nobility which most decidedly was "marrying a sealskin wife, on a coonskin salary."

But after a month more or less, when the time came that Sheero must return to Muscat, it appeared that his spouse did not care for any, more probably that her father refused to let her go. So Sheero lived for two more years in Muscat by himself, earning ten cents a day or less and sending a little of it to his wife. A few months ago he decided that this was not good enough, and that he would go and live in Baloochistan, where he could set up his home. He hoped that the girl's father could locate him somewhere. Apparently, however, the prospect of having the couple settle down on the estate was regarded as unattractive, and rather than gain a new son, the family decided to give up their old daughter, and to our surprise, Sheero and his bride have just arrived in Muscat to set up business there. We decided that Sheero has a higher I.Q. than we supposed, for in this way he and his wife have at least freed themselves from the pestilent in-laws who ruin more homes in Arabia than they do in America, and that is a good many. And there is no doubt that he has a very nice wife, so we hope that she may make of him a real sealskin husband. She probably will, too, for Sheero has a lot in him, and his smile is worth more than most husbands' whole capital stock.

It must be admitted, of course, that the men carry some burdens too. We see lots of things in the little group of houses just back of the mission house. Our group prayers are set for an early hour, but this particular morning before we prayed a competitive carnival began. A quarrel was evidently on between one of the men and his wife. This particular wife was notorious as a loud speaker, and there was nothing in her entire horizon that she did not quarrel with, whenever the whim struck her.

It appeared that regarding some ring or other there had developed a difference of opinion. They became extremely angry. "You are no man," said the gentle lady; "your beard does not do you any good," the idea being that he might just as well have been a woman. There is a streak of the ludicrous in this insult coming from a woman's mouth, but this was not noted at the moment, for in the men's universe that we call Muttreh this is the worst insult that human beings recognize.

The man embarked immediately upon a vigorous effort to demonstrate that his beard did do him some good. The wife in the meantime had armed herself with a big stone to keep the husband off, but this was quite ineffective, and after a brief wrestling match, he was sitting on her prostrate form, and pummeling her vigorously. The curtain was rung down at this point for over fences and across fields we neighbors converged on the scene of conjugal felicity and dragged him off. He protested that his wife had said to him unendurable things. No one disputed this, but he was admonished that domestic discipline must be kept more private and a trifle quieter.

No one seemed the worse for the experience, indeed the atmosphere was greatly cleared by it. The woman showed no bruises, nor other injuries, her punishment having evidently been more official than anything else. No one was offended by the outside interference. Indeed it was evident that the man was anxious to be dragged off. He did not want really to hurt his wife, and he had at least satisfied his honor. As for the wife, who can say? But at least she went after some excitement and got it. Telling men that their beards do them no good, is recognized in Muttreh as one of the most strenuous of outdoor sports.

A few days later the couple quarreled again, and this time the man divorced his wife and went away and left her. He went away for the date-stick hut was hers, not his. We were inclined to approve heartily of this action on the husband's part, for living with such a wife would be worse, we thought, than a sentence to Sing Sing. We were wrong. It was not a week till he came back and begged his wife to take him on again. He found life tasteless and insipid without her. More important she was his only visible means of support. Such a prompt remarriage is contrary to orthodox Mohammedan law, but trifles like that are disregarded in Muttreh; I imagine that they are still living together, and doubtless a good time is had by all.

But it is a mistake to fix our attention too constantly on the dreadful catastrophes, and the regrettable features of the present situation. Those things will change some day. It is the little group of Christians which is being created in Arabia that will change them. Even now many families, perhaps most, get off to a good start. The women have to carry the burdens, but they do it well. It is true, moreover, that in Oman their burdens are not quite so heavy as in other parts of Arabia. Women remaining unmarried are not common, but they do exist and have a recognized place in society. Such women sometimes teach school, which certainly seems natural to those of us coming from the West.

There are a good number who, after divorce or the death of their husbands, do not remarry. It is difficult for such an unattached woman to earn her living, for sewing is poorly paid and basket weaving is even worse. Life for such a woman is likely to be semistarvation. A fair number manage it, though. Next door to the Muttreh hospital is such a family. Four women live together and support themselves with no masculine assistance: great-grandmother, grandmother, mother, and daughter. Two of the husbands died, and a third divorced his wife and left. The little girl has not yet been married. The four are a happy family together. One of them makes and sells local sweets, and evidently she has great capacity in that work, for the home is one of moderate comfort. But groups of this kind are rare. In the usual family the husband works hard all day to earn a few cents, and the wife at home spends this for something to eat and wear.

The families are desperately poor. The daily wage does not amount to more than ten cents a day, probably, and every such family with which I am personally acquainted loses nearly or quite a quarter of such a theoretical income, because of unemployment. And the thriftless spirit and practice of the community make a bad situation worse. The ease, indeed the avidity, with which the average Baloochee gets into debt fairly takes the breath of a Westerner away. To be debtless is a disgrace in that topsy-turvy community, and to pay a debt is one of those unreasonable things which a harsh government at long last may require of innocent and long-suffering subjects.

At the present moment the land owners in Oman are not getting rich. Prices are so low that many of them are losing money. Our only prosperous class are the merchants, and by no means all of them. Many of the merchants go to the wall, and bankruptcy declarations are fairly common affairs. But there are a few of the merchants who have made themselves millionaires in this land of great poverty. That seems a grotesque impossibility in a land of free markets like Oman. A free market in a country as poor as Oman will doubtless produce merchants of ability who are well off, but it will hardly produce millionaires.

The fact is that the market is not so free as it looks. Men sell for prices far less than the highest, and buy for prices far above the lowest. They do that almost universally, and for a very compelling reason. They are in debt. Our cook is in debt up to his ears, indeed over his head. He has been that way all his life, I imagine. A third of his salary is mortgaged ahead of time, every month, by government order, and more would have been, except for our stubborn insistence that the man be allowed something to live on. When a cook is in debt, his employer pays more than she should for everything that she buys. Her cook is not a free purchaser. He has to buy where his debt attaches him.

The same compelling reason dictates the merchant to whom the land owner sells his dates, and the fisherman his fish. It is skill in inducing and exploiting debt which makes men millionaires in Muttreh, and because it makes a few men millionaires it makes a great many men paupers. The dreadful network extends through the whole community. Our Indian moneylending spiders are past masters in the art of weaving this fatal net around the entire community. The Baloochee flies walk into it with the greatest willingness. The land owner is in debt to the wholesaler. Therefore he sells to him and at a severe disadvantage. The small merchant is in debt to the large one, the retailer to the wholesaler, and the private citizen to them all. There is no free market in Oman. I do not suppose that ten per cent of the transactions of the Muttreh bazaar are free transactions.

This is regrettable enough in its strangling effect on trade in general, and in the burden it puts on the moderately well-to-do. But in its effect on the poor and the laboring class it is utterly disastrous. An appalling percentage of their meager earnings must go to the payment of their debts, and at rates of interest which often reach fifty per cent. Clear-eyed honesty in business simply disappears from the earth. Babies go hungry, and their mothers with them, and family life is crushed under a load which is heavier than it needs to be in this country where inevitable poverty and suffering are bad enough.

It is the children whom the doctor has principally in mind when he demands a better economic arrangement for the families of Muttreh. There are lots of them, and they do not have a good time. The babies are not so badly off as long as their mothers keep them on the specially prepared baby food, which only mothers can manufacture. They are round and fat and happy, and as pretty as pictures. Malaria is their most serious trouble, that and bad eyes, which the flies give them. The second and third years are much harder and diarrhea and dysentery carry many of them off.

The children's clinic in the Muttreh hospital is a great place. The Muttreh babies are the prettiest in the world, almost, and without question the world's greatest fighters. They are a juicy lot too, and half a dozen little pools decorate the cement floor when the morning's work is over. It is their Christian duty to take castor oil and quinine solution. Many disciplined Caucasian adults balk at such an assignment, and so do these babies. However, they have businesslike mothers, and a Baloochee madonna giving castor oil to the small and very precious rebel in her arms is a real picture. First she lays him down on his back, between her outstretched legs, and sits gently but most efficiently on his active feet. Then squatting in position, she nimbly pins his arms down with her bare feet, one foot to each arm.

The child having been fixed in place, three points down, she sticks a finger of her left hand into his mouth, and pours the castor oil in alongside of it, with her right. Even then, if the baby is in an argumentative mood, he can put up a good fight, spewing out of his mouth this hideous unwanted thing. But that does not do him much good. It is caught by the mother's hand, which with the baby's immobilized face makes a very fair dish, and the medicine runs neatly back into the mouth that has just rejected it.

Eye treatments are simpler. The doctor at one end anchors the child's head between his knees in a first-class scissors grip. The mother at the other end takes care of hands and feet, and a good time is had by all, while the eyelids are everted and painted with stinging medicine. The child sings a fine tenor solo while this is going on, but that is about all he can manage. However, eye treatments are not very painful, and they extend over a long period. If the operator can turn on an adequate grade of charm, many of the youngsters come to look on this as a fine game, and take their treatment like men.

The orificial bean is the most difficult problem of all. A pea-sized stone will do nicely, but best of all is the long slippery date pit, an object which is always available for the experimentally inclined child, who doubtless will be the future Einstein of the country. But in the meantime this investigation of the cubic capacity of the nose and ears gives the doctor some bad times. The potential scientist has a bad time of it too, before he is through, and his bean fished out. But beans, diarrhea, castor oil, and all, the Muttreh babies are a nice bunch, and he would be a stony individual who did not enjoy working with them.

The doctor directs the treatment of all these alluring limbs of Satan, but the clinic languishes and almost disappears when he is its central figure. When Mrs. Harrison mixes some feminine charm with the castor oil, the waiting room is too small. Under her persuasion, the young men of four and five who come with their mothers learn to accept eye treatments as an opportunity to demonstrate their hard-boiled masculine texture. The little girls take whatever she gives them just because she puts a smile on it, like a red cherry on top of a salad in the restaurant. The world over, a nice attractive nurse, with hypnotic feminine eyes, is the essential feature in a children's clinic.

In Oman the family works against many handicaps. Free divorce is the worst. Many a woman comes carefully into the office when no one else is about to ask for some medicine which she can give secretly to her husband, and restore to its former vividness his early infatuation. Such a woman sees divorce on the horizon, and divorce is the indoor sport of men. The women of Arabia do not want it. It throws them back on to the matrimonial market as inferior second-hand goods, and their capacity to allure is far, far down. If they are encumbered with children, the situation is still worse. No wonder they come and whisper their need for a love philter. The doctor wishes he had one to give them.

The men come in much larger numbers but not for love philters. No man has ever asked me for such a thing. Nor have I been asked, except perhaps once or twice, for a tonic so that business responsibilities could be better handled. But in dozens and hundreds, and it would be thousands if it were encouraged, men come to ask for some medicine which will increase and intensify their capacity for the physical preliminaries of parenthood. Faded and aging in his physical capacities, such a patient wants to become again the youthfully virile and dominant male. We do not have that medicine either.

Divorce and polygamy have ruined many of the families of Arabia, but not all of them. The doctor above all others knows what family life among the Arabs can be. Nothing anywhere could surpass the devotion and loyalty with which wives care for their sick husbands. Our Muttreh hospital is composed for the most part of small individual rooms, with just this in mind. They are family rooms, and here where women care for their sick husbands, we see many beautiful things.

The loyalty of husbands to their wives is almost as splendid, if only they have been able to resist the temptations to stray after pretty faces and lovely soft bodies along the way. Shereefa and her husband were such a family. They have remained a beautiful memory.

Shereefa was brought in to the hospital from a distant village, for she was the victim of a serious disease, and it was evident that unless surgery could offer her a way of rescue, she and her husband would soon be separated. She had ascites of an unusually severe type, and its cause seemed utterly obscure. Operation showed an extremely adherent fibroid packed into the pelvis. Its removal was followed by such a hemorrhage as I have seen only once or twice in my life. We were too slow in getting it under control, and, in spite of all we could do, twelve hours after the operation Shereefa died. Whatever else she carried up into the next world, her husband's kisses went with her, deep witnesses to a love which would follow her until he could, and in her ears like beautiful music, I am sure it went over into the next world at least a little way, "Shereefa, Shereefa."

A family doctor must make himself one of the family, granted that they wish it. When we fail, and death always defeats us finally, it is no part of the doctor's task to run away. It is not easy to sit and watch death make sport of our best efforts. It is harder, indeed almost the hardest thing in this world, to sit and see our limitations and mistakes bear bitter fruit, when it is the operation that we recommended and performed which proves fatal. But we do well not to claim omniscience even with our admirers. The price of brotherhood is to be a brother, and there is no time when brothers are needed quite so badly as when ties are broken, and good-bys said, and the world becomes desolate and empty.

The family physician concerns himself with men's souls as well as their bodies, therefore much of his work must be with mental maladjustments. To have cancer of the stomach is bad enough, but to think that you have it is almost worse, and the Arab has a vivid imagination.

Fish is the staff of life in Oman. The same word which is used for bread in Mesopotamia, and for rice in Bahrain, is used for fish with us. Digestive disturbances are common in Muttreh as elsewhere. So perhaps twice a year we see patients who have fish in their stomachs. No cooked fish this either, but an actively swimming, live one. It may be an imaginative fish, but there is nothing imaginative about the trouble it causes. In America it would be a frog.

No doctor is deceived when a patient tells him that a fish is swimming around in his stomach, but the treatment of such a case is tiresome and unsatisfactory. The most troublesome case is the one where the fish is only part of a real disease picture. We have such a patient now. His habits are sedentary, and he is fat. His digestion is good, but with some flatulence. This gas distends his abdomen, and embarrasses his heart just enough for his imagination to get hold of, and he is the next thing to a bedridden invalid.

The obviously unstable personality is not uncommon. Years ago in Bahrain a patient with a large tumor of the neck was on the operating table, the operative area had been anesthetized with Novocain, and was draped and ready. As the knife was picked up to make the incision, the patient jumped from the table with a shout and ran earnestly around the room from one to another. His voice and personality were completely changed, and he insisted that the operation be abandoned. He had come all the way from Mecca, he was anxious for everyone to know, to stop the dangerous affair. Twelve hours later the man snapped back to normal, and wanted the operation, so the next day we did it under chloroform. Visiting spirits from Mecca make less trouble that way.

In and about Muscat, there are frequent *dhikrs* where this splitting of the personality is the intended and usual result. The name of God is chanted in unison for hours until the state of frenzy is succeeded by one of trance. Having arrived at this thrilling point after hours of hard work, various marvels are reported. Eyes are taken from their sockets, cleaned, and put back. Children's heads are cut off, and put back on again, with no injury to anyone. Swords are driven through the bodies of the devotees, with neither pain nor hemorrhage resulting. These of course are the reports of onlookers. Skeptics are not invited.

However, sometimes skeptics see the end results. Early one morning, six men brought to the Muttreh hospital a participant in such a seance. He and his friends had put themselves through this psychological third degree the night before; but for him the charm failed to work, and the dagger with which he stabbed himself did go in. The hole in the abdominal wall was not large, indeed less than an inch in length. On seeing the wound, his terror must have been great, for he forced out on to the surface of his abdomen an incredible mass of intestines, perhaps ten feet of them; and, half-strangulated by the narrow aperture, they swelled up to twice their normal size. In an effort to keep the rest inside where they belonged, his friends covered the extruded bowels with mud and bandaged the whole mass into place tightly with a long cloth. This was bad enough, but to make matters worse the dagger in making its small hole had cut a large artery, doubtless the deep epigastric, and the man was nearly exsanguinated.

It took gallons and gallons of saline to wash the mud off from the intestines, and one stitch to stop the bleeding. We lengthened the tiny incision a little so that the intestines could be replaced more easily. With glucose injections his shock passed off and he made a good recovery. His bowels were moving normally, and the small opening which had made all the trouble healed by first intention.

This unexpectedly favorable outcome did not altogether please him. His companions of the trance fraternity felt that he had let them down very badly indeed. They expected and, I think, rather wanted to see him die. The diagnosis of an unstable personality was stamped unmistakably on his features, and he scarcely cared to recover to face his community's disapproval. However, on the seventh or eighth day, he began to cheer up and look forward to life with some anticipation. The fates were against him. An embolus, probably from the traumatized veins of his intestines, carried him off.

We have learned to have lots of respect for the disruptive effect of the emotions and instincts in a place like Muttreh. A leading member of the transplanted Indian community there, came one day to consult me about his sister. She was far gone with tuberculosis. The question was whether pneumothorax had anything to offer her. She was so advanced a case, that I felt quite sure that the effort would be useless, but still she was a unilateral case, and against my better judgment, I put in ten or fifteen c.c. of air. She died perhaps five minutes later.

The scene which followed this catastrophe, I will have to live a long time to forget. There must have been a hundred women in the company, shrieking and tearing their hair, and in other ways manifesting their vociferous grief. I stayed with them for fifteen or twenty minutes, not because I was wanted, for these were Shiah Mohammedans, and with them the participation of an infidel doctor in death scenes is not cared for. This was one of the few instances which I have seen, where I was afraid to leave, lest it be interpreted as running away and thus invite some additional catastrophes. It was an extremely wild, irresponsible crowd, and their individual sanity was at least fifty per cent gone.

After a little time they carried the girl off and buried her, the brother superintending the ceremonies. He dropped in for a minute on his way back from the cemetery to express his thanks for what we had tried to do. He was obviously much broken up over his sister's death, but he had known it was coming for months. I myself felt very badly over what had happened and told him so.

That was four o'clock in the afternoon. At six there came a hurry call for me. The call was to the great mosque, for in one of its anterooms this man had fainted away. That is the only time that I have ever entered this mosque. Outsiders most emphatically are not invited there ordinarily. He was conscious when I arrived, but his blood pressure was down, quite surely below a hundred, but the atmosphere was so hostile that it was out of the question to introduce a blood pressure apparatus into the scene. I was allowed to listen carefully with the stethoscope. Nothing appeared to be wrong, except the shock of his grief and worry.

The family was present in force, and utterly refused to accept any medicine from me. A friendly pharmacist of their own persuasion was in the crowd, and I turned the case over to him. This agitated man did not relish his responsibility, but I reassured him. All that was needed, I felt sure, was to get the man home and in a warm bed. Hot water bottles and hot coffee constituted the whole of my recommendations, inasmuch as even from him no medication of any sort was acceptable. I suggested that the foot of the patient's bed be raised for an hour or two, as helping to raise the blood pressure a little, so far as the brain was concerned. I urged that he accept the case without hesitation, for I insisted, "These cases never die. Grief over the sudden death of his sister, was aggravated by the scenes which followed her death, but that is all that seems wrong. Men do not die of pure grief."

I was wrong there. At eight a much agitated messenger came to ask that I come immediately to his house, where he had been taken, as I advised. He was worse. The pulse was inperceptible, and the man had been unconscious for some time. The stethoscope detected a mere flutter. He died a few minutes after my arrival.

I imagine that if we had been permitted to give the man intravenous glucose with ephedrin in it, and adrenalin perhaps in addition, in small doses repeated every fifteen minutes for as long as required, the dreadful collapse in his blood pressure could have been arrested. But perhaps nothing would have done any good. The influence of the mind over the body is a profound thing. I have never seen another case of that sort, but since that experience we try not to bring a case up for operation until any profound fear that he feels has been allayed. Operations tax the blood pressure a good deal in any case, and we try to see to it that fear and terror are not added to the burdens that are carried.

Cases which actually die from an emotional upset are extremely rare, of course, but the Oriental lives very much in a world of his imagination, and this has to be taken into account when studying his symptoms. The particular obsession of the Omanee is his anal region, to which he devotes an appalling amount of attention. *Boaseer*, i.e. piles, are the bane of his existence, and of the doctor's almost as much. Genuine hemorrhoids are common enough, but incomparably less so than imaginary ones. Indeed *boaseer* is a sort of demonic conception and to it is ascribed nearly every ache and pain which enter into an average man's experience. If at any time in the recent or remote past half a drop of blood has followed a constipated movement, the diagnosis is clinched.

Recently we operated on one of the modernists of Muttreh for piles. There was nothing imaginary about his large and juicy masses, and he spent a very uncomfortable night after the operation. Every unattached and semi-attached gossip in the neighborhood supposes that it is her duty to visit such an invalid's house, and talk cryptically about the dark and mysterious disease which caused the operation.

This particular patient did not care for women of that type anyhow, and under the circumstances it took all of his self-control to remain civil to his wife. So he assured the ladies that he needed no discussion of either the cause, characteristics, or cure of his *boaseer*, and with some abruptness he sent them all home. One of the women concerned explained afterward that this showed a most unfortunate peevish lack of stamina on his part. She was operated on for the same trouble a little later, and was proud that the neighbors were always welcome.

The family physician in Muttreh devotes most of his time to the Arabs and the Baloochees. Not all of it though. He treats boils, and it is the Europeans who specialize on boils. Dr. Hosmon gets a new crop every year. I went down to India a few years ago as a deck passenger, and slept on a very rough but handsome bed-cover which I had recently bought from the Bedouins. Every protruding bony eminence of my anatomy which rubbed against that hair shirt bedspread, developed a most gorgeous boil. I did not know that a nondiabetic could have so many. I remembered when it was too late, that students of bacteriology produce boils in guinea pigs by rubbing bacteria into their skin with a stiff brush. Boils are not trifles. It is easier to get them than to get rid of them, as is true of many evil things in this world.

We have most astonishing epidemics of colds in Muttreh. "The hottest place where white men live." How can anyone catch cold in such a place? How indeed? The impression is that we do not catch the cold, so much as the cold catches us. If only that told us something about getting rid of them. Mohammed, our engineer, can catch a cold on half an hour's notice at any time by sitting in a draught. Doubtless it is a matter of congestion to begin with, but it is an infection before he gets through with it.

Some of these colds develop into pneumonia, and occasionally such pneumonias are deadly fulminant things. Three years ago we saw an especially bad case where from the beginning of symptoms to the death of the patient scarcely thirty-six hours elapsed. I have never seen pneumonia like that except in the great flu epidemic. We waited with a great deal of apprehension, but no further cases developed.

The family physician lends a hand whenever opportunity offers. He sends for the catalogue of Beirut University, for a boy who wants a modern education. Something went wrong and it took months to get it. He devotes an hour quite frequently to mending up family relationships and trying to postpone the day when divorce will tear up so many beautiful things. He arranges to have the Muscat national anthem sent to the State Department in Washington so they can get ready for a visit of the Sultan. He helps to get a tennis club started in the city, knowing that tennis will do the young men more good than any medicine.

But it is Mrs. Harrison who confirms the weak bonds and strengthens the feeble knees. Every week she has an official reception, and dozens and scores of the hard-pressed wives and mothers are there to get a little reinforcement, and sometimes the still more important personal advice that adjusts them better to a hard world. And these receptions are followed up by lots of visits among those who are so poor that they have little to eat, and that greater number who are starving for the things that are more important than the bread that men try to live by.

There are many women who get a helpful word in connection with those receptions and those visits, but they get more than that. They see the vision of their innermost souls objectified before their eyes. No wonder lots of them come. That sort of work is a taxing thing, but as for reinforcing the family life of Muttreh, these receptions are the most important contribution that we make. They have little to do with medical practice but lots of the things that we do in Arabia have little to do with either the pill or the scalpel.

VIII
COMMUNITY HEALTH

THE FIRST THING I learned in Muscat was that the people's health was very poor. The second was something even worse, i.e. that the fundamental cause was poverty. "Within limits," says the Commissioner of New York City, "health is a purchasable commodity." Having no money, the Omanee cannot purchase this extremely precious thing. Three inches or less of rain a year spells poverty of a desperate and inescapable sort.

Ten and fifteen years ago we used to get patients from the Shergieh country whose very appearance frightened us. For ten years their country had practically no rain at all. The gardens died and the people moved away. It takes a long period of semistarvation to drive an Arab away from his home to Zanzibar or Bahrain or Muscat, where he swells the already overcrowded ranks of casual labor. Men and women from Shergieh died in the hospital from the most trifling causes. One fine old man came and had his hernia mended. He scratched his leg in some sort of slight accident. The resulting infection was a trifle, but it was to his final home that he went when he left us. Another contracted a slight diarrhea from unsuitable food, which he had bought in the bazaar. A month later he too was dead.

We gave these men cod liver oil, and we fed them milk. We tried every means that we knew to build up their resistance, but when resistance has been broken by a starvation extending over years, there is no known way in which it can be re-established in a few days.

The city of Muscat is not suffering from particularly bad times just now. As years go, this has been a good one. But all our years are bad. The only difference is that sometimes, as in Shergieh, they are worse. So far as I know there is no clinic in Bombay or Calcutta where as many chronic leg ulcers are treated as in the little hospital in Muttreh, where we serve a community of not over ten thousand. Coolies with bare feet carry the community's burdens in India just as they do in Muttreh, and those feet get scratched and bruised in the same way. A normal man pays no attention to such trifles, but in Muttreh we have very few normal men, and trifling scratches lead to trifling infections, and trifling infections grow into formidable ulcers under our very eyes. Seventy-five, and even a hundred ulcers come in for attention in a single day.

Infant mortality is very high. Dirt and the lack of all sanitation are the principal causes. Babies who cannot walk hold a green date in their soft little fists. They chew cheerfully on this indigestible thing. Diarrheas and dysenteries are the commonest diseases. But all these handicaps put together do not succeed in disposing of all the babies. The Baloochee sections of Muttreh are simply full of children, and apparently the whole of Oman is destined to become a province of Baluchistan.

The Arabs have lost their grip. Hardly one of the old Muttreh families is left. Inland the process has not developed so far, but a Baloochee section is to be found in practically every one of the great oases, and their numbers steadily increase. Nuchl is "full of Baloochees" and in Bedieh they form a third of the population.

The doctor who works in a city of extreme poverty such as Muttreh has to listen to a great many pessimistic arguments to the effect that poverty being what it is, the great excess of babies might better be allowed to die. It is a poor intelligence which tries to save them from an early death, for they will simply be thrown against the immovable wall of limited food supplies, and have to die later when death is a more painful affair. When there is food for only a thousand children, it is simple folly to work day and night so that fifteen hundred will survive their infancy to struggle in a futile way for life as children. Five hundred of them are destined to an early death in any case.

The problem, we are assured, has been illustrated for us by the large community of pariah dogs which wander the streets of Muttreh and all the coast towns. These dogs pair off in a rough way into couples, and such a couple raises two families a year, averaging perhaps four to a family. Thus the canine population is multiplied by four each year, or would be if all lived. The fact is that nearly all die, and the dog population remains stationary.

Some years ago the Political Agent in Bahrain decided that this dog community was a pest, and a menace to the city. He decreed its annihilation. The dogs were killed in scores and hundreds, and the canine population was reduced to perhaps ten per cent of its former density. But it proved impossible to root out the last fraction for they ran away and hid in the wilderness outside the city. The effort was finally given up, and the small fraction of canine Bahrain which remained after the massacres restored the city of the dogs to its former population in perhaps a year's time.

The parallel is fallacious and the conclusion wrong. The food supply of the dogs in Bahrain was doubtless more or less fixed, and population expansion impossible. Nothing could be less fixed than the food supply of Oman. The streets of Muttreh are full of children, and those children will conquer and fill Oman. It takes lots of energy and a good deal of brains to extract a living from such a country. Most difficult of all, it takes some co-operative capacity. The Arabs presumably possessed all these qualities once. Inland Oman has many oases whose water is led through underground tunnels for miles before it can be used. Such a tunnel is a very considerable engineering triumph. I have never seen such a watercourse that was not hundreds of years old. We can be very certain that only a mere fraction of the water underneath comes to the surface now. Some of those bright-eyed babies in Muttreh are going to find and develop new watercourses. The Baloochee community is doing that already in a small way. There will be new gardens, and if some of the mistakes of the Arabs can be avoided, there will be a new Oman and a better one.

What has happened to the Arabs? They have occupied Oman for a thousand years, and probably much more than that. Some of their deterioration is due unquestionably to the fact that they chose to live by the labor of slaves rather than by their own. Two hundred years of that will ruin any nation. At least it has ruined Oman, and now with moral standards gone, energy gone, and the large families gone, Baloochees who are willing to work are coming in and pushing out the Arabs who are not.

There is another cause which must have operated at least in the recent past. Like ancient Rome, modern Oman has been a dreadful center of malaria. How many hundred years or thousand this has been true I do not suppose that there is any way of knowing, but the situation now is obvious enough.

When the hospital was built, no areas of standing water were left, and so we did not screen the office. That was in the days of our ignorance. The landscape gardening left no pools, and the nearest well is a hundred yards away, but the mosquitoes of the whole section found under the office desk a "fine garage" to quote our hospital philosopher. We used to "flit" this dark cave vigorously every morning, and I have counted five hundred dead mosquitoes left behind on the tiles. A far greater number flew out and escaped when the storm of flit began. These mosquitoes bit my feet so badly and so constantly that I developed a sort of mosquito eczema, different from anything I have seen elsewhere. It took years to get it cured.

We screened the office, of course, but the houses that the people live in are not screened. Most of them, unfortunately, are not capable of being screened. Patients must be visited in their homes, and there one learns what an incredible pest the mosquito can be, and how serious a handicap malaria is to a city like Muttreh. The spleen index is high. If recent immigrants are excluded, and only those ten years resident in the city counted, I imagine that it would run between seventy and a hundred per cent. Even the Europeans who live in screened houses have malaria occasionally, for it is impossible to stay inside all the time. I have myself averaged an attack every six months for many years.

The Missionary hospital exists to serve the community, and this is the one thing which the community needs. Poverty makes the problem extremely difficult. We teach the use of quinine, and none of the blessings of modern medicine compares with that bitter drug in the contribution which it makes to Muttreh. But even its help is little enough. During the spring and fall seasons when malaria is at its height, the effect of a thorough course of quinine lasts between a month and six weeks. That is not because too little has been given. Increasing the dose will not prolong the fever-free period. Eighty grains of quinine in sixteen doses, distributed over three days, will do all that any larger quantity will do. So far as practical results are concerned, it kills the parasites which are present in the patient at that time. But the patient goes out to furnish breakfast, dinner, and supper to fifty, or more likely to five hundred, mosquitoes a day, and in five weeks he is back with a new crop of parasites to be killed. Atebrin and plasmoquin give no better results, as indeed it is impossible that they should.

A small number of the intelligentsia are learning to use mosquito nets at night, and this helps a great deal. It is at night that the dangerous mosquitoes take most of their meals. But mosquito nets cost money and they wear out quickly. Moreover they rob the sleeper of his last breath of wind on hot nights. I have myself rejected them at times, and endured the mosquitoes outside rather than suffocation inside.

For many years great stagnant pools of water have furnished evil sights and smells behind both Muttreh and Muscat. The government is developing a feeling of responsibility on such matters at last, and the pool behind Muscat has been filled and drained, but with no perceptible effect on the prevalence of malaria. This was a great disappointment, but it should not have been. The pool badly needed filling and draining. It was an offense to the eye and a worse one to the nose. But such a pool is not nearly as important a source of mosquitoes as many suppose. The pool behind Muttreh lasts for months, following the rains each winter. However, it becomes so salty after a little time that mosquito larvae cannot live in it. Bahrain, with much the same malaria problem as Muttreh and Muscat, put through a very radical sanitary program, and there is not a stagnant pool left in the whole place. But malaria is still present, and as much of it as ever.

It is the water jars in the houses that do the mischief. Water is man's most treasured possession in Arabia. The jars are never entirely emptied. The effort, indeed, is to keep them moderately filled, for the price of water fluctuates; and, by having a large jar filled, it is possible to avoid the high peaks. The sanitary engineers scratch their heads over this aspect of the problem. Dr. Russell of the Rockefeller foundation tells me that even in India the malaria problem still defeats them.

The second public health problem in Muttreh is that of intestinal diseases, and the wayfaring man though a fool knows that it is the millions of flies which are responsible. A very intelligent contractor was taking tea with the missionaries, and a fly made a forced landing plump in his cup. Without a word he rose and threw the tea away. His host expressed pleased surprise at this reaction. "Well," said Faqueer Mohammed, "I see them in lots of unsavory places like latrines. I do not know where this one came from."

He might have put the case more strongly. He had made a very good guess as to where that fly came from. But where they come from in the first instance was for years a complete mystery. The ground is utterly dry. There are no manure piles worth the name anywhere. Nevertheless the city swarms with incredible myriads of flies.

There is another item in the situation that the wayfaring man though a fool can not err about. Every open space is a public latrine, even though there is no more privacy than in the public square in front of a U. S. Post Office. There is great resulting offense to the eye, and still more to the nose. Granted the existence of the flies, the spread of intestinal disease is inevitable. The marvel of the situation is that such diseases are not more common than they are. One day with the idle curiosity of the small boy, I broke up a little pile with a stick. I wanted to see what it looked like inside.

I learned a great deal. I discovered that these little piles of human feces scattered thickly over every unoccupied area are not only the places where flies get Flexner bacilli on their feet. They are also the stations where Flexner bacilli get taxis to carry them around.

Every six-ounce pile of feces lying there in the open sun is visited by six hundred female flies during the first six minutes of its existence, and supplied with the utmost promptness with the eggs which later will turn into maggots. The outside surface dries down under the pitiless sun into an astonishingly impervious protecting skin, and the moisture inside is retained for a period of time sufficient for the maggots to mature into flies. Two or three days after its deposition, that six-ounce pile of feces is exactly six ounces, more or less, of wriggling maggots, not a few hundred, but literally several thousand. When they break out as complete flies, nothing is left except a curious powdery trace to mark the pile's location.

This simplified the problem. Those piles of human feces are the source of the bacilli, and of the flies that spread them. If we can corral them in properly protected latrines, the problem of intestinal disease in Muttreh will be solved. Moreover, the matter of locating the necessary latrines is simple enough. Wherever the sensitive nose is offended by the typical Muttreh odor, and the eye discovers hundreds and thousands of these little piles disfiguring the landscape, that is the place for a latrine.

Occasionally we spend a minute or two regretting that God did not make of us a sultan or a sheikh, or some other sort of dictator. A pirate captain might do, but lacking that sort of authority, we decided to trust to the power of a good example. We put up two public latrines opposite the hospital where they were very badly needed indeed, for it is a camp ground for caravans from the interior, and actively used for inartistic purposes.

A vigorous protest was immediately forthcoming from the local religious authorities. Such a latrine would make the location smelly and disgusting and contaminate the mosque a hundred yards away. We asked, in a mild sort of way, whether the present atmosphere was regarded as sweet with perfume. It was regarded, we were assured, as satisfactory. But we told the worried puritan that we intended to take care of these latrines, so that the atmosphere and the appearance of the vicinity as well would be improved. It hardly seemed possible to us that it could be made worse. It took a good deal of persuasion, but finally the religious authorities allowed the experiment to be made.

Other prominent figures among our neighbors joined in the debate, and finally the governor of the city came out to inspect these innovations. By this time they were in place and functioning nicely. The governor had traveled to Bombay and other advanced places. He declared the latrines to be a good work and commended us. That settled it. We heard no more from our critics.

The pits were dug at a cost of perhaps two dollars each. We cannot bore nice round holes at ten cents apiece in this stony country. The pit is lined with rough masonry and lasts for a year or so before it fills. Then it must be abandoned for a new one. A nice rectangular narrow opening above was made with dressed stone slabs, and a tiny room of date-stick construction gave the necessary privacy.

The nicely dressed stones were promptly stolen. They were replaced and stolen again. Then we made a gigantic cement top for this latrine pit, which four men could scarcely carry. That stayed in place.

The date-stick room above lasts about a year. It is picked away a stick at a time to burn as fuel, but it only costs about twenty-five cents to replace, so we do not worry over its gradual dissolution. A new one looks better anyway, and we regard it as distinctly an advantage to replace it after a year.

We have found it necessary to give these latrines a good deal of supervision. At night they serve merely as lighthouses indicating the locality intended for latrine purposes. Unless the vicinity is cleared of litter each day, the room itself becomes unusable. Even in the daytime matters have to be watched. I found Walook, who has charge of the latrines, in a vivacious quarrel with a tinsmith who had discovered that a latrine throws a most acceptable shade. He set up his shop in this cool and attractive patch next to the latrine, and, the wall being semitransparent, this made impossible any use of it for its intended purpose.

But through evil report and good report, the latrines have been doing good work. The public square in front of the hospital is a different place, and the people can pray in the mosque with uncontaminated air in their lungs. Officials have come to inspect these improvements, and now there is discussion which we encourage and foster looking toward the possibility of establishing similar comfort stations at critical points throughout the town. One of these days Muttreh and Muscat are going to be cleaner cities, and there will be almost no flies, and very little intestinal disease.

Public health measures receive cordial support from the general public, and it is a pleasure to record one first-class success which stands to the credit of Oman, entirely unassisted by modern medicine. Leprosy appears to have been common in Oman in the past, but it has been almost wiped out. Next to Dubai is a little village which is the leper asylum for the entire Pirate Coast. Once a week lepers may enter the towns and beg. The charitable support these indigents in a fairly adequate way, and most of them have donkeys to ride on.

In Muttreh a similar group of about two dozen collect from the Bottina and from near-by places in Oman, and are allowed to live in the public square in front of the hospital, granted only that they put no roof over their heads, so the disinfecting sun can shine down on them. Each digs a long shallow hole, like the first installment of a grave, and this is his home. During the day, while a leper is away begging, his cooking utensils and other meager possessions are arranged neatly in this shallow trench. His bedding weighted down with stones at the corners is placed over them. Their quarters show a pitiful resemblance to a graveyard, and I am afraid that the lepers feel that this resemblance goes much deeper than mere appearance. But the lepers are allowed much freedom of movement, and they have a fair amount to eat. At night after they have come back from their various excursions, a dozen or even twenty cheerful little fires gleam through the night, and there is a real community life developed. One Christmas we gave them a rupee apiece, and they asked with much feeling that a comrade in arms, absent at the moment of this unexpected good fortune, be not omitted from our count. We left a rupee for him too.

From the standpoint of the community this was a good arrangement. Nearly all of the patients are old burned-out cases and almost no new cases were seen. The disease was in a fair way to disappear. Recently, however, increased immigration from Baloochistan has brought in many new cases, and it looks as if some definite action would have to be taken, if we are to prevent a very great increase in the prevalence of leprosy in Oman.

Oman has another credit mark in preventive medicine, but this mark is not more than a B-minus. Smallpox used to be a devastating scourge. Pockmarked faces are common everywhere. The people believe in vaccination, but they neglect it most dreadfully, a large unprotected population of children grows up, and then a terrible epidemic sweeps the community.

A good deal of intelligence is shown in keeping the disease out of these towns. In Dubai when a case appears he is promptly hustled out of town where he is placed in a freshly built hut, and a pockmarked slave is sent to take care of him. If he recovers, he must stay there till the last trace of eruption is gone from his skin; and then, after a bonfire of all his clothes to the last stitch, he must take a swim in the sea, and, upon covering his nakedness with absolutely new clothing, he is admitted to society again. The necessary food, and finally the clothing required are brought out from the city and deposited at a good distance from the hut, from which depot the pockmarked slave carries them to the patient.

If this rule were combined with even a fair observance of vaccination, it would work very well indeed, but large numbers of children are vulnerable in every one of these towns most of the time, and the resulting epidemics are very severe. Six years ago an epidemic like that started in Muttreh. Thousands of unprotected children were ready to die like flies. But the medical missionary was a new factor in the situation. Bahrain sent down in a military plane all the dessicated vaccine they had. That took care of some hundreds. Cables brought vaccine from India in unlimited quantities. We vaccinated babies in hundreds and before we were through, in thousands. It was the privilege of a lifetime to stand between those bright-eyed babies and that devastating plague. I do not think that Muttreh lost a dozen children. Muscat, two miles away, declined to be protected, and they buried hundreds. Abood, one of the Mission school boys, was a victim who did not die. Both of his eyes are gone, and he will never be anything except a burden on the community.

No discussion of the Muttreh public health situation is complete without some mention of eye diseases. Throughout Oman the blind number thousands. Ragged and hungry and hopeless, they sit along the Muttreh streets in dozens. When we arrived in Sifala, seven days inland, the first contingent to come for treatment was such an array of blind old men as appalled us. Trachoma is the usual cause. It is terribly common and, if neglected, it can cause complete blindness. Glaucoma is the next commonest cause, but glaucoma affects old eyes rather than young, so it is not so important. Hundreds are blind because of the smallpox epidemics of the past. Gonorrhea has caused some blindness. When a baby is born through an infected birth canal, he is in very great danger indeed. But in Oman this is uncommon. I have not seen a case.

Glaucoma we can do nothing for. Smallpox is being overcome by means of vaccination. The problem is really that of trachoma, and it is one of the greatest of the health problems of Oman. On our recent trip to Sifala we operated on over a hundred eyelids which were being curved inwards by their chronic trachoma. Probably every one of those eyes was saved. They need much further treatment before the lids become normal and this treatment they will not get. But their vision has been saved, and we take lots of satisfaction in knowing that we have been able to accomplish as much as that.

But the children around us in Muttreh, what about them? Hundreds suffer from trachoma, more girls apparently than boys, perhaps because they wash their faces more often, and dry them on dirty towels. There are plenty of houses in Muttreh where the boy who does not wash his face is safer than the girl who does. Trachoma is a very contagious thing. Often we find all the children in a house infected.

And of all the diseases which we see, the treatment of trachoma is the most slow and tedious. It is not remarkable that the children get tired of coming to the clinic day after day for treatment. They often stay till improvement is marked but not at all permanent, and then they disappear for a long period. After some months they turn up again, as bad as ever, and we have to begin all over again. It is a matter of months to treat trachoma, and the patience of the sufferers is measured in weeks or perhaps in days.

The hospital has devoted lots of time to the problem of trachoma. Surely if we have any conscience at all, here is a disease that we must do something about. Moreover we can offer a cure to nearly all of these sufferers, if they will only come patiently for treatment. But it takes an incredible amount of patience, and they simply will not do it. If the new derivatives of prontosil fulfill their promise, and put into our hands the possibility of a prompt cure of trachoma, their contribution to Muttreh will be very great indeed.

In Arabia a hospital usually gains its reputation by some special line of work which it does really well. Muttreh has such a reputation, not built on its eye work, unfortunately, but on its work for ulcers. Not duodenal ulcers. Those are the luxury of the nervous and over-driven Westerners. Muttreh's ulcers are out in the open where they can be seen, occasionally on hands and arms, but usually on feet and legs. Some of them are enormous, and when of long standing, their odor is likely to be a long-range lethal thing. Abdullah came in from Oman with an ulcer which measured four by six inches. Only the swollen condition of his leg made such dimensions possible. It took us four months to floor that ulcer over solidly and well. A local Baloochee developed two ulcers about four by three inches, one on each leg. One of these healed well inside of two months. During that time the other increased in size and in spite of all we could do eventually caused his death.

We know surprisingly little about ulcers. Barring only the modern operating room, every scratch and cut in the world is liberally supplied with dirt and bacteria immediately the skin is opened. Fortunately most minor injuries of that sort heal up promptly, in spite of the dirt. In Muttreh a good number of them do not heal up. Infection sets in, and, as it spreads, the skin involved dies and we have an ulcer. This process may be very rapid and at the end of seven days the ulcer may be three inches across. Usually the process is much slower than that. It is unusual for active infection to persist for more than three weeks. The size of the resulting ulcer depends of course on the rapidity and duration of the process. Eventually a defense reaction sets in and the infection is overcome. Then the process of healing can begin. Many ulcers come in when still small, and the average of all cases is about half an inch across. Dozens and scores however measure one and two and even three inches in each dimension.

In treating ulcers, first of all we need something that will assist the local defensive processes, so that the infection can be overcome promptly, and further increase in size prevented. The Arabs attempt this in various ways. The skin of a freshly killed kid may be bound on such an area. Often this seems to help a great deal. A commoner remedy is a paste made from the fresh leaves of the *neem* tree. This paste is applied thickly to the spreading ulcer, and the infection is supposed to clear up at once. In our hands it usually does no such thing, which is a pity, for we need an effective agent very badly. Many cases seem to be helped by the pure putridity of the necrotic mass which covers the ulcer. On removing the dressing from an especially redolent case, we usually fine a nice clean granulating surface below.

Of these products of Arab imagination, we have tried a number, adding a few of our own. We hoped great things from powdered charcoal, but it failed us, even when we added charred hair to it, so that it might possess the value of putridity as well as absorptive capacity. *Neem* leaf mush we worked on for a long time, but we finally gave it up in favor of saturated Epsom salt dressings. It must be admitted that doctors working in the

East turn easily to Epsom salts when they have nothing better to suggest.

The *neem* leaf mush however gave us a useful idea. United States babies with severe digestive disturbance are given scraped apple. If scraped apple quiets the infection of the small ulcers which make trouble in dysentery, it seemed reasonable to imagine that it might have a similar good effect on larger ulcers of the leg. Apple powder for the purpose is commercially available, so it was not difficult to try it. It seems to be a great success. Ulcers come in infected and still spreading. We immerse them in raw applesauce for a few days, and this seems to defeat the microbes completely. Treating ulcers with applesauce seemed positively sacrilegious to my friend, the chief of the Muscat Oil Commission. He asserted that hereafter he would not be able to eat applesauce with his roast pork. I urged him to come over and smell the ulcers on which the applesauce was placed, and then he probably would not even want the pork.

After a few days in applesauce, when the infection has disappeared and the ulcer is clean, it is time to start getting it covered over with epithelium. We have an effective agent for this. Cod liver oil as a dressing for ulcers is easy to take, and over it the leg is bandaged tightly with an adhesive elastic bandage. Such ulcers heal rapidly. One of our best ones, over an inch in diameter was healed and dismissed inside of three weeks. Once applied, the elastic adhesive dressing is left on for two weeks. The patient often objects to this, regarding himself as badly neglected. The odors of Araby the blest are apt to hover about such a neglected leg like an aureole, but we are Jesuits: the end justifies the means.

Lately we have added to our ulcer equipment a Pavaex machine as it is called. Into a beautiful glass boot the patient sticks his leg, and there it is subjected to rapidly alternating suction and pressure. This has added greatly to our reputation. Certainly now we are doing something for our patients, even if the dressing is not taken off for two weeks. The machine itself is a temperamental thing, and like some people it has to be petted a good deal to keep it working. Under its influence the ulcers make very rapid progress, and the patients vote it a huge success.

As described above, the ulcer is trouble enough. Some of them make more trouble still because the last tiny area of ulcerated surface simply refuses to floor itself over with epithelial tiles. Abdullah, our champion case for size, was an illustration. In less than three months we had him almost cured. Only a tiny ulcer remained perhaps a millimeter across. His leg balked at this point, and the whole wound broke down so that a month's steady work lay ahead before he was completely cured. It is here that our Pavaex prima donna promises to make her greatest contribution. Stimulated by the soft click-clack of the machine, the paving gang keeps steadily at work till the job is finished.

Our antimalarial work and the hospital's efforts to do something to lessen the incidence of intestinal diseases are services rendered to the entire community. No more democratic institutions exist in the world than the mosquito and the fly. But the ulcers on which we have spent so much time and effort are diseases of the city's coolies, *hamalees* as we call them. The hospital has not been able to make any contribution to the productivity of Oman.

Probably it never will. There are a good many things that we would like to teach our patients and all their friends with them about what they should consume. That belongs to the future. But between the production and the consumption lies the distribution system, and we feel that the Muttreh hospital is to be considered as a very essential cog in that machine. The *hamalees* would surely agree with us.

The distribution system of Oman is important, for everybody has a lot of one thing to sell, and a little of many things to buy. Every date gardener eats some of his own dates, and every fisherman some of his own fish, but only a little. He must sell most of them.

The buying and selling are done in the market. One is ready and waiting in any town that may be selected. A market has three parts. Permanent shops are maintained with large stocks of goods. Nonperishable commodities are thus kept ready in quantity for any purchaser. The second feature of a market is free space where any citizen who has something to sell may sit and offer his wares to the passer-by. Women offer their needlework, and the Bedouin his clarified butter. The mango grower sits for a few weeks behind great piles of his special fruit, as do the purveyors of vegetables, and tomatoes, and similar things, each in its short season. The third feature of a market is permission for itinerant auctioneers to offer special articles to the highest bidder. The cries of such passing hawkers are in the air continually.

The markets are free. Men sell where prices are the highest, and buy where they are the lowest. Every sort of article is admitted. Dates and fish, rice and coffee, cloth and needles, thread and buttons, cement and lumber, building stone and plaster. Nothing is excluded. Here are the shops of the blacksmiths, the coppersmiths, and the tinsmiths; the carpenters, the potters, and the tailors—each with his product to offer to the public. Here sit the beggars offering the public an opportunity for charitable self-expression, and here are gathered the donkeys and their keepers, waiting for someone to hire them. In a different place are the camels, and off by themselves, like the lordly aristocrats they are, the motor taxis under a shed of corrugated iron.

The market constitutes the distribution system of Oman, not one market but dozens, one for each of the towns. The complete system includes also a network of transportation lines which extend to the very limits of the country. Camels bring dates and other products from far-distant places. In Muttreh we see caravans that have been on the road eight days and even more. Back to the inland cities the same animals carry rice and kerosene and coffee, as a return cargo. A thousand camels in one day have knelt down outside the gate of Muttreh to be unloaded.

From points not so far away come dozens and hundreds of industrious donkeys, bringing wood and alfalfa and fruits of various sorts. Often they too bring dates, and like the camels they take back to their home ports what the steamer calls "miscellaneous cargo."

Like the Bottina gardeners with their bullocks, and the Bedouin shepherds with their goats, these carriers live in intimate partnership with their donkeys and their camels. It is a partnership of deep sympathy and understanding. On our trip to Sifala we simply hired such a returning caravan to carry us as their return cargo. We used to watch in the early morning while the camels were called back to camp. Each one had a personal name, and some of them came from long distances when they heard the morning call to breakfast and work. Each ate a lump of dates, and had his back scratched and his saddle rearranged carefully before the work of the day began. It is by means of long hours and hard work that men and animals working together in this way manage to extract a very meager living from an unfriendly world.

But of all the burden bearers by means of which the market functions, the most important are the human carriers who work within the market itself. From the steamer's lighter to the shore, from the caravans' resting place to the warehouses, from the market to the houses of the community, it is men who carry the burdens. There is a great deal of this work to be done, and almost nothing can defeat these tremendous workers. When we moved, our piano traveled a full mile without a pause, like a curious square centipede, with about fifty legs. The men assured us that the piano was an easy job.

Distribution is thus the work of two classes. Commodities must be bought from their producers. They must be sold to their consumers. This is the work of the merchants. There are a few of them, and they are well-to-do. The hospital does a small amount of work for them. These commodities must all be carried from their point of production to the market, and from the market to the consumer. That is the work of the carriers. There are many of them, and they are very poor. We do a great deal of work for them. Their legs have ulcers and we treat them, and their children are underfed and anemic, with trachoma in their eyes and itchy wanderers in their hair. Knox Memorial is their hospital.

The markets with their network of transportation lines cover every corner of the province, and form a very efficient distribution system. The fishermen of necessity live next to the sea, far from the people who want their fish. Nevertheless practically everybody within fifty miles eats those fish. Nor does the matter of getting his fish to their ultimate consumer give the fisherman a moment's concern. He drops his catch into the hands of the waiting distribution system, much as an American drops his letter into the postbox. A buyer meets him as he steps from his little boat, and a hundred feet away are the donkeys which will carry some of his fish inland. Near by are buyers who are anxious to take some of his fish, so they can be salted and dried for the connoisseurs in Ceylon. All that the fisherman has to do is to sell the fish.

It would be difficult to imagine a more efficient and economical distribution system than this one. It needs some drastic revision of the rewards which the merchants receive. That should be a revision downward. The greater need is for a revision upward of the rewards which the carriers receive. The hospital is happy to contribute its share toward the maintenance of the system. It is proud to be reckoned as their special institution. Noobie is absolutely fond of their ulcers, and we have won a great reputation in treating them. But they are an evil symptom, a sign of cruel underpayment of the men who carry the community's burdens, and all that the hospital does is simply a futile palliation till that underpayment is corrected.

We have another star in the crown of our local reputation. We do hernias, some of which have already been described, in their strangulated form. They are common in Arabia. Whether more common than at home, it is not possible to say. Arabs ascribe these hernias to various causes, from a bad smell to excessive sex indulgence. The orthodox pathology of the country, however, considers them due to "wind," though just how this operates to produce such an unfortunate effect I have never heard explained. The fact seems to be that as men grow older their skeletal structures weaken, and hernias develop. Hard laborious work is certainly not the cause of most of these hernias. Some are large and some are small, and some are pure imagination.

Like its colleague, the hemorrhoid, the hernia is a conception projected by the imagination into our inner regions. No end of disagreeable symptoms are ascribed to these "internal hernias." To the Western mind with its absurd demand that some concrete reality be behind a disease concept, it would be extremely interesting to discover just what such an internal hernia might be. The Arab is troubled by no such thirst for scientific precision. When out of sight and mysterious, hernias, like Plato's celestial numbers, do not have to correspond to any earthly pattern.

Small hernias are easy to operate on, but even with them some recur. The large ones are much more difficult. As we saw in Chapter IV, they may be enormous in size, reaching almost or quite to the knees. Such a patient needs relief very much, for he is a real cripple. Unfortunately, in these cases a permanent cure is often very difficult to obtain.

We have worked a good deal on the problem of hernia. From 1880, when Bassini proposed the operation which still bears his name, until now, a great number of operations have been proposed. They all aim to cure the patient by rearranging his own tissues. Lately it has been found possible to put in permanent reinforcing patches of ox fascia, and for some time we have been mending hernias in humans, just as a garage man mends a tire, by putting a patch over the weak area. It has taken nearly fifty years to arrive at this profound conclusion, which the automobile mechanic, we will imagine, discovered within fifty days.

Many patients come in to be treated for hemorrhoids. For the imaginary ones encouragement is sufficient, provided the dosage is adequate, and frequently repeated. But there are plenty of large juicy masses for which psychotherapy is very unsuitable. These we treat with the clamp and cautery. The cautery irons are heated in a gasoline flame, a plumber's torch being very convenient for the purpose. Surprised to see such a blow torch in the operating room, a visitor wanted to know what it was for. "We use it," I said, "in operating on hemorrhoids." He did not know hospitals very well, and horror spread over his face. "Gosh," he said, "not that." I assured him that all it did was to heat the cautery irons. We have many of these cases to treat, and the results are good, but like everything a doctor touches, they bristle with question marks. The coast cities are full of hemorrhoids. I know of no exception. Inland, in the desert regions, they are almost unknown.

Most diseases interest us because we see many cases. Appendicitis because we see none. That statement must be modified now. Through the past twenty years, appendicitis has been practically unknown in Arabia. Doubtless it is still unknown in the inland districts. But on the coast, where contact with civilization is closer, it is no longer rare. We have seen perhaps half a dozen cases this past year. Many questions arise. Why are primitive peoples free from this disease? That of course is an extremely stupid question. They are free from appendicitis because they are normal folks. Why do civilized nations all suffer from this peculiar disease, and to make the question more pointed, what is happening now in Arabia which is bringing appendicitis in?

In Muttreh at least we are not eating civilized food. The poverty of the people makes that impossible. So far as customs house figures show, Muttreh is eating much the same food as has been used for the past hundred years. We listen to fifty or a hundred radios, but it is difficult to suppose that appendicitis is caused by that. We read newspapers, and play tennis and hockey.

There are some other results of civilization which may not be so innocent. The malignant western spirochete is taking the place of the much tamer Arabian variety and the type of syphilis is changing. Smallpox is disappearing. Acute articular rheumatism is gradually coming in. The world even in Arabia is moving at a faster tempo, and nervous tension is unquestionably higher than it used to be, though mild still, judged by Western standards. We are using more sugar than we used to, and it is possible that the rice which constitutes such a large fraction of our diet is more thoroughly polished than it used to be. The doctor who speculates on the cause of appendicitis in these days must of necessity postulate some dietetic deficiency as the fundamental cause, and a specifically educated micro-organism as the excitant.

Wounds and fractures give us a good deal of work. The Baloochee and the Arab both find it difficult to turn the other cheek. The Arab carries a big curved knife in his girdle as part of his dress. A respectable man will scarcely be seen on the street without one. It is not a very effective weapon for stabbing, at least if penetration is the object. The Baloochees carry a smaller and much wickeder knife concealed under their clothing.

The doctor mends the holes. When victims come in promptly, we try to keep these wounds clean, like surgical incisions. Generally we succeed. Scalp wounds are usually caused by other weapons. A wood cutter next door quarreled with his neighbor and had a tremendous gash cut in his scalp with an ax. It was as neat and smooth as a surgical incision. He had a very high-grade skull. It was not even cracked.

There are elaborate rules for the assessment of damages in such cases. The *Kadhi*, i.e. the local judge, measures the depth and the length of the wounds carefully. The longer and deeper the hole, the greater the sum which must be paid. More than once his officious assistant has come into the operating room with a small official stick to measure the wound, so damages could be correctly estimated. In such a case we boil up a hospital stick, and take the measurements with that, the *Kadhi's* man looking on and directing the survey.

Sometimes accidents happen far from the hospital, and days elapse before the patient can be brought in. Such cases never stay clean. All that we can do is to wash them clean, and handle them as ulcers. Three years ago two Hindu merchants were attacked by robbers in Seeb, and stabbed in a feeble sort of way in a dozen places. In self-defense the merchants embraced the robbers most affectionately, and, because they hung on desperately, the robbers could not inflict any wound that was an inch deep. This courageous bit of pacifism saved their lives, for help was attracted by their cries before they could be killed, and incidentally before the robbers secured any loot. Unfortunately they lay unattended for nearly forty-eight hours before arriving at the hospital. They lost a great deal of blood, and their wounds all became infected. Moreover one of them nearly died from hiccoughs which the shock and exposure brought on, but they both finally recovered.

The worst case of neglected accident of recent years was a compound fracture of the femur, due to a falling wall. The man lay with several inches of his femur exposed to the air and the dirt for four days. When he arrived at the hospital, the condition of the whole thigh was unspeakable. His external saphenous vein solidified with phlebitis, and an embolus carried him off.

Venereal disease is common everywhere in the Orient and Muscat is no exception. Moral standards here are the lowest of all Arabia. Muscat was the center of the slave trade and is still the center of such slavery as remains. Slaves have no rights. Men and women must hold themselves ready to serve the demands of appetite and instinct, especially if they are physically attractive. Such attitudes wreck the soul of society, and they make their contribution to the surgical clinic.

Gonorrhea is common enough everywhere, though

perhaps in few places quite so common as in Muttreh. Further to the north its chronic and severe manifestations are very rare. There the patient is treated with hot drinks, and in ten years I think Bahrain furnished only one stricture for us to treat. But in Oman it is reckoned as necessary to treat gonorrhea with various local applications inserted with the help of smooth sticks, and wires. A Bedouin from the mountains came in recently passing all his urine through two sinuses in his perineum. It took a month and more to put his plumbing in order. Such a patient is a real surgical problem, and the risk of infection is considerable.

Stones in the bladder we see, but for the most part these are importations from Iran and from Baloochistan. We are likely to treat half a dozen such cases in a year, and some of the stones are of large size. Most of the patients are children, and three years ago we operated on a baby of a year and a half for a stone in his bladder which was so large that it seemed almost certain that it began while he was still an unborn traveler with his mother. Just what etiological factors could be operative in such a case, was a matter for much active speculation. The baby, however, did not speculate. He was very well satisfied to get rid of it.

We owe a good deal of our surgical reputation to spinal anesthesia. In Oman general anesthesia is not popular, and when a patient is found dreading an operation it is usually the anesthesia which is in mind, and not the post-operative discomfort. General anesthesia is not popular with the surgeon either, for no anesthetist with expert skill is available, and when too much is given, we all turn to, to give artificial respiration. These efforts are nearly always successful, but the delicate aseptic setup is ruined. It is ruined just as badly when not enough chloroform is given, and the patient rises up to kick out of the way the whole aseptic field.

Local anesthesia is first class for the surgeon and lends itself to the development of careful and accurate asepsis. I was a great devotee of local anesthesia for years. But local anesthesia is hard on the patient. No one enjoys being a pin cushion even for fifteen minutes. A major operation is a real ordeal.

Operating on the lower part of the body, i.e. on those parts which are below the umbilicus, we scarcely ever use anything now except spinal anesthesia. The prospect of smoking a cigarette comfortably while the doctor mends up his hernia is very alluring to the Omanee. There used to be a fairly acute twinge of pain connected with the induction of such an anesthesia, but we have succeeded in eliminating that, and now we assure our patients that we will cause them no more pain than a mosquito bite. There was a time, too, when the headaches which followed this type of anesthesia were so severe that all its advantages were neutralized. We have eliminated the headaches too.

Years ago, when our experience with spinal anesthesia was just beginning, we were called on to operate on a Bedouin chief in Kateef for old osteomyelitis of the tibia. It was a gunshot wound, neglected for years. All that was needed was the removal of a small sequestrum of dead bone. The chief himself was a smallish man, but his wife was a tremendous Amazon, of a hundred and eighty or two hundred pounds, and with a spirit to match. I suggested that she remain outside, but she would have nothing to do with such an idea. She remained inside, and watched everything that was going on with very alert and untrustful eyes.

It did not go on very long either. Under her very eyes her husband's legs had become so influenced by this black magic injected into his back, that they were both paralyzed. To make matters worse the paralysis of the well leg was greater than that of the sick one. She saw the doctor take up a wicked looking little knife, doubtless to cut something off completely. At this critical point she came up silently but irresistibly from behind and embraced me affectionately, pinning my arms helplessly to my sides, and out she carried this dangerous practitioner, black magic and all. She handled me with the practiced ease of a mother of two-year-old children, and when I was disposed of, she carried her husband off to safety, in the same style.

But that was a long time ago, and I did not expect anything like it again. To do the Omanee justice it must be admitted that we have not seen anything like that in Oman. But we have come to the conclusion that some patients are not suited to this sort of anesthesia. One of the many Indian merchants in Bahrain came in to have his hydrocele operated on. Spinal anesthesia is very satisfactory for such cases, but in those days the puncture was still a painful procedure. This particular patient also found the elaborate preliminaries very frightening, and that made matters worse.

We did not realize the state of mind at which our patient had arrived when we began to work. With what was doubtless a sharp twinge of pain, the needle slid into place. The patient was sitting on the edge of the table, with his legs hanging over. He gave a great shout, jumped down, and ran for the door. Spinal fluid was dripping from the needle, for we had placed it accurately at the first throw. His shirt came down over the dripping needle as he ran.

I was not considered much of a runner in the university, but I did better that afternoon. I was on the wrong side of the table, and the door was not far away but I made a fast end run, and caught up with my fleeing patient as he was opening the door. I did not argue the matter nor try to stop him. All that I was interested in was to hoist up his dirty shirt, and recover my needle. The vision of him running around the streets of the city with spinal fluid dripping out of the needle made me sit up in imaginary alarm for many days afterward. However, he did not get away with it. I recovered the needle, and the man suffered no ill effects. The current was from within outward, and I suppose that no bacteria got in. I wondered how much headache he had afterward. According to our present ideas he should have suffered severely, but he probably did not.

We see hopeless cases in Muttreh, a good many of them. Eyes ruined by glaucoma are common. Limbs paralyzed by poliomyelitis common enough. Worst of all are the cancer cases, which always come too late. In the early days of the hospital we saw so few cases of this sort, that we imagined cancer to be almost unknown in Oman. Now the reputation of the hospital has extended further, and we wonder whether certain types of cancer are perhaps more frequent here than at home. Cancer of the stomach certainly is not rare in Oman. I must have done a dozen palliative operations on such cases. In a case from Birka a few years ago, such an operation afforded over a year and a half of comfortable existence.

Epitheliomas of the external skin are a very benign thing in Oman. They are common, and surgery gives excellent results. Only once has such a cancer defeated us. The socket of his eye had been invaded, and in spite of the removal of all the contents of that orbit, and some of its bony wall, the cancer recurred, and eventually caused the patient's death. Cancer of the breast is external too, in a way, but such cases never come in early enough for an operation to be attempted. We see about a case a year. They are dreadful cases, and we are thankful that there are no more of them.

Hydrocephalus is a distressing disease. Every few years we see a case, always far advanced, the head distended to enormous proportions by fluid contained in the ventricles of the brain. We have never seen a case except in very young children, under three rather than over, with their little faces, and enormous heads, and abnormally quiet behavior. Such children are hopeless cripples mentally, because the stretching of the brain leaves a mere sac enclosing the mass of fluid within. However, no one has yet ascertained to what degree the brain of such a young child might recover its functions, if the condition could be relieved.

No one has been able to do much for these cases, but every disciple of Cushing's, even the least in his father's house, lies awake on occasion turning over in his mind the problem they present. It is a purely mechanical problem. All that is needed is a way of escape for that dreadful mass of fluid. Surely our ingenuity ought to compass such problems.

An especially pathetic case was recently brought to Muttreh, and we added our name to the list of those who have worked on the problem. The large intestine absorbs fluids, and so far as we know, that is about all it does do. So we speculated that the power of cellular habit, being strong, if some of the mucous membrane of the large intestine were incorporated in the wall of the brain, it might absorb some of that troublesome fluid. The absorption of a few drops a day would probably be all that is needed.

It is not particularly difficult to do this. A fair-sized patch an inch long and half that wide was removed from the large intestine, and the opening repaired. The patch was washed nice and clean, and placed between muscles for ten days to render it completely sterile. At a second operation it was sutured gently into the wall of the distended brain, with the specialized mucous membrane lying next to the fluid. We did not succeed. The child died a few days after the second operation.

Surgery requires equipment, but it is relatively permanent, and once started a moderate sum each year for repairs and improvements eventually secures a good layout. Sometimes ingenuity will take the place of money. We provided ourselves with a very fine operating light, by having the carpenter cross three six-foot beams at more or less equal angles. Each of the six ends carries a forty c.p. light, with an inverted enamel dish for a reflector. The most expensive light devised to date can hardly surpass this simple arrangement, and it cost less than ten dollars. But most of our surgical equipment has been provided by friends at home, our most recent addition being the Pavaex machine for the scientific pulling of ulcerated legs.

The Muttreh hospital is a great place. In it the patients have a good time, and they get well. The doctor has a good time too, and he learns steadily. What success could be greater than that?

◇◇

IX

THE DATE GARDENERS

OMAN IS A rough mountainous country, about three hundred miles in length and a hundred in breadth. Traveling for eighty miles from Rusail to Sifala, we could survey the country for perhaps ten miles on either side of the slowly moving caravan. We saw about a dozen oases. An oasis always means a spring of water, but many of them are very small. Rusail contains only a few hundred palms.

The rainfall is an inch a year, perhaps two inches, and, even if it were perfectly conserved, the area which could be cultivated would be small enough. It is not perfectly conserved. Indeed, so far as men are concerned, it is not conserved at all, but without any help nature saves a good portion of it. In a gravelly country like Oman, very little is lost by surface evaporation, for the rain as it falls sinks immediately into the underground water courses. The amount which is recovered for agricultural purposes is considerable. Land under cultivation must approach one per cent of the entire area, if the gardens along the coast are included, and if this is true, we probably recover and use in irrigation several per cent of the actual rainfall of the country.

The rain runs off the mountains into these underground water courses. After the springs among the mountains have taken their share, the water flows on toward the sea, to make another contribution there. The mountains do not drain directly into the sea except at the two ends of the Hajar range, where their feet are dipped direct into the Indian Ocean. Along the intervening two hundred miles, between the sea and the foothills, there is a coastal plain which varies in width from twelve to thirty miles. This plain receives the drainage of the whole mountain area, and there never has been a drought so severe and prolonged as to interfere with its underground water. No surface streams are to be seen, and the plain is as dry as any stony *wadi*, but a thin jungle of trees and shrubs shows that below the surface water is not far away.

While we were visiting in Sohar a hundred and twenty miles from Muscat, we became very well acquainted with this plain. Its trees are trimmed with the greatest care up to a point about ten feet from the ground. This was the more surprising because in that section the plain is in the hands of the Ajman Bedouins, than which none are more truculent and untamed. The mystery was solved for us by a camel which came by and, seeing some juicy leaves well up above his head, stood on his tiptoes figuratively speaking; by stretching himself to his utmost limit of elasticity, he managed to get them. Many thousand trimmers of that sort are at work all the time. They look thin and bony enough, but the trees are surprisingly well groomed and modern looking.

This plain furnishes wood for fuel to all the near-by towns. It is forbidden to cut trees down, but dead limbs may be gathered, and dead trees taken away. On our trips to Birka and Nuchl we often see the Bedouins at work gathering wood, and meet donkeys and camels bringing it to Muttreh for sale. Further up the coast we found two ports where merchants of large acquisitive energy export it to points further away. Many shiploads go to Kuwait and the ports of Persia. A large sailboat will nearly always be seen out in the deep water being loaded.

But the real importance of this plain does not lie in its wood nor in the pasturage which it affords to camels. A third of the people of Oman live in it. The whole plain doubtless has most excellent soil, washed down through the centuries from the mountains. Every family in Arabia could have a garden here, if only water was available. The plain supports only a few nomads, but next to the sea, running practically without interruption for two hundred miles is the outstanding date garden of Arabia. There are no flowing springs, but fresh water is close to the surface, and irrigation is possible by means of wells. This great garden is called the Bottina, which may be translated as the inner territory, the reference perhaps being to the mountains which enclose it.

Hundreds and thousands of wells have been sunk in this garden area. They are the most important things in that little world. The law takes note of the boundaries of a man's land, but common conversation simply reports him as the possessor of one or more wells. Attached to the well is a garden of probably a hundred date palms, though some wells care for double that number. It is easier to maintain the garden if the channels are kept short, and less water is wasted, for the soil is very sandy. When the garden is larger and channels become longer, a second well is dug.

Large trees are planted next to the well itself. In Birka and Seeb, as well as in many other places, these are usually mango trees, and their fruit in season as well as their shade the year through make the well a most inviting spot. In the channels near the well the women wash their clothes, and in the shade the men sit at appropriate times to gossip and take a nap. The beauty of a garden centers in its well.

The only pumping apparatus that has proved successful for these wells is the bullock. Fuel for this engine is raised in the garden itself, so the expenses are low. The bullock is man's partner in the struggle for existence, and this fixes the boundaries of the cultivated area and the type of life lived within it.

Close to the sea, fresh water is only eight to ten feet from the surface, but, as the land rises toward the foothills, the water in the wells is further and further from the surface, and when the depth of the wells reaches thirty to thirty-five feet, cultivation stops. From a depth greater than that, water cannot be drawn for irrigation, if a garden is to pay. The date gardens usually extend back from the sea for only half a mile, though there are places, as in Birka, where they are two miles deep or even three. Unfortunately there are places also, where they shrink to nothing.

When the hospital, after the long period of delay, was finally established, the first effort was to organize the work so that the sick of Muttreh could be taken care of. That took some time, for making bricks without any financial straw is not the easiest thing in the world.

But we had no desire to confine our services to the little city where we live. The whole province of Oman is the field of the Muttreh hospital.

Oman stretches out from Muttreh in several directions. The Bottina was taken up first because it wanted us. The other districts did not. The days of universal acceptance were twenty years in the past. The Bottina has always been friendly. When the arms traffic was abolished and Oman revolted from Muscat twenty-five years ago, the Bottina remained loyal. I am not sure that this was a spontaneous and deep loyalty. Like all the rest of Oman, they suffered severely when that traffic disappeared. But the mosquito fleet could reach and influence the coast. The result is that for the past twenty-five years Muscat has not been the capital of Oman as she desires to be. In actual fact she has been the capital of the Bottina.

Traffic between the capital and these coast towns has been active and cordial, and in recent years Henry Ford and his crew of local assistants have united them more closely than ever. We were not at all surprised in the early days of our Muttreh work, to receive a very friendly invitation from the governor of Sohar urging us to make his city a visit. He promised the best quarters that the place afforded, and every facility for our work. He also promised us lots to do.

We held a council of war and decided that it would be well to devote a month or six weeks each year to this sort of work. There are ten towns of a thousand and more population, on that coast, and dozens of villages besides with many hundreds living in them. The population of the Bottina cannot be less than fifty thousand,

and probably not over a hundred thousand, according to the best guess that we could make of the uncounted multitudes.

We made the trip in a sailboat, Sohar being a hundred and twenty miles from Muscat. That has a romantic sound, and if the weather would co-operate a little such trips might be very pleasant affairs. Sometimes the wind does help out most accommodatingly, but not usually. I know of few things more wearisome than spending four days in an open sailboat, and traveling only a hundred miles during that time.

We transferred the hospital bodily to Sohar, or as nearly so we could manage. We worked for days to get the medicines into boxes, and the surgical apparatus packed up in mobile shape. We used an ordinary pressure cooker purloined from the kitchen as our sterilizer. It works very well indeed, and transports easily. A formidable battery of primus stoves was taken along, and a tin or two of kerosene, for it is not always possible to get supplies in these faraway places.

We made two trips to Sohar. On one of them we had as our guest, Dr. Suthers, who teaches missions to the Methodist intelligentsia in Ohio. Suthers was a good sport, and he did not complain, though he had a right to. We drew a bad card on that trip, and it remains a sore memory even in my hard-boiled soul. The first day out we did pretty well, and by night we were fifty miles on our way. It would have shown more judgment on our part to tie up for the night and sleep on shore, for there was not a breath of wind. We did not make a hundred yards' progress during the whole night, but Americans are always in a hurry, and we wanted to get along; so we stuck to the wicked little ship in the hope that her sail might fill out before morning, and get us somewhere.

If we made any progress that night, it was in Christian patience, and I am very uncertain about that. The tiny ship did not belong to Dr. Suthers' denomination, nor to ours. She was a "Holy Roller," the adjective in this case being a mistake. There was no breath of wind, but the water is shallow along that coast, and from the outlying sea there was a steady roll which I have never seen surpassed. We were rocked in the cradle of the deep all night long. First on one side and then on the other, that satanic boat tried most earnestly to drop us into the sea. There were no rails, and only by hanging on to everything in sight could we avoid being pitched into the dark waters. We tried lying crosswise, and we tried it endwise. We tried it lying down, and we tried it sitting up, but it was equally strenuous in all positions. By morning we had decided that there is a good deal to be said for walking as a means of transportation.

Nevertheless we had a good time when we did get there. There were hernias to do and lots of bad eyes to take care of. We found all three varieties of malaria parasite in Sohar, just as we had found them in Muscat. A very attractive Bedouin boy brought in his brother, who was suffering from an old neglected gunshot wound in his leg. He looked like a bad risk, and Bedouins from that part of the world have hasty tempers. However, we talked the situation over carefully with his brother, who is one of the world's noblemen, even if he does belong to the Ajman tribe of Bedouins. After the amputation the boy made a fine recovery, and we decided that the tribes of that part of Arabia are not so bad as they have been reported.

Coming back we stopped for a month in Musena'a. There we found a tremendous amount of work. We straightened out over a hundred eyelids and had a whole yardful of hernias and hemorrhoids. An especially alluring small boy with a stone in his bladder was one of the major features of that small hospital where each patient built himself a little date-stick hut and we lived as a small colony together.

The stone boy eventually made a good recovery, but a bad infection followed his operation, and he required an enormous amount of care. His mother and father pulled him through, with such loyalty as only mothers and fathers know. Mohammed was left behind to watch over the final convalescence of the patients, and especially to continue the necessary treatment of this stone boy. This special attention was much appreciated by the family, and Mohammed was frequently their guest at meals.

One day he was horrified to see them kill a large and well-nourished cat who had been making a nuisance of himself with his fine tenor solos at night. Mohammed was not especially fond of the cat, but the circumstances surrounding the execution made him suspect that it was the intention to eat the animal. Cautious inquiry proved the suspicion correct, and the matter was made worse by a cordial invitation to come on the following day and join in the feast.

Mohammed is a Christian now, but in those days he was a Shiah Mohammedan, and the Shiah Mohammedans are particular about what they eat. Their prejudices do not run along exactly the same lines as our own. There is no special aversion to dirt, but animals designated as "Nejus," i.e. unclean by religious law, are abhorred with an abhorrence that we of the West find it difficult to understand. Cats are not in the official list of eatable animals, and the shock of this invitation was so great that for two days Mohammed could scarcely eat anything at all. He had been entertained off and on at this hospitable home for a long time, and he was greatly concerned lest other forbidden things might have contaminated his stomach.

The Bottina people as a whole are a loose-jointed class religiously. Nowhere else in Arabia, as far as I know, will the people eat shark meat, but the Bottina fishermen take the shark in their stride, without flicking an eyelash. Near Birka I saw a gigantic shark being towed half a mile to the fish market, by a very triumphant fisherman. How he had been secured, I did not learn, but his size was unusual. He must have been ten feet long. The fisherman waded along through the water up to his waist, in a very cheerful mood. Why should he not be cheerful? He saw in prospect a whole handful of rupees. "Are you going to eat him?" I called out. "Sure we are going to eat him." He looked at his gigantic victim and added philosophically, "They eat us, and we eat them. Everything depends on who gets the other one first."

The Bottina can be depended on for unexpected experiences. One of the sheikhs sent for me. He felt that he needed an operation. Examination showed an epithelioma on the side of his face the size of a dollar. He had carried it around for ten to fifteen years. There is nothing very difficult about excising such a growth, though

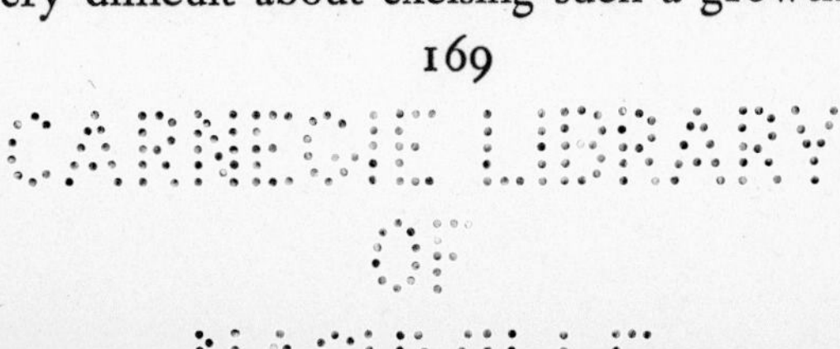

the blood vessels run a high figure per linear inch. However, in this case it looked very difficult indeed for the sheikh. "No," he said, "I cannot come to the hospital in Muttreh. It is impossible." That seemed unreasonable, for the hospital is only thirty miles away. Inquiry elsewhere gave us more information. This sheikh is a notable figure. Many years ago, so the story goes, he fell in love with a businesslike woman who was managing her father's estate. Falling in love with a woman you have seen is a scandalous business in any case, and for a powerful sheikh it is unheard of. However, the lady replied that she did not want him, would not have him indeed at any price, nor could he carry her off until he had killed both of her brothers, as well as some other male protectors.

This matter the suitor attended to without delay, and returned shortly to press his suit, this time with complete success, and they lived happy ever afterward and had plenty of children. However, eventually I saw this family at home, and I am afraid that the glamorous story will have to have its wings clipped. They have had no children, and the sheikh has been equally unfortunate with his other wives. Nor am I certain about the other romantic details. But such a man does not live a monotonous life, and it appeared that it was indeed impossible for him to come to Muttreh and lie down in a strange hospital in the midst of his enemies. So we brought out from Muttreh a pan full of instruments and a basket full of sterile dry goods, together with some local anesthetic and an assistant, and arranged for the use of the same operating room that I imagine the Paleolithic splinter extractors must have used long ago. There was a very nice one next to the garden well, and under this tree we set up our working plant. A mat on the ground was the operating table, and a sterile towel spread out close to it was for instruments. The doctor waddled around on his knees like a penguin, after having washed his hands for an incredible time with soap in a series of dishes.

The operation went very nicely and received much applause from the interested audience. Transplanting about fifty pinch grafts of skin from the near-by shoulder excited the most interest of all. I explained to the old warrior that I was making him a new garden, planting alfalfa in one part and eggplant in another. All the grafts took except those in one corner. The old chief took lots of satisfaction watching the grafts grow till they coalesced. He studied himself in an old mirror carefully whenever the bandage was removed. "Sahib," he said one day, "you should have planted alfalfa down in this corner too. The eggplant didn't any of it grow."

Treating patients in the great clean outdoors is an educational enterprise of much value. No damage is done if dozens and hundreds of our friends look on. They learn many things which it is good for them to know. Nothing surprises them quite so much as the astonishing way in which the doctor insists on washing his hands before the operation. In one dish after another he scrubs and scrubs and consumes much valuable soap, long after all imaginable dirt has been removed. Too much in awe of this formidable adept in questionable arts to ask him any questions, they usually wait till the assistant is washing his hands. "Why do you wash your hands such an incredible amount?" "It is this way," replied Suroor, a dark brown comedian of large capacity. "I wash them with this great diligence, in the hope that eventually they will become white like the Sahib's." An appreciative grin went around the attentive circle, and after that they were not so timid and discussed the matter with me.

We learned a great deal on these trips. We saw in the first place what an incredibly laborious struggle the cultivation of the Bottina gardens is. These gardens used to be organized in great plantations, and the melancholy remnants of those days of glory are everywhere. Cement watercourses are no longer used. Great tanks crumble unrepaired. Fine houses are tumbling to ruin, deserted and broken. The gardeners themselves are spiritless and discouraged. When I visited those splendid establishments twenty-five years ago, I entirely missed the essential difference between the Bottina and the splendid gardens of the mountain oases. That is to say, I entirely missed its significance. In the mountains, the water comes to the surface through flowing springs, and all that the gardeners have to do is guide it to the roots of the trees. In the Bottina it has to be lifted to the surface from wells that may be thirty feet deep, and the labor required is very great. That was true twenty-five years ago, just as it is now, but in those days the number of slaves was so large and each man and each animal had such moderate hours of work, that no one appeared to be very busy.

It is a different story now. The water must be lifted to the surface level, and the amount needed is appalling; for the ground is sandy, and the people are too poor and too discouraged to build cement runways. They do not even repair and use the old ones. A man and a bullock work together, partners in perhaps as grinding a struggle for existence as the world affords.

It is a genuine symbiosis, with deep sympathy and understanding between the two. The same sort of symbiosis exists between the wandering Bedouin shepherd and his goats, but that is a partnership of freedom and wide ranges, even if it does mean constant hunger. This is a dreadful partnership of hopeless imprisoned drudgery. The bullocks are surly animals, with much hostility toward strangers who walk unannounced into their horizon, and their partners come to be like them. The same garden nourishes the bullock and the man who works with him. The water which is their common life, they pull out of the well together.

The man furnishes the brains, and no mean fraction of the pulling power. The bullock furnishes the power and much of the skill. A rope runs over a high pulley, and the water is drawn up in a great skin bucket the size of a washtub. I measured the capacity of a large one, and it held twenty-five gallons, which means that it weighed two hundred pounds. The man and the bullock walk down a steep incline cut in the earth, as they pull this heavy weight up to the surface. The pitch is steep and they haul the bucket up with only moderate exertion. The harder part is climbing back to the top of their little hill to be ready for the next descent.

The bucket is ingeniously shaped, tapering off at the bottom into a slender funnel about five feet long. This tail is doubled up against the side of the bucket while it is in the well, but when the surface is reached a second rope straightens out the funnel so that the water is automatically discharged into the waiting tank. In this way it is possible for the man and his bullock partner to go up and down the treadmill without interruption, hauling up a tubful of water every forty-five seconds under optimum conditions. Four hours of this is all that either partner can endure. During the hot season most of such work is done after sundown, and the whining squeak of the pulleys can be heard all through the night.

An ox and two men can care for two hundred date palms. Hours are long and the work hard. While one man works with the bullock, another must guide the water to the roots of the trees. Each tree stands in the center of a five-foot circle with a small mud wall to retain the water. Alfalfa and similar crops are walled off in squares. In the sandy soil of the Bottina the palms should be watered twice a week, but in the off season, when no fruit is developing, once a week is all that they get, or even less than that sometimes. Once or twice a year the ground is stirred by a little wooden plow. At least it should be, and once a year it should have a certain amount of manure worked into the soil. Last year's fronds must be cut off and cleared away each spring. They can be sold as fuel or as house-building lumber. There are accessory crops of which alfalfa is the most important, but dates are the support of life as well as its intolerable burden. Not many men pay for their right to seventy years on this planet with such unrelieved and constant labor as the Bottina date gardener. "You must come to the hospital for treatment," I told a gardener who was suffering from an unusually severe ulcer. He lived only two miles way. "Could you possibly send me the medicine here? I have to work."

This would be bad enough if the wages of the Bottina

This is the kind of reception Dr. Harrison (tallest figure, in center) gets when he makes a medical call in the hinterland of Oman. The car is equipped as a dispensary, and one day each week Dr. Harrison spends in treating the population of the interior back of Muttreh.

Yankl, a typical small oasis nestling in the sun-baked hills of Oman. Water is abundant, so alfalfa fields flourish outside the date-palm area.

cultivators were adequate and their living conditions good. The facts are shockingly otherwise. Date culture in the Bottina is an utterly discouraged and disorganized profession. Absentee landlords own the gardens and disheartened tenants try to work them. The dates are poor in quality, and the care given the trees has so deteriorated that the average crop per tree is below thirty pounds. Such a figure tells a very bad story of insufficient water and indifferent care. Scores and hundreds of gardens have been abandoned by their owners, and the rows of gaunt dead tree trunks give an impression of desolation and death scarcely surpassed by the whitening skeletons of the desert.

Throughout the Bottina a cultivator gets four *rials* a month, and that is thirty *baizas* a day, which is four to five cents in our money. He has no permission to grow small crops for himself, for the landowner needs all the water which is brought to the surface for his dates. It it not easy to establish a reliable standard by which we can judge the sufficiency or otherwise of such an income, but in Muttreh fifty *baizas* a day is regarded as the irreducible minimum for the maintaining of family life, and prices in the Bottina are not very different. It is not in the contract, but without question the cultivators do find part of their food in the garden, otherwise they would starve.

We have a very good friend among the small garden owners in the Birka area, and we frequently drop in to have a meal with him, which meal we are careful to pay for, because at the moment, the gardeners are in no position to entertain expensive strangers. Hafidh owns this garden which in its glory possessed a hundred date palms, if not more.

The price of dates has sunk lower and lower, until now Hafidh is on the road as an itinerant *hakeem.* He treats the sick of all varities, but his speciality is trichiasis. He ties two tiny pieces of wood on to the eyelid, enclosing a liberal bit of skin between them. They are clamped so tightly together that the enclosed skin dies. The hope is that this removal of a small strip of skin will uncurl the lid, and save the eye. Hafidh has earned a good many rupees in this way, but I am afraid that the eyes have not been much benefited. He insists that it is no longer worth his while to cultivate the garden, for even after careful cultivation the returns are so small that the family simply cannot live.

There is truth in this, of course. The price of dates has dropped so low that very little money can be earned in that way. Unfortunately, this family and its deterioration, illustrate also another very common feature of Bottina life. Hafidh has a very impressive family of large and extremely able-bodied sons. With their white gowns and their impressive-looking daggers, their erect carriage and fine black beards, they might be a group of provincial governors. Each of them has a family too. The garden has great possibilities, or at least it had possibilities once. There is a good well, and the water is not over twelve feet from the surface. It would not have been necessary to pay for any outside help, and food for the five families could have been raised easily. The one thing that is true of all members of this group is that they will not work. If they possessed slaves, they would be glad to order them around, but to attempt the laborious job themselves is unthinkable. Not one of them will touch it.

So they did the only thing there was to do. They hired an old Baloochee to come and work with their thin, feeble old bullock and pull some water to the surface day after day to keep the date trees from dying and provide a little crop. I feel sure that the trees in that discouraged garden will not produce ten pounds per tree this year. Indeed, I doubt if they produce five. And it will be only a few years till that garden passes into the hands of some energetic Baloochee who is willing to work like a slave, and his wife with him. And the elite of the community, in which class Hafidh very earnestly reckons himself, will mourn the increasing deterioration of the country.

The Bottina cultivators live near the seashore fortunately, and all of them catch fish on occasion, for the sea is full of fish, and they are hungry. As might be expected, a small community has developed which does nothing but fish. If ninety per cent of Oman's population raise dates, and ten per cent rear goats, we must supplement this with the statement that a fraction of one per cent catch fish. Visiting aliens like steamer officers, regard Muscat as the fisherman's paradise, but fishing as a sport is something that the Omanees know nothing about. It is one of the ways of earning a meager living.

Catching fish is an art and science by itself. There are dozens and scores of different varieties. Nets are used for some of them, and of the nets themselves there are many kinds. I saw one that must have been over a mile long. For the hook and line there are deep-sea fishes and surface fishes, and the wind and tide have to be consulted in all this, if a good catch is to be expected.

Finally, no matter how many things are consulted, the catch is the most uncertain thing in the world, alternating between feast and famine with a fine impartial caprice.

Men fish in groups of three to a dozen, in a boat which is rented for the purpose. Twenty per cent of the catch is the rent of the boat. It is a laborious and poorly paid sort of life, but by common consent vastly preferable to that of the Bottina date gardener, or even that of the Bedouin, in his democratic utopia of baked starvation. There is adventure in it, and unlimited scope for the instinct of the gambler. In addition there is usually enough to eat. Frequently enough there is danger. Only a few weeks ago, as I asked the prices and the catch of the day, I found the whole fishing fraternity concerned about a boatload of five colleagues unheard of for days, and probably lost without a trace. A storm two days previous was the explanation.

The fisherman has three markets. The first is, of course, the local community which simply lives on fish. In Seeb and Birka and all the towns that we visit in our outside dispensary work, the event of the day is the afternoon fish market. Dozens of varieties are offered for sale, and apparently every man goes home at night with either a small piece of a large fish, or a large string of small fish for his supper.

But the fisherman's market extends further than the local community. Coming back from our trips to neighboring towns, at sundown we always expect to meet dozens and scores of donkeys and camels carrying part of the catch of the day to inland points. Great fires are built at sundown, and the fish are broiled thoroughly.

They keep longer before spoiling. The donkey is the more rapid traveler, and for the far distant points they are used. They travel hard all night long and are able to reach points that are fifty miles inland, so that the absorptive capacity of the fish market is greatly increased. The fish develop a formidable astral body toward the end of these trips and can be detected a long way off. American palates would not be tempted.

In addition to this sale of fresh fish, many are dried and salted, and exported in various directions, but principally to Ceylon. Just why the Ceylonese prefer Muttreh fish, no one seems to know, but we are glad that they do. Last year they ate four *lacs*' worth. The fish are dried in Muttreh, and Muttreh has a reputation all over Arabia for its inimitable smell. The smell, however, is due to the entrails and refuse, which are not properly disposed of. The dried fish themselves are of good quality.

Of late years one of our energetic merchants has been exporting great quantities of tiny dried minnows to Germany. There the chickens eat them. Trade with Germany is difficult because of their unwillingness to pay for such things except in goods which are difficult to dispose of in Oman. Still, a good many tons of these tiny dried fish have been sent, and the life of the hard-pressed Bottina cultivator has been distinctly brightened by the accessory income that the trade has brought.

But the fishermen are a small community, and even the added income which the appetite of the German chickens has provided is a very slight help. The Bottina is a date-raising community, and the level of life is set by the price of dates. For years that price has been so low that even the garden owners make little or nothing, and numbers of them are moving away. We all hope and believe that the extreme level of poverty in the Bottina is essentially abnormal, and therefore temporary. Oman is not a land of hard-faced landlords. It is a land of much brotherhood and comradeship. The landowners themselves have their backs against the wall, and the condition of the tenants is bound to be bad.

But in the meantime the men that do the work are starving to death. Thirty *baizas* a day for an entire family, with no opportunity to raise small crops for themselves means exactly that. And because the cultivator gets thirty *baizas* a day, the tree produces thirty pounds a year. That literally is about the present average throughout the discouraged and broken Bottina country. There is no reason why the date palms of the mountain oases should produce more than the Bottina trees, but they do. They averaged in a large garden which I investigated 117 pounds a tree, and the fundamental reason is that their cultivators get 117 *baizas* a day caring for them. As a matter of precise fact, counting the small crops that the mountain cultivators are allowed to grow for themselves, they probably do get very nearly that much.

The one thing that requires doing in Muscat is restoring the position and morale of the Bottina cultivator. It will not be difficult to treble the present production of dates if a comfortable living is provided for the cultivators as a result. To accomplish this will probably prove difficult, for human society is a complicated, elastic sort of thing, like a soft balloon which, when pushed in at one point, swells out an equal amount at another. One thing, however, could be done by government fiat which would help very substantially. A law could be laid down by the Sultan giving to every cultivator the irrevocable right to cultivate small crops for himself, and punishing drastically any interference with that right. If this were sent out with the teeth of royal determination in it, the whole Bottina situation would be lifted to a new level overnight.

There are other things which might help. The Bottina is greatly handicapped by inferior varieties of its date palms. Some old trees are replaced by new sprouts each year, and, if a steady effort were made to see that the new plants were of the better and more profitable varieties, in the course of the years a better crop would result. We need, too, to find out what is the best and most economical means of raising water from the wells. If some crude-oil engine or other machine could be developed which could make irrigation profitable from wells seventy-five feet deep, the area of cultivation could be doubled.

But the important thing is improving the lot of the cultivator. Suitable machines, if such exist, will be brought in. Experiments are being tried even now which seem to offer some promise. The Persian wheel is being tried out by one of our officials, and the centrifugal pump by another, but it is the cultivator rather than his tools who needs improvement. If we can feed him decently, put his children in school, and give his family some red cloth with which to celebrate their feasts, the country will rejoice and blossom as the rose.

No one who has seen the Bottina can work in Muttreh without carrying the Bottina burdens on his mind, and speculating occasionally on means for lightening them. In the meantime we decided that a trip a year, such as we had been making, was simply playing at the job which God had given us to do. It was our task to help the hard-pressed cultivators now, so far as we could, and these trips were not doing it.

We decided to see what could be done by means of weekly clinics held fifty miles from Muttreh. A day a week we devoted to this purpose, and it was the hope that several points, perhaps three, could be reached in one day. This would make it possible to reach the date gardeners with an antimalarial service which would make a really significant contribution to their pitiful condition. Friends at home provided a Ford motor and set it up with four driving wheels instead of two. This tank for service in Arabia excited lots of surprised comment in America, when it was driven from Chicago to New York on its way out, and more comment still when it arrived in Muttreh.

We have learned a fair amount about sea travel since embarking on the policy of one tour a year to the far-distant points. That, however, is a small thing compared to what we have learned about land travel since instituting our weekly dispensary service with the Ford tank. A road in Oman is any long, slender piece of land over which a Ford car can be driven, pushed, or otherwise persuaded to navigate. Even a Ford cannot climb the mountains, so we have to wander carefully around the stones in the *wadis*. A stone the size of a piano or larger stops even a Ford. Many of these towns can be reached along the sea, and the coast is a great temptation. If it were not for the millions of crabs that dig their little underground houses along this road, we could use it more. These citizens shift their lodges frequently, and when a large colony is encountered, we have a terrain with about the consistency of porridge. A man walking over such an area will sink in halfway to his knees at every other step, and there is no known motor vehicle which will not stall and try to bury itself there among the crabs. Nothing remains then except to summon help and have twenty-five to fifty men chant merrily as they pull the motor out of its troubles, extracting a considerable fee from the owner for the service.

We wore the six-wheeler out. The soft sand defeated it. The engine was not heavy enough to drive four wheels when they were all bogged. The dispensaries were maintained, but it was by means of paying a whole lot of subsidies to the villages, as the price of frequent rescues. We replaced that car with a light Ford V-8 phaeton, dressed up with nine-inch tires. That was real medicine, and we have paid only two or three subsidies in the four years since. Those nine-inch tires opened the road to Kuriat. We forced our way through the unpenetrated *wadi* one afternoon and were welcomed almost with banners. The government came up to that challenge and cleared the road, so that taxis now run to that point whenever they are asked to do so.

One day, while we were still driving our six-wheeled tank, an hour before sundown we burned out the clutch. That is an incurable disease, for most of us do not carry spare clutches. In this part of the world, no taxi cares to be caught out lacking a spare rear axle, or an extra crown wheel. An extra front spring, they always carry, too, but even they trust their clutch.

It was evident that there was nothing for it that time, but to sleep *in situ*, and send in word for a taxi to come and rescue us. We were forty miles from home, and forty miles is a long way when legs are the only available motor. Walook was with us, and him we parked in the car with a little money to keep starvation away, till Mohammed could come back with a new lining for the clutch and drive the machine home. It was necessary to leave someone with such a car, or every removable thing would be missing inside of twenty-four hours.

The rest of us walked five miles to Seeb, where Mohammed assured us he could find the sister of one of his wives. It was dark and the world was cold and silent when we got there. We found no sister, but only her empty hut, which seemed like adding insult to injury. However, the neighbors told us where a different sister might be found, so we were left there in the empty house, while Mohammed fared forth on a donkey to find her. After an hour the two of them returned and with them two luckless chickens which they had caught. The chickens seemed to realize that their life expectancy was short, and this fact they mourned. Some eggs had been secured too, and a little flour. A few date sticks were picked off the edge of our date-stick house, and a fire was soon cooking some food. Theater supper was served at twelve, and not a bad one at that, with stewed chicken, flat bread, and eggs.

The winter wind was cold. I did not know that it could get so cold in Arabia. The cracks in our little house were of about the same dimensions as the date sticks which separated them. Our host was solicitous concerning our fate, and a man was found who offered to ride to Muttreh thirty miles away; the following morning he would send a taxi to get us. With a good donkey it can be done. We paid him his fee and planned to pay him a little more when we met him later in Muttreh. I think that he probably regarded this as the easiest money he had seen for a long time. He belonged to the fraternity which believes that "only saps work." We never saw him or our money again.

Our hosts brought a cotton-padded quilt, under which Mrs. Harrison and I tried to keep each other warm, with most indifferent success. Mr. Pennings was with us, and he wrapped himself up in a still more ragged and ancient specimen of the quilt-maker's art. When morning came, he remarked that Oman was certainly a hard field, and we agreed with him. However, Mrs. Pennings, untrustful soul that she was, did not wait for any messenger with an S.O.S. in his hand. When we failed to turn up by morning, she promptly sent out a rescue party in a taxi, and by ten o'clock we were back at home working in the morning clinic as usual.

We spent a lot of thought and put a lot of work into those weekly clinics. Thursday we expected to find life a little different, and we were not disappointed. We never did sleep out in the desert except that once, but it took hard work sometimes to prevent it. One morning on our way to Birka I broke a tooth out of the crown wheel. There were some critical cases in the hospital, and I was extremely unwilling to be marooned abroad that night. We were forty miles from home when it happened, but we drove back thirty miles, and made the rest of the distance on a donkey. Before we were through we had torn four teeth out of the crown wheel and driven one of the pieces through the gear case, as well as broken a cog in the gearshift assembly. It took two hundred rupees to repair the damage, but we did get home.

But the clinics themselves were a great disappointment. The date gardeners for whom the work was planned did not come, and after several years of this effort we reluctantly concluded that our job was still most emphatically not being accomplished. There were various reasons. In the first place it was sometimes impossible for the cultivators to devote even this much time to getting the quinine, or other medicine that they needed. As a matter of fact, however, through the winter that argument does not hold. There are very few cultivators who cannot spare a few hours then to get something if they really want it.

A much more important reason was that many of these men owed money to the government. Their taxes were unpaid, and they dared not show themselves in the towns under any circumstance, for fear of immediate arrest. These taxes on the date palms, are a new thing, and very keenly resented. For the most part they have remained unpaid, to the great embarrassment of the royal treasury. Some active riots occurred in one or two places, for the men were determined not to pay.

But the most important reason was that the date cultivator, working at his hopeless drudgery, as a partner with the bullocks, comes to share the bullock's outlook on life; and, while he appreciates an obvious blessing when it is put directly in front of his eyes, there is not enough spirit and initiative left in him, to drive him half a mile to get it, no matter what it is.

We decided to embark on a new line. Kumbar came back about this time from a long absence. He had been lent to Dr. Storm for a trip around the southern coast of Arabia. Kumbar is our outdoor contact man. He was born to be the leading mixer in the country. I venture to guess that he has never met anyone of whom he was afraid or anyone he did not immediately like. Moreover he has accumulated a good deal of experience in the hospital. He can give an intravenous injection, very well indeed, and he has some judgment in the administration of quinine. Noobie had been moved up into the ulcer room so Kumbar was not needed there. We decided to see if Kumbar could get the date gardeners to take the quinine they needed, if he carried it to them right where they sat, so to speak, and put it in their mouths.

He could. The assignment delighted him, and it delighted the date-raising fraternity just as much. Every Monday morning Kumbar fares forth on his little donkey with his saddlebags crammed full of quinine and Epsom salts. He carries a set of tooth forceps, and equipment to wash and treat ulcers, and he leaves behind with such patients the salves and bandages they need so they they can carry on by themselves when he is gone. Quinine he dispenses in great amount. Other things more sparingly. Aching teeth he pulls with much skill. Fifty-six was the record for one week.

Kumbar wanders from one date garden to another, from Monday to Thursday. He ends up at one of the weekly clinics of which there now are four, each a monthly affair, and each functioning chiefly as the climax to Kumbar's wanderings of the previous four days. This itinerant service carries Muttreh quinine to the gardeners for sixty miles in one direction, ending at Kuriat and Hail Ghaf. In the opposite direction the trail ends at Nuchl, which is seventy-five miles from home.

The date gardeners suffer from very bad eyes in some areas, and it was the plan to have Kumbar note carefully those who needed a trichiasis operation, or some other simple surgery, and once a month we would send Mobarrek out with him, to do small operations. In this way we hoped to make a real contribution to a very bad eye situation.

Kumbar found that our impressions regarding eye diseases were correct, though areas differ, and the average was not so bad as we had feared. In Billa, a small garden center about sixty miles from Muttreh, he found dozens whose eyes would be lost unless their lids could be operated on. He arranged to have them ready and waiting, and the next week Mobarrek went with him, expecting to have lots of work to do.

It embarrasses the clinic in Muttreh very badly indeed to have both the boys gone, but we managed to get along for the four days involved. After all, the date gardeners' eyes are important too. But although most of the patients in question were men this time, it was the women who ruled or at least it was they who exercised the feminine prerogative of changing their minds, and not a single individual was willing to be touched when Mobarrek turned up all keen and bloodthirsty, and prepared to be a high-caliber public benefactor.

This somewhat ludicrous denouement of a very rosy enterprise has been repeated a number of times since;

and, while we have succeeded in rescuing a dozen eyes or thereabouts in the course of the last two years, it is not possible to wax very enthusiastic over any contribution that we have made, up to date, to the gardeners' eyes. Mobarrek is not a very good salesman, for all that he is an unsurpassed medical assistant. Evidently the cultivators do not want his contribution, even if it is brought to them right where they sit, and put into their mouths, or rather into their eyes. So, at the moment, we meditate on teaching Kumbar to do eyelids. Evidently we need to have a first-class book agent selling this particular article.

That sounds simple, but in reality it is far otherwise. Minor surgery in general, and trichiasis operations in particular, are tricky affairs, with lots of pitfalls, and some of the post-operative episodes are serious. It will take months of hard work to do it, and the eyelids will not be as well done by a considerable margin. They say that there was once a baseball manager who chose his men from candidates who had natural ability as batters, and trained everything else into them; so we will have to take the one man we have who is a natural salesman, and train all the rest into him. It is not true of the rest of the Arabs, and especially not true of the free and untrammeled Bedouins, but the Bottina date gardeners, whose partners are the bullocks and whose life is dark and unrelieved drudgery, accept the best that we can give them, only after we have overcome lots of sales resistance.

We hoped for developments in other directions. There are several points where it is easy to leave the Bottina and travel to the near-by towns of inland Oman. Since the rebellion of twenty-five years ago, when the inland country repudiated the Sultan and all his works, the missionaries have been shut out of that country along with all other white faces. Both Dr. Dame and Dr. Storm have made medical tours into the forbidden country, but neither succeeded in leaving an open door behind when he came back. It was the hope that Kumbar, as a purveyor of quinine, might hypnotize a door or two; and then, after he had prepared the way, we had plans for a fortnightly dispensary in at least one of these near-by places, which is, as a matter of fact, seventy-five miles away.

Kumbar did his part of the job, and we started such a dispensary in Nuchl. Nuchl is an important place in one of the three or four largest oases of the whole inland country. Things ran very well indeed for a month or so, and the people really appreciated what we could do for them. There is no partnership with the bullocks in the mountain country, and the difference is felt immediately. Some of the friends of the mission of twenty-five years previous appeared, and we seemed to have entered a very promising door indeed.

The religious leaders however, were not pleased, and so after perhaps two months we were abruptly asked to discontinue our visits. Evidently we must teach Kumbar to hypnotize his victims more thoroughly. The opposition, however, did not last, and as this report goes to press we have received a most cordial invitation to come back and set up our shop again.

In Oman, as in the rest of Arabia, everything depends in the last analysis on what the people want. Sometimes it takes a good while to overcome the opposition of the religious leaders and the sheikhs, but, if any demand is kept steadily active, it is eventually granted. Mrs. Harrison was part of the force that set up work in Nuchl, and the women were very sure how they felt about our coming to Nuchl. I was very confident that this exclusion order would be revoked, for out in this part of the world, what the women want they get, and even the most hardy of the mullahs do not like to pit themselves against the feminine vote.

At the end of several years' experience we feel that we have made a considerable contribution to the date gardeners of the Bottina in the way of quinine distribution. The numbers that are reached are considerable, amounting to several hundred a week. It becomes more difficult than ever to tell the truth in our statistical reports, may the man perish who invented them. What is the total number of treatments given in the Muttreh hospital in a year? I am not sure that giving a man Epsom salts by the hand of an itinerant assistant like Kumbar should be dignified by such an impressive term. Nor is it easy to invent a better one, and the figure at the end of the year is so large that I am afraid our friends at home will suppose that the tiny Muttreh hospital has grown to half the size of the Massachusetts General.

Nothing could be more obvious than the fact that the date gardeners of the Bottina need some word for their minds and their hearts inside as well as quinine for their bodies outside. Christ came to bring deliverance to the captives, and certainly these men are captives. The prison that encloses their souls seems far more dreadful than the hungry emptiness of the Bedouins or the aching ulcerated legs of the *hamalees* in Muttreh.

Up to date this has completely defeated us. None of these men can read or write, and our efforts to distribute copies of the Gospels and illuminated editions of the parables have amounted to little or nothing. Some years ago, Mr. Van Peursem came with us on a medical tour to Sohar, and on the outskirts of that city and other Bottina towns he held stereopticon exhibitions. A good part of our audiences were made up of the date cultivators from near-by gardens, and by this method he seemed to get over the wall that encloses the minds of these men, and let in at least some of the Christian message. Unfortunately Kumbar cannot read or write, but perhaps, if we armed him with a machine of this sort, he could minister to men's deeper needs at night just as he ministers to their more obvious and superficial needs during the day. Certainly if Christ came to preach the gospel to the poor, to bind up the broken-hearted, to preach deliverance to the captives, and to give sight to the blind, then His message must be for the Bottina date cultivators. It is evident, though, that we have not yet learned how to deliver it.

X

REACHING THE BEDOUINS

MOST OF US see Oman first through Muscat. That is because we travel in steamers. Bombay trades with Sur and Sohar and Khabooreh by means of sail-boats. About twenty-five thousand people live in these distributing centers, and it is around them that the political and commercial affairs of the country revolve. But these cities are neither large nor important, and the real soul of the country is not to be found in them.

Oman's only resources are its sunshine and its rain and its soil, and the balance between them is poor. Of sunshine we have enough for two countries and of rain not half enough for one. Of soil we have mostly stones. The visitor looks at the Oman landscape with astonished pity. "Why do people want to live there?" a man asked me once. Short of the Genii of the Arabian Nights, who could extract a living from this wilderness of baked mountains? A goat would starve in that arid barrenness and dreadful heat.

That is a mistake. Goats do not starve there. They can live, and camels with them. Because goats and camels can live there, men can. Over that rocky landscape from which the visitor recoils with a feeling of horror, nomad

Bedouins roam with their wives and babies. With them are goats and camels with their wives and babies. It is a real and profound partnership. The man contributes brains and leadership, and, with his rifle, protection. The goat contributes a capacity for survival that seems utterly undefeatable. He can gnaw a living off the bare rocks, and not a living for himself merely, but with something left over to keep the man alive as well.

During the winter when a little rain falls, there is a good deal of forage to be found in the *wadis* between the high bare mountains. The trees are not large but they come to be quite green. The *wadis* near Muttreh are really beautiful after a rain, and the goats and camels have a fine time. One wonders sometimes that their numbers are no larger.

Six months later the world burns like a furnace, and every green thing is dry and dead. The goat has no difficulty even then in finding dry forage. Certainly none of the *wadis* in the vicinity of Muttreh are lacking in it. But a goat must drink at least once in two days, and lacking water dry forage does no good. Everything depends on the wells, i.e. on the wells which do not dry up in the summer.

From one well to another the Bedouin wanders with his goats and camels. It is unusual for the flock to number over fifty, and these little flocks are often met by the traveler. The goats hunt for their breakfast on the tops of the highest mountains, and at the bottom of the deepest valleys. As our caravan was slowly winding its way through the *wadis* on the road to Sifala, we were usually under the eyes of some of these wanderers, often so far up on the sides of a great canyon that it was difficult to make them out. Whenever goats were seen we knew that their shepherd was not far away. Often we heard him singing cheerfully to himself and his goats, as they wandered together over their bare and rocky world.

This naked and hungry existence which the Bedouin and his goats enjoy in the desert is a far more meager living in point of food than that which the gardener and his bullock partner laboriously extract from the Bottina garden. But it is a free existence, with a cheerful disregard of hungry destitution which is one of the great triumphs of the human spirit. A little goat's milk plus the small allowance of dates they have been able to exchange for clarified butter in the bazaar, that is their whole diet. For clothes they possess a garment or two, in utter rags.

In the vicinity of Muscat, the Bedouins are supposed to be of a very civilized and urbane variety. They are shepherds with little flocks of goats. They scarcely know what houses are. Along the road to Seeb we see little verandas of a rough sort put up in front of a deep hole in the side of a mountain. That is the home of the Bedouin shepherd and his family, and of his goats as well. A copper utensil or two for cooking, and a skin for water is all the furniture which he possesses. If times have been good, there will be a red quilt for a bed. As for all the other things which we regard as necessary, they simply are not there; but if liberty and equality and fraternity are the supreme values of life, we have here some of the richest people on earth.

With their lean hard bodies, and their thin aquiline faces, there seems to be no limit at all to their endurance. On our recent trip to Sifala, the caravan was overtaken by rain, and a small tent which we had taken along was literally a lifesaver for the town Arabs which were in the party. The Bedouin camelmen however were not greatly interested in the tent. Sitting through the rainy night, and letting the sun dry them off the next day, was a common experience which called for little or no comment.

They walked through the heat of the day with nothing to eat, and this, too, seemed to be the regular thing. Even when the night came it was coffee that they wanted first. Apparently it is difficult for a Bedouin to eat till he has started his gastric juice going with some coffee. Each night we watched the caravan cook build a tiny fire, and brew some of their bitter refreshment in an earthenware coffee pot. That was the first course always. They would bring some of it around for their guests to drink.

The Bedouin sells goats, and goat's hair as well, and some hides. His best market for goats comes at feast time, when everyone wants to eat some meat, however bare the rest of the year may be of such luxuries. There is clarified butter too, which he sells as cooking fat. It is brought to the market in tiny water skins, which were doubtless the skins of small kids. He makes and sells dried cottage cheese, which is nourishing and full of vitamins. It is full of hair too, and the hair is more visible than the vitamins, so that it would not sell in an American market. We were surprised a few months ago to find bones being collected by the Bedouins and brought in to Muttreh. They must have picked up quite a number of rupees in that way. It appeared that a

European buyer had appeared who wanted these bones for fertilizer.

Coming in from Kuriat a few weeks ago we met two tiny Bedouin boys bringing in wood from the wilderness. The smaller of the two could hardly have been over ten years old, and his brother was scarcely larger. With their sharp little intense faces, they were hurrying their loaded donkeys on toward Muttreh, where they would arrive the following morning and get perhaps a rupee for the two loads. By the time they returned it would be an enterprise of three days. No wonder they looked strained and drawn and curiously old as they earnestly joined in the never-ending struggle for existence that the desert enforces on every one of its children.

The Bedouins supplement their meager living of goat's milk and dates with the sale of wood, bones, hides, and anything else that comes to hand. A more substantial accessory activity for those who own camels is transporting dates in season from the oases to the coast cities. There is a good deal of work of this sort to do, and as we travel to our outlying dispensaries we expect to meet a number of such caravans. A caravan of camels is the slowest and most superciliously dignified thing in this world.

But in spite of all these incidental things, the Bedouin for the most part lives with his goats. He guides them and protects them from enemies, of which there are a good number. Even close to cities like Muttreh, the mountains are full of jackals and foxes, while the more dangerous human thieves are never absent. He wanders all day long with them over mountains and *wadis*, and shows them where the best food and water can be found.

In return he lives from their milk and meat and skins and hair. Each lives with the other, and from the other, and for the other, partners in the freest and hungriest life in the world.

The Bedouin sees the world through eyes that are different from our own. When we opened the road to Kuriat with our motor, it was by a narrow margin that serious trouble with the Bedouins of those parts was avoided. I was much interested in this reaction, for the motor does not do them any harm, and all of them have seen such machines in Muttreh. But the motor was a new thing, and new things are not wanted. They had an instinctive feeling, I imagine, that eventually this new and hideous animal would compete with their precious goats for the meager supply of grass and forage that the mountains afford.

But the deeper reason why they did not want the motor was that it stood in their eyes as a representative of ordered government. Bedouins differ in many things, but in this they are all alike.

Anything that looks like regulated order is most cordially hated. Even their own tribal organizations are loose and irresponsible. When the recently organized Muscat petroleum concession sent a pair of engineers to investigate the possibilities of the territory behind Khabooreh, they found plenty of excitement. The chief of the tribe in question was their guide and chaperon, but that did not keep the tribesmen from killing one man and wounding another before they were pacified.

Their conception of property is not the same as ours. Anything movable, particularly if it runs around on hoofs, is the property of anyone who can get it, or, rather, it is the property of anyone who can keep it. The national sport of Arabia is raiding back and forth between the different tribes. Years ago I met a most benevolent-looking old sheikh in Sharga and was greatly intrigued by his appearance. Abraham, I feel sure, must have looked like him. He had my father's own eyes, than which there never were any more twinkly and delightful.

My obvious interest in this old patriarch alarmed my friends, for it appeared that they regarded him as a bandit of the first order. He was a member of the Ajman tribe, which, I gathered, was sufficient to condemn even Abraham himself, had he been there. I warmly repudiated this idea. Those eyes could not belong to a bandit of the Ajman tribe. I was wrong.

"You are not a member of the Ajman?" was my somewhat ill-advised question.

"I certainly am." There was a tinge of nettled pride in the answer.

"But you do not take part in their raids, and robberies."

"Of course I do. What sort of man do you think I am?" Evidently the case was hopeless, but I continued.

"Your beard is white already. If you keep up this sort of life, you are likely to die from a bullet in one of these raids." Then he floored me completely.

"Well, I surely hope so. I certainly do not want to die just lying sick in a bed."

To an enemy the Bedouin can be vindictive and cruel. At least that is his reputation. It is a pleasure to testify that to a friend he can be loyalty itself. We were taken into Sifala by an ordinary caravan of Bedouins, but we found them to be extraordinary men. We liked each other so well that we made arrangements to be brought back by the same company. The trip was a hard, fatiguing one, but it did not seem so to them. If we asked for a drink of water, they were quick to bring it either from an available spring or from a water skin.

The caravan was halted at noon whenever the convenience of the strangers dictated, even though they would have found it more convenient to keep steadily on till night came. We were their guests and nothing could have surpassed their consideration and kindness.

Coming back we had to carry a thousand *rials* * with us, and the lure of such a sum seemed dangerous on that long road, which was to last four days before we came to the better-known and presumably safer country close to Muscat. So we asked Sheikh Eesa for an official caravan leader who would represent him as the ruler of the country.

It would be difficult to imagine a more perfect gentleman than the Bedouin caravan leader who was sent with us. He came on a beautiful riding camel, which he cared for with the utmost attention. His first question, indeed, was whether we had any medicine which might benefit its one blind eye. We marveled at his efficiency and earnestness. He roused the camelmen in the morning, and helped get the packs in place on the camels' backs. He brewed a tiny pot of coffee immediately the day's trek was over, for him and for us. He marked out the road and determined the stopping places.

His teeth protruded, and his shirt badly needed wash-

* A *rial* is a Maria Theresa dollar worth now about twenty-five cents.

ing, but Mohammed was a very handsome figure on his splendid camel and we were proud to be headed by such an important official. In easy and natural courtesy he was a typical son of the desert. It would not have embarrassed him to meet the king, and he did not feel himself superior to the meanest camelman of the caravan.

Yet Mohammed was a child, a typical desert child. When we arrived in Muttreh we gave him a good reward, a little more than was expected, for we felt that his service had been outstanding. He went to the bazaar and spent it all, and came back to beg for some more, "just a little," so he could get back home carrying to his children a memento of his Muttreh visit. We felt that such naïve trust must not be disappointed, so we gave it to him, and like all children he received it gladly.

The hospital has no means of reaching these wanderers in any regular way, but Kumbar visits them in their camps occasionally, that is, when such a camp happens to be close enough for him to reach. The Bedouins in the vicinity of Birka have a semipermanent collection of tents within five miles of that city. These tents are made out of date sticks, and are nearly as mobile as those from cloth.

We visited this center of goats and camels and men one morning and were enthusiastically received. The reflection of the faces in the shiny sides of the automobile excited as much interest as the medicines. We decided that they did not have mirrors in their dressing rooms. We had a few teeth to pull there as well as other ailments to treat. Very little quinine was called for, however, which means that malaria is rare. It was something of a surprise to have any teeth to pull, for teeth among the Bedouins are proverbially well preserved, their diet of milk doubtless being the cause. But if caries of the teeth is rare, pyorrhea unfortunately is not.

Gunshot wounds constitute the favorite disease of the Bedouin. New ones and old ones, though it must be admitted that we do not get the new ones. Those are treated at home. Such patients are handled in a vigorous way, and while hemorrhage and infection carry off a large number, more recover than might be expected. The gunshot fractures are the most serious, and these are handled exceedingly well.

Such a patient is laid on the sand, and his fractured member fastened in place by driving little stakes along each side and lacing the limb down with leather strips. When the limb is thus thoroughly immobilized and the patient with it, a hollow is excavated underneath the patient, for a bed pan, and a tent is erected over him to keep off the sun. The man stays in place till he is well, or rather until his fracture has united. That is a matter of weeks and months.

Cases without fracture are less serious. They are bandaged and poulticed and eventually come in to the hospital for the removal of fragments of dead bone which could not come away of themselves.

Another disease common among the Bedouins is the so called Madura foot. It is due to an organism very similar to actinomycosis. It is a disease of the desert, usually of the feet, for the Bedouin is a barefooted individual. The progress of the disease is slow, but nothing stops it. The great swollen foot with its dry sinuses looks absurdly like an enormous potato. It is a pathetic and hopeless thing.

Dr. Mylrea of Kuwait has found that prolonged treatment with bismuth causes very marked improvement in these "potato feet," and since that discovery we have all been anxious to find a patient willing to remain under treatment for a long time. The hope is, of course, that if treatment of that sort is prolonged sufficiently, we can bring about a complete cure. But a Bedouin is about as patient as an American tourist, and it is difficult to keep him in for six days, to say nothing of six months.

Recently one of these nomads came in to the hospital in Muttreh, suffering from a very bad Madura foot. We explained very enthusiastically our hopes for his foot, if he would stay for six months' time. He was filled with enthusiasm at that moment, and cheerfully promised to stay for six years if necessary. He had the run of the hospital or at least of its verandas, and occasionally he saw someone from home. Homesickness overcame him after he had been with us for a few weeks only. His foot did show distinct improvement, but we could not be sure that he was even on his way to a complete cure. One of these days he will turn up again, with the process so far advanced that an immediate amputation will be imperative, and that will suit him much better, for within ten days he can return to his bare and beloved rocks, where his goats, I dare say, are lonesome without him.

Our exact scientific world, the Bedouin is not acquainted with. He is just as likely to bring to the hospital a purely imaginative disease as a Madura foot. Recently a woman was brought in by her husband because her pregnancy had lasted two years and the baby had not put in his appearance. It was an ordinary pseudopregnancy and there was nothing solid at all as the basis for the abdominal distention. I explained this to the lady, and Mrs. Harrison was given the job of convincing her that the baby was pure imagination. This proved to be a difficult piece of work. When told that every normal pregnancy terminates at the end of nine months or thereabouts, the Bedouin husband explained that among them this was not the case. One of her friends gave birth at the end of a five years' pregnancy!

We did not get to first base with her on this line, and examination showed a marked grade of retroversion. So we agreed to explore her abdomen as she so greatly desired. Her husband was present and after careful inspection he agreed that no baby was hidden in there. We corrected the retroversion, and everyone went home satisfied.

The Bedouin can change his mind, too, especially if some new and unexpected phenomenon disturbs his composure. On one of our trips to the Pirate Coast a boy with a most tremendous hernia turned up at the last minute. His reached for an inch and more below the knee, which is a very unusual size. He was practically incapacitated by this enormous handicap, and very anxious to have it mended. There was no time to attend to it in Abu Dhubbi, where we were at the moment, so we offered him passage with us to Bahrain. There we would be glad to fix him up.

It was a hard trip for him. The weather was rough, and the trip took about ten days. He had never been on the sea before, and the slightest motion made him utterly seasick. Only those who have been there know how miserable we all are when first introduced to this particular tribulation. One day when he had reached the stage where he wanted to die, and the urge to vomit overcame him, he did not make the necessary exertion and move ten feet to the edge and feed the fishes. He picked up a tin cup lying near him and filled that. This happened to be the drinking cup for the crew, the only one they had, and inasmuch as they were Shiah Mohammedans they were extremely fastidious about such things. There was a tremendous uproar over this *faux pas*, but the seasick Bedouin lay quietly and let the storm blow over. They did not throw the cup overboard either as they loudly declared they would have to do, but found some way of adequately purifying it for further use. After all it was the only one they had, and none of us was in a position to replace it.

We finally arrived, and once on shore our guest traveler felt better. He came into the hospital and was duly installed in a bed. The operation was set for the next day. That was a bad mistake. We should have attended to it that day. During the intervening time something frightened him, and when night came, he picked up his bedding and other small belongings, and disappeared. We have never seen him since nor found out what frightened him. Perhaps seasickness lasting for a week had reduced his nerve to an abnormally low point.

These people from the desert are less bound by convention than town Arabs. A vicious vesicovaginal fistula case came in two years ago, and stayed with us in Muttreh for nearly two months. She was not frightened when told that the operation would have to be performed by a man. The enormous opening was an inch and a half across, and after three operations there was only a tiny opening left. This, however, did not do her any good for she leaked as much as ever, and she decided at this point that she had had enough, and left. What cannot be done in three weeks' time for a Bedouin, had better be left unattempted.

Among them women have a better position than anywhere else in Arabia, and sometimes such a woman is absolutely chief of her clan. Such a woman came in to Muttreh asking to have her cyst removed. It was an enormous affair, and the history given indicated that it must be an ovarian in origin. It was so large, and the abdominal distention was so great, that nothing could be ascertained by examination. She declined to be operated on in Muttreh at the time of her first appearance, but turned up a year later when I was working in Sur. It promised to be a difficult case, and at the moment I would far rather have postponed it, for we had just lost a goiter case, and the atmosphere of the place was chilly. However this lady would have nothing to do with the idea of delay. She needed the operation and wanted it. There was no doubt about her needing it, so it was undertaken.

We had a bad afternoon of it. The cyst was hepatic in origin and utterly irremovable, and the patient did badly on the table. The operation was watched by four or five sons, the wildest-looking audience I have ever demonstrated before. But the patient did not die, and we were able to remove the greater part of the cyst, repairing it so that it took a good while for it to grow again to its former size. The patient made a recovery that was at least moderately satisfactory to all concerned.

But the Bedouin, for all that he is unacquainted with

some of the things that we know, is also acquainted with some of the things that we do not know. Some years ago a very popular Chinese merchant in Muscat was murdered. He had lived among us for a long time and was much liked. He bought shark fins from the Muscat fishermen, sending them to China where they serve as soup bones. He paid a good price and was regarded as a valuable community asset.

The courtyard of his little house was a dusty place, and every door was locked immediately the crime was discovered. The authorities sent a hurry call for some of our Bedouin friends, whose reputation as trackers was great. The chief tracker sat and studied the available tracks for a little time, and then ordered that every possible suspect come and make tracks in a level dusty area which he carefully prepared. The crime had been committed by a barefooted individual, which was a great mistake from the criminal's point of view.

Half of the population of Muscat, more or less, came and made tracks in the soft dirt for this wise old Bedouin to look at, but none of them interested him and he assured the Sultan that they were all innocent of the crime. Were there none who had remained away from this examination? There were none except the slaves in the royal palace. So the slaves had to come. "That is the man," said the old Bedouin, as one of the more truculent and troublesome of this group made a nice print for him to look at. The slave confessed to the crime and told where the money was hidden. They executed him a few days later.

Not all of the Bedouins are capable of being used for this purpose, with a man's life hanging on the decision, but they all learn this book of the desert to a degree that seems uncanny to us. One morning, as we traveled from Sifala back to Muscat, we found that three of our camels had wandered so far away during the night that they could not hear the breakfast call in the morning, so the whole caravan had to wait.

A Bedouin youngster was with us, fifteen or sixteen years old, one of the most perfect gentlemen that I have even seen. His smile was worth a five-dollar bill. He was as keen as a whip, and he went out and tracked the wanderers several miles and brought them back. The ground was stony and rough, and to my eyes utterly lacking in any tracks at all. Off that hopelessly illegible slate, that boy picked out the tracks of the three camels that he wanted, and followed them for miles in and out between the bushes and rocks. He brought them back, and grinned with great pleasure when we praised him for his achievement, as boys do the world over when they have been able to do better than their elders.

When we were sent to reopen the Muttreh medical work, it was the inland tribes and cities that we had particularly in mind. Coast cities are a dubious mixture always. The soul of a country is always better than its coast. France is better than Marseilles, and Oman is better than Muttreh.

But we found it extremely difficult to execute this commission. The inland country did not want us. Among the Beni Buttash, Bedouins close to Muscat, we have not even been able to get Kumbar in with his quinine. From the sheikhs further inland it has also been impossible to get an invitation. The hospitable cordiality and kindly comradeship of twenty-five years previous were vividly in mind, but times had changed. We wrote letters trying to arrange for medical tours but invitations were not forthcoming. Mr. Dykstra and I drove our six-wheeled leviathan through untamed *wadis* to Rostock and discussed the matter with the Imam in person. He was considerably surprised, I think, to find that we had succeeded in calling on him. He was personally cordial, too, but this strenuous wooing did not elicit an affirmative answer. No permission was given.

We learned on this trip what we had believed before—that the people themselves do want us. The Bedouins from that inland country, and the oasis people as well, come to the hospital in good numbers, and after they leave, they serve as advertising agents in their home communities. All the caravans from the inland country bring their dates, their wood, and their pomegranates to Muttreh, for there is no other port where steamers call. It is the emporium for trade of inland Oman just as it is for the Bottina.

The inland Omanees are all earnest Mohammedans. The flood of materialistic unbelief which has swept over Iraq, India, and Egypt has not reached them, and their confidence in the validity of religious conceptions is undisturbed. Most of them are Abadhees, and that means that religion costs something. Abadhees may not smoke tobacco, and in the inland districts this religious tenet is lived up to with scrupulous care. However, this particular product of the theologian's brain has been rejected by the Bedouins. All the Bedouins with whom I have come into contact smoke, and for the most part a brand of tobacco which I must say goes far to explain the prohibition of the practice.

The Abadhees, too, are emphatic in their teaching that the beard must be left untouched, and the sheikhs of inland Oman, with their long white beards reaching halfway to the waist, are very fine, dignified figures. The irreverent and unbelieving youths have stories about these beards. An old and dignified patriarch, as he and his wife slept together, felt some itchy irritation connected with his luxuriant beard. He called his wife to investigate, and she, running her fingers through it, was stung by a scorpion who had made his nest there. There are a number of reasons why this story is not true, the least of them being that scorpions do not live in dry, hairy places. But as showing the attitude of the younger generation, it is a true and excellent story. There are worse ones, as for instance, the one concerning the fat mullah whose skin lay in folds like a double chin. Its recesses had never been washed. When he died, then they had to be washed, for, however dirty a man may have been in life, in death he has to be cleaned up. When they lifted the folds apart, a small snake was disturbed. His home had been there for years.

The Abadhees are also very sure that the mustache must be kept so closely clipped that it might as well be shaved. This is supposed to reduce the dangerous pride of the human soul, which they regard as a religious matter of importance, as Sheikh Eesa of Shergieh assured me very warmly one day as I sat in his reception room in Kabul.

However, it became evident that it was not religious differences that kept us out of the inland country. Our patients in the hospital could talk religion over with us in a most friendly manner. They do not regard their own religious observances as disturbed by the presence of someone of a differing practice. Matters of importance, like quinine for fever, need not be interfered with by differing habits in prayer.

It was the political situation that excludes us. When inland Oman revolted and repudiated the authority of the Sultan, twenty-five years ago, the different sheikhs assembled, as their religious law provides they should, and elected a general ruler whom they call the Imam. Oman is a turbulent individualistic province, and the Imam has had a strenuous time. The first was assassinated after a few years, but the dissatisfaction with him appears to have been a personal matter. There have been rebellions, as a year ago when a small chieftain tried to transfer his allegiance to Muscat. This luckless man came to Muscat and was royally entertained by the Sultan. What presents and promises passed between them outsiders were not informed, but on his return he wrote to the Imam repudiating that official's authority completely. This manifestation of free and independent self-expression brought punishment down on his head, and several dozen men died before the war was finished. He remained "inside the iron" for some months, and was only released when he promised to repent of his sins and be adequately loyal. Two of his partisans, old friends of ours, dined with us in passing from Muscat to their own country. Forty-eight hours later one was dead.

Coming from Muscat, we are reckoned as of Muscat, and Muscat is feared exceedingly, not because of its religion, for Muscat does not have much religion anyway, but because of its taxes, of which it has a great many. Taxes have increased steadily through the years and bear heavily now, not because they are of any impressive proportions in themselves, but because the country is so poor and prices are so low that even light burdens seem heavy.

Twelve years ago, Mr. Wingate, the British consul, won laurels from Simla, and gratitude from Oman, by arranging for an official recognition of the Imam's government by the Viceroy of India. In this way he made an official peace possible, and the country became quieter. It had been reckoned in a state of rebellion before this time. The Imam has rested more easily since that administration.

But the inland country as well as the Bottina have to use Muttreh as their commercial capital, so in actual fact they pay in customs to the Muscat government, a heavier tribute than anything they are asked to pay to their own. All of their foreign relations are mediated through the Sultan. Many of their citizens travel, particularly to Zanzibar, and Muttreh has to furnish passports to all such wanderers. There have never been lacking those who look forward with much desire to the day when the whole of Oman can be united into one country again. The Imam feels all such sentiment very accurately, for with the re-establishment of the united kingdom his position and honor will disappear.

It is this which makes our entry into the inland country so difficult. We are looked on as representing the Muscat government, and insofar as we leave behind a pleasant impression, by so much is the way prepared for the dreaded reunion. Even now, when the doors are opening a tiny crack, it is not the Imam who is letting us in, but some of the more powerful of the sheikhs, who are technically under his rule but who, as a matter of fact, are the support which makes his rule possible. Our recent permission for an inland visit came from Sheikh Eesa of Shergieh, and whatever the theory of the Oman government, Sheikh Eesa is in actual fact a more powerful figure than the Imam, and the same is true of Suleiman bin Hamyeer of the high mountains around Tenoof.

◇◇◇

XI

MOUNTAINS AND OASES

IF BARE MOUNTAINS constituted the whole landscape, wandering Bedouins would be the whole population. Oman then would probably have about the population that Muttreh has now. The traveler who views the country from the top of Jebel Achdhar, sees nothing which would suggest the possibility of a garden or field anywhere. It is an utter wilderness of dry and barren rocks. The one or two inches of rain a year are insufficient for any agricultural plant. But flowing springs are found in the desolate *wadis*, and by their means men irrigate fertile gardens and form a community many times larger than that of the Bedouins. Wherever such water has been found, the graceful date palm appears with its feathery top and grateful shade. The date palm is the outward and visible sign of an inner and spiritual grace, for in Arabia water is the grace of God, His gift of life to man.

Wherever an Italian goes, he plants a grapevine, and wherever an Arab lives, his home is sheltered by a date palm. The Bedouin lives with, for, and by means of the goat. The oasis Arab lives with, for, and by means of the date palm. I have often asked these men why they do not diversify their crops, and give attention to some other promising trees. They do not know why. Doubtless in Arabia the date palm will support more human life per square yard, or rather per barrel of available water, than any other plant.

The country as a whole is an empty desert, and the fierce heat of the stony earth is only one degree less than that of the pitiless sun from which all death comes. The oasis which grows up around the flowing spring is a very beautiful spot, a real abode of peace. The wayfarer who comes out of these desolate blackened *wadis* to couch his camel at sundown where water has brought greenness and beauty will never search in a book for his description of heaven.

The amount of water which an oasis needs is enormous. Some of the springs are very large. In Somail the gardens stretch between the mountains on either side for fifteen miles. Even smaller places like Hajar, where only five thousand date palms are found, require very impressive amounts of water. Where does so much water come from? The Arabs speculate on various sources, the Euphrates river a thousand miles away being a favorite. But it is the rain that furnishes water for these springs, as impossible as that seems. We have seen the proof these last two years, when, because the rain stopped, the springs went down and some of them nearly disappeared. On our last trip to Habibieh, the lime trees and the pomegranates were dead, the date palms barely alive. Only a trickle of water came from their splendid spring, and unless the rains are better this year, those gardens will have to be abandoned, and the people move away.

The oases are narrow, stretching between mountains, sometimes miles in length, but rarely more than half a mile in width. The actual bed of a *wadi* cannot be planted with date palms, for perhaps twice a year a rushing torrent runs through to the sea and, as we saw in Sifala, anything unfortunate enough to stand in the water's path is swept away.

In this mountain world, everything depends on the springs, and they are given careful attention. The Suakim spring is led through underground tunnels for five miles and then through an above-ground channel for another mile before the water is used. Wells are sunk every hundred feet or less, following the line of flow planned for the water. Their depth is such that when the bottoms are connected by a tunnel the resulting channel will have a gentle slope but one adequate for a vigorous flow. The walls and the tunnels are lined carefully with stone so that it is a comparatively easy matter to keep the underground courses clear.

I have never seen or heard of new watercourses being opened. Those that are to be seen now are obviously scores and probably hundreds of years old. It is evident, too, that Oman society has lost a large part of its capacity to co-operate in these community enterprises, which must have characterized it once, for even maintaining the present watercourses is difficult.

The Suakim date gardeners explained this to me at some length. Their watercourse requires a thorough housecleaning every ten years if the flow is to be kept up. So much is indispensable. It might better be done oftener. For some years the matter has been agitated, and, because of the steady diminution of the flow, before long it will be imperative. But such a matter is arranged with great difficulty, for the cost must be divided between a number of owners, all of them living a long distance away, and interested in the garden only for the profits that it yields on money they have invested in it. Housecleaning will cost eight hundred rupees when it is finally taken up and attended to. In the meantime the shortage of water presses heavily on the gardeners, for their private small crops have to be given up first. The date palms which give the owners their profits suffer last of all. Every time that we go to Suakim, we pass two abandoned gardens where the flow of water has been lost altogether, probably because of this neglect of the channels.

The oases that these springs make possible are some of them real cities. Somail is the largest, and its gardens stretch for miles and miles between the mountains. Nuchl is nearly as large, Rostock and Nezwa as well. Four or five thousand people must live in each of these magnificent oases, and years ago, when an American expert in date culture visited Oman, he stated that in his judgment, the care and cultivation of dates had reached a higher point in Somail than anywhere else in the world. The best varieties are cultivated, and the highest prices are secured.

There is no partnership with bullocks here, but a fine aristocratic hospitality, the pride of Arabia. Men have only to guide the flowing water and care for the growing trees. Hajar is a tiny gem among the mountain oases. A fine spring waters five thousand palms. The average of one of its large gardens worked out last year to 117 pounds per tree. The water supply is studied with care, and used more thriftily than in the Bottina, while everywhere there are cement runways to prevent waste. No effort is made to cultivate more trees than the available water will care for. It is a pleasure to turn from the thirsty gardens of the Bottina and, after traveling across the stony desert for twenty miles, to reach the gardens of Wadi Maowel and Nuchl. There the date palms in their well-nourished greenness seem almost consciously happy and contented.

There are scores of these oases scattered through the mountains of Oman. Indeed, counting the small ones there must be two or three hundred. Most of them are very small. The Arabs estimate the inhabitants of these mountain gardens as double the population of the Bottina, and I know of no estimate with any better foundation. If the Bottina is considered as having a population of a hundred thousand, Oman oases may perhaps have two hundred thousand.

Living conditions are better by far than in the Bottina. Some of the gardens are cultivated by their owners, and even when tenants work for an absentee owner they are much better treated. The fundamental law is that the cultivator receives one spray of dates from each tree. This means the best spray, which is often as good as any other two. It works out to about an eighth of the crop, and in many places the cultivator's share is so reckoned. This afforded about sixty *baizas* a day throughout the year in a garden which I investigated, and, in addition, the cultivators of these mountain oases have permission to raise small crops of their own. This includes vegetables, alfalfa, and even bananas. When the water supply is adequate, this is a good arrangement, and among these people one finds bright clothes for feast days and schools to teach the children to read. In Suakim all the children that I was able to find were in school. Some of these places must have a very high percentage of literacy.

But when the rainfall drops and the flow in the springs diminishes, the standard of life goes down with it. The schools and the bright clothes disappear. In a very bad year there will be barely enough water to keep the palms alive, and none at all for the cultivator's private crops. Then distress is very great. If the drought continues for a long time, even this small supply disappears and the people move away.

That has happened in a great many places in Oman. Between 1910 and 1920, Shergieh went through a drought that simply depopulated it. Forty or fifty years ago Wadi Maowel did the same. Our friends in Effie, one of the richest oases in all Oman, tell of the time when the place had to be abandoned utterly. Long years of drought finally drove them all out. Later renewed rains brought them back, and they have seen days of great prosperity since. There is no community in Oman which does not feel the menace of drought continually hanging over it; and, when a single year passes without rain, as happened recently in Muscat, peoples' faces are grave, and their hearts full of fear. Without water no one can live.

The hospital serves Muttreh first of all, but only for the sake of reaching Oman. That is a large order, for Oman is a large province. It takes a caravan ten days to travel from one edge to the other. The hospital has been working now for ten years and through all this time we have been trying to get into this inland country. Political and religious reasons conspire to keep us out, but disease microbes and gunshot wounds conspire to get us in. People get sick out in the far-distant corners. They are no sicker there than in Muttreh itself, but sometimes it is pretty hard to get to them.

One day a letter came from Suleiman bin Hamyeer. He is a powerful sheikh. Along with Sheikh Eesa of Shergieh, the fortunes of all Oman are in his hands. His father, Hamyeer, was notorious. He and Sheikh Eesa attacked Muscat twenty-five years ago. They took the city and looted it nice and clean. The chinaware and Indian brassware that they took back with them are scattered all over Oman. I have seen pieces hidden away in the most unlikely places. But the British rescued Seyyid Feisul, the Sultan, when he was a prisoner in his own palace. Hamyeer went back home and continued to rule his mountain kingdom.

Hamyeer's son, Suleiman, is an urbane gentleman whom it is a pleasure to meet. He has kept all his father's territories, and is a greater man than he. He is not happy, for his efforts to raise a fine family of boys have not been very successful. His only son was ill. Could I come at once and see what could be done in the way of treatment? The messenger who carried the letter would make all arrangements.

That sounds good, but the little boy was a long way off, on the other side of Jebel Achdhar, the tallest of all the ranges of Oman. Some of its peaks are nearly ten thousand feet high.

However there was no way of making the problem any less. The hospital owns no airplane. So we marked a week off from the calendar of hospital work, and called in Mohammed our chauffeur. Were the tires in usable shape? Scarcely, and the new ones still weeks away, but he would see what could be done. Very well, then, tomorrow morning early. They were a pathological lot of tires, with the red inner tube showing through in one place. We suffered from ruptured aneurism more than once before we were through, but tires can be mended. They are a tough lot.

In spite of its lame tires, Mohammed thought he could push the motor through to Awabi. That is halfway to Tenoof, and it saved us three days on camels. An especially vicious puncture kept us on the road overnight, but we did get to Awabi. Taxis have been there many times since, but it was the hospital car that opened that particular road. We took Noobie along and left him in Awabi with the motor. Everything movable, or rather everything removable was taken away and secreted in a sack, the sack being the responsibility of the sheikh of Awabi. Noobie camped with the car for three or four days till we got back.

Suleiman's messenger was with us, and his word was sufficient to bring for inspection various donkeys of the place, so we might select the best for our particular journey. These donkeys are tremendous animals. I have seen nothing like them anywhere else. They look like half-grown mules. However, the donkeys did not surprise me so much as their extraordinary saddles. I felt sure that the local saddlemakers must have suffered from bad dreams when they made those. They were enormous double humped affairs, as if the effort was to imitate a north Indian camel. The rider was deposited between these two enormous humps, which were big and firm, and over a foot in height.

I protested against these extraordinary creations of a perverted artistic instinct and was briefly informed that these humps, fore and aft, were there to keep me from falling off. This was the unkindest cut of all. Did they think that I was so drunk as that, or would become so on the trip? They grinned at this and became more communicative. Evidently I had not been over the road before. I admitted that I had not. After I had seen it once they assured me, I would understand why these saddles were necessary. I wondered what sort of road lay ahead of us, but decided to accept the saddlemakers' effort as read. It appeared that there was no great hurry. The climb over the mountains would not begin till after midnight, when the moon came up. We were to travel three hours first to the foot of the mountain. There we would wait.

We had a nap at the foot of the mountain, and shortly after midnight I had my first lesson in the use of these remarkable saddles. We mounted, each in his hollow between the two humps. After a few miles the serious climbing began. My critical spirit evaporated. It was dark with a niggardly sliver of a moon. The impression was that we were going up an almost vertical cliff. Riding on the back of a cat as she climbs a tree would give much the same general effect. I sat on the hump behind and clung earnestly to the hump in front, and wondered why they had not been made larger.

Those donkeys were extraordinary animals. The path was a pure mental concept, running through the midst of an utterly chaotic rocky waste. The donkeys followed it by means of their noses, which were down close to the ground all the time. I did not know that the donkey had such a well-developed sense of smell. The climb was terrible. My donkey would struggle upward for perhaps thirty seconds, climbing almost like a cat. Then he would rest for an equal period, puffing desperately to get his breath. This was kept up steadily through the entire night, till with the sunrise we came up on a plateau and the going was somewhat easier.

It was an uncanny night. The path, visible only to the donkey's nose, had a most dreadful predilection for the edge of any precipice that was available. In the darkness the sheer drop might have been five thousand feet, and, as daylight eventually showed, it was in literal truth five hundred and often more. Sitting on a puffing donkey as he struggles up over enormous boulders and around great rocky masses, and stands up on his hind legs to reach for his footing on the next level, is a delicate business at best. When it is spiced with a black and bottomless abyss only inches off to one side, the mental effect is very vivid indeed. We had enjoyed only the most rudimentary of naps before we started, but no trace of sleepiness assailed my brain that night. I held my breath when the donkey did, and sometimes when he did not, and, as the saying goes, tried to wink both of my eyes at once lest his balance be disturbed in critical places.

Daylight came and with it magnificent scenery. A peak off to the right was just under ten thousand feet in height. The clouds were sometimes below us. The rocks were of many and vivid colors. We saw several varieties which would have made superb building stone. Straight ahead rose two gigantic pillars, perhaps five hundred feet in height. I speculated as to whether the road went to the right or to the left, and was astonished to discover very soon that it went straight up and over. Here we had to get off, for even these climbers could not manage this stairway cut in the solid rock, with riders on their backs. The staircase seemed endless, but at last we arrived and were on the top of the world.

There remained the task of descending, for Tenoof with its small patient was down in the *wadi*. Going down was almost worse than going up the night before. No trace of a path was to be seen, but the donkeys went cheerfully along, and smelled one out. If only the path had not run so consistently close to the edge, it would not have been so bad. It was a nervous job. My donkey would hump up his back, as if trying to sphericalize himself, and make a neat little jump for it, landing with his two front feet on the spot he had selected with a jar that almost addled the brain of his rider, though it did not appear to addle his own. His tiny landing field was often not more than a six-inch circle, and when it was placed temptingly next to the edge of a thousand-foot precipice, the nervous tension in the atmosphere was considerable.

The donkey made dozens of successful landings with his infallible little hard front feet. I did not see him slip two inches. When the descent was a foot or over and the rider's whole weight came down astraddle that blessed front hump, the jar was something to be remembered. I trembled lest the surcingle underneath break under the strain, and there were literally dozens of times when, if that had happened, I would have completed the descent without benefit of clergy, medics, donkeys, or anything else. But the surcingle had been planned for just such jumps and it did not give way.

In Oman the fly is a pest, and there is no situation of which he is not a part. Every rider carried on his back a dozen to fifty of these annoying insects. They rest peacefully in place through the night, and have a most diabolical capacity of appearing at just the wrong time to look for some breakfast. Our attention was sufficiently occupied already, landing time after time on those iron front feet, till I was dizzy and almost nauseated. To that was added the imminent possibility of pitching bodily over the precipice, if those infallible hoofs should slip for six inches.

But the worst was yet to come. When I had one arm wrapped fondly around the rear hump, and half my weight carried on the other arm braced against the hump in front, when the donkey was sphericalizing himself for his neat little jump down on to his six-inch landing field, and when everybody's breath was held for the fierce resulting jar, that was the time when my fly companions would start out to look for a drink. My eyes were always their first object of investigation. I suppose that to a fly the eyes must look like beautiful pools for an afternoon drink. Emotion I feel sure is not reflected there for, if it were, no fly would have dared to drink from such poisonous lakes.

It was impossible to brush them away, but the eye can be closed. One or two barely escaped with their lives. Unfortunately the nose is also a tempting drinking fountain for a fly, or at least it deserved investigation, they thought. It is not possible to shut one's nose, and my most savage effort to blow the offending insect away from the nostril proved futile. I developed an ability to direct a formidable hurricane in his direction, by properly curling my lower lip, but he hung on teeth and toenails, and I was not able to dislodge him that way. If he had gone clear in, it would have been easy to blow him out direct, but he simply tickled the vestibule, delicately reducing me to a sort of incipient insanity. By this time the donkey had decided to jump, and, released from the necessity of hanging on for dear life, a hand could be spared hastily to brush off the devilish little flies, even though the jar left only a minimal fraction of my brain functioning.

We arrived before the sun went down. It took an hour or two to rest the dizziness and nausea out of my system. For once I was glad of the inevitable delay before an Arab meal is ready. We were ready when it came. The boy was a congenital syphilis case, but we outlined a course of treatment which made him a different boy for that year. It was only a temporary victory however, for he died the following year. The most discouraging feature of this kind of work is that after a hard trip like this one the benefit to the patient is so slight that it hardly seems worth while. The father appreciated our coming though, and we left a warm friend behind when we departed. We decided to take it in one march, and we reached Muttreh thirty hours from the time we left Tenoof. There was a taxi waiting to take us to a sick baby when we arrived, but that was only a malaria case, and it was easy to fix him up. It was one o'clock by this time, and the opportunity for a nap was very welcome.

Special trips like this to individuals were the beginning of our work for the inland oases, but only the beginning. We try to make a trip to some faraway center once a year, spending a month in the process. The inland cities are our real objective, but it has not been possible to visit them; so we go to points in the Bottina, or to Sur, which is a port lying in the opposite direction.

Twenty-five years ago some of these inland districts were touched by missionary tours, but up to this year Shergieh has consistently refused all the offers of kind-hearted outsiders to come in and contaminate them. However, everything changes if we wait long enough, and one day a letter of invitation came from Sheikh Eesa, who rules that desolate rocky desert.

It is a ruined land over which he rules. Thirty years ago, the oases of that district were among the finest in Oman. We saw in Sifala the ruins of a five-storied house, and there must be a dozen that used to have three. Sheikh Eesa is the greatest of all the independent Oman princes, the greatest ruler that Oman tribes have had for many decades. He ruled a great country. But from 1920 to 1930 the heavens closed. From what the Arabs tell it seems doubtful if an inch of rain fell in all that period.

The springs dried up, one after the other, for there is no spring that does not depend on rain in the last analysis. The date palms died. A few did not die. There were places where wells were sunk and water found, and with great labor men and animals pulled water to the surface and kept a certain number of the palms alive. The five-story house fell into ruins, and its noble neighbors with it, for men moved away to Zanzibar, and to Muscat, and anywhere they could. Some of them did not move. They died with their gardens. Year after year, the ruin became more complete. The desperate semistarvation that the survivors went through made them marked men and women wherever they went.

But in 1930 the rains came again, the gardens were replanted, and some of the refugees returned. Now, nine years later the gardens are beautiful to see, and the springs are flowing. The houses have not been rebuilt, for the price of dates has been so low that even with plenty of water it is barely possible to make both ends meet. No surplus is available for fine buildings, not even for repairs. It is a very saddening experience to walk through streets and streets of old, ruined houses, abandoned and empty. A few servants live in the remaining tumbledown rooms. Nevertheless these oases are full of promise, for the gardens are green with splendid young date palms, alfalfa, and barley, and the future is with the gardens, not with the broken and abandoned old houses.

Sheikh Eesa still rules in Shergieh. He is an old man now, erect and thin, with a huge nose and a falcon's poise. He is dignified and quiet in speech. He brought his country through its days of tribulation, and he watches it now with a father's solicitude. Last year only a little rain fell, and cold fear spread through the hearts of the people, but this year the rains have been abundant, and everyone is happy.

Sheikh Eesa decided to allow the alien doctor to come in. Just what brought him to this decision, he probably is the only one who knows. The year previous he accepted the Sultan's invitation and came to Muscat on an official visit. Such a gesture of friendship was something new, and the community applauded. It was only twenty-five years since he took Muscat and looted it. The grandson of those days rules at the present moment so Muscat was glad to see Sheikh Eesa come and visit them as a friend; but there were plenty who distrusted the friendship of this eaglelike man. The Judge of Muttreh and I were guests at the great official dinner, along with a hundred and fifty others. We walked home together, and he muttered to himself. "That man is an enemy, inside his heart he is an enemy."

During this visit, I went to see the regal old Sheikh in his garden *mejlis*. He was cordial in a cautious way, and evidently fond of a dignified joke. I explained that I would be glad to make a medical visit to his country; but he did not warm to the suggestion, and I was very doubtful of the outcome. It was evident that he wanted to protect his isolated kingdom from suspicious Western influences.

However, the best part of a year later, this letter came from him, a letter as lean and uncompromising and direct as its author. I might come, he told me. Previously this had been forbidden. Now it was permitted. I think that this will stand as the chilliest invitation I ever received for anything. Even so he was afraid that he might be interpreted as excessive and compromising in his enthusiasm for my visit. On the outside of the envelope, in addition to the conventional address, was written, "Peace is to those who follow the right path," this being a standard Arab phrase indicating a high degree of spiritual disapproval.

I grinned over this letter. We get used to being handled with tongs like a dangerous disease germ. In the old days in Nejd, the spirit was lots worse than this. We carried the letter to the Sultan, who gave his permission, and all hands fell to and got things ready.

Getting ready for such a trip is a real piece of work. What we need is some way to melt the hospital down for convenience in transport, or perhaps it might be better to saw it up into small pieces. It was necessary to carry on camels over a seven days' journey into the stony wilderness everything small and great that we would need in that lonely place. Unfortunately our buildings have to be left behind, and with them all apparatus which is too heavy for the Omanee camels. The camel men on such a trip always complain bitterly at the weight of the boxes we ask their tiny camels to carry. Further north in central Arabia, and most of all in Mesopotamia, the camel, as the Arab says, is first cousin to an elephant, but in Oman he is first cousin to a mouse. The camel men felt that our boxes were related to elephants rather than to mice, and I am afraid they were right. Abdullah, the official cook, with his kitchen utensils, had the heaviest box of all.

It takes days of work to get the bottles packed into the big boxes, and the surgical instruments and dressings into packages, and all the necessary supplies assembled. In such an empty country as Shergieh, the local market furnishes scarcely anything that an outsider cares to eat, so we carried some rice in addition to all the other things. We even took along half a camel load of kerosene.

It took twenty-one camels to take up the white man's burden, we humans numbered nine, and constituted a respectable fraction of the total load. We were joined by seven camels more, driven by friends of our camel men, and going to the same place. The resulting string of twenty-eight animals made quite a show, stalking majestically along over the landscape. I timed this formidable procession. It took three minutes to pass a given point. That ought to indicate that a potentate of some weight was traveling through the empty waste. The shadow and the substance are likely to be very different in Arabia.

This trip was unique in one respect. Mrs. Harrison was with us. It seemed a reckless thing to do, for Shergieh is the most untamed of all the Oman provinces, and has been the most hostile. But we were thinking of the future. A permanent entree is the one result that such a trip aims at, and she was more than fifty per cent of our resources in this effort to get our names erased from the Index Expurgatorius. Like all the rest of the world, these redoubtable Abadhis are ruled by their wives. So we determined to get her there if the thing could be done. She had never traveled on camels before, and I was not much better. Tours there have been, plenty of them, but it was ten years since I had used camels for the purpose.

We decided to shorten our sojourn on the swaying backs of these ships of the desert three days, by sending the caravan ahead, and then overtaking it with a motor three days out from port. Four days is a lot less than seven, when it is spent on the back of a camel. The motor, however, had trouble. Its first load, consisting of half the hospital staff, went on ahead. In that particular *wadi*, the motor is still a dreadful apparition to the Bedouins, who surrounded it upon arrival and fired into the air to produce an attitude of proper anxious acquiescence on the part of the boys. The motor was then "arrested" and put in jail. Kumbar has charge of our caravan work, and rose to the occasion. He spent a strenuous night proceeding by forced marches to the castle of the ruling sheikh. This was none other than the man whose "eggplant failed to grow." He ordered the immediate release of the motor.

So the motor returned, and lights were reported as green all along the road. We started for the caravan ourselves. A pressing invitation was waiting for us. We must come and take dinner with the sheikh. Following the disagreeable incident of the motor we were glad to accept. On donkeys we cut across a corner and over a mountain pass around which the camels had to detour. We were to rejoin the caravan the following morning. The sky looked cloudy, and the air was damp; but the country had seen hardly one raindrop in two years, and in any case the rainy season was over. We saw a number of tiny oasis gardens along the road. Every one of them was dead.

But the drought was over. Our arrival was the signal for rain to begin. It rained all that night, and the following day, and the night following that. That was some rain. The *wadis* are rivers after a heavy rain. Unless the *wadis* run, a rain has not done much toward replenishing the underground watercourses on which the springs depend.

The following morning we woke with a low roar in our ears. It was mixed with shrill cries of joy from the early risers who were out in the rain to see the *wadi* run. The rushing torrent was seventy-five feet across, the first time in five years that so much water had been seen. The people told us with much joy that without another drop it would be two years before there could be any shortage. The community passed from discouragement and want and toil to comfort and comparative ease, in one night. No wonder they rejoiced. "Your feet are green," they said.

But the rain was only started. Through the day it continued. Reports came in from distant points. The rain had fallen everywhere. "By noon," said the people, "the *wadi* Kharoos will come in." That is a large tributary to the *wadi* we were watching. The forecast was correct. At about noon the branch flood arrived, and the noisy torrent seventy-five feet wide became a river two hundred feet across. As that mass of water rushed down the *wadi*, there were places where the waves were six feet high. The flood cut into the corner of a garden which had been planted too far out. Two palms were washed out and floated helplessly away. The great flood lasted till night.

We were imprisoned for three nights in the house of our hospitable host. All the houses of that little town are made of mud bricks, and rain is hard on that sort of house. Several fell in. Some of the pillars of the castle where we were staying suffered the same fate. However, our corner held. Every roof in the castle leaked, except ours.

Finally we got away, and our string of twenty-eight camels filed solemnly along through the *wadi* bed, which only the day before yesterday was a raging torrent. The *wadis* are the roads in this part of the world. The caravan paths wind back and forth through them. The gardens, too, are in the *wadis*. All life and activity is found there. They are the circulatory system of Oman. The mountains are a total loss.

Traveling in a caravan is not as romantic as some folks suppose. The first day we spent eight hours on the backs of those deliberate and supercilious beasts. I cannot believe that anywhere in this world a harder substance exists than the vertebrae of a camel. It is a contagious hardness, and all the cushions and blankets which may have been put in place become hard by noon, so that through the afternoon one rides on a hard board. This, of course, is an index of inexperience. Ten years between camel rides is too long an interval. Abdullah, the cook, has seen lots of this kind of travel, but like myself it had been a long time since he practiced. He was full of sympathy. "Everybody's back aches tonight," he said. But it was not my back. My own aches were two in number and two inches in diameter. They were eight inches lower down.

The camel has a low I.Q. His predecessors through the centuries have chosen a path which snuggles most affectionately up against the thorn bushes. The rider who goes half asleep from the monotony of the landscape and the fatigue of the ride is likely to repent when repentance does no good. I have never seen a camel scratch himself on one of these thorn trees, but his rider extends up thirty inches into the ether, from the apex of the camel's back, and it is well to guide him a few feet out of the path sometimes.

Camels are a peevish and jealous tribe. We started out with my own mount tied in the caravan just ahead of Mrs. Harrison's. Thubbian, who carried her, was a peaceable creature with no hostility toward anything except her own numerous ticks. But Naseer, who went ahead carrying me, was a more aristocratic breed. The third morning the caravan leader made a mistake and reversed their positions. Naseer plunged ahead and then she fell behind. Her dignity had been insulted, and no service was to be had out of her till her old pre-eminence was restored.

Camels are sentimental, too, though to look at them, no one would suppose it possible. One of our Bedouin companions was a venerable old patriarch. He dropped out of the caravan and went over the mountains by himself on foot, on some errand known only to himself. We did not see him again till sunset. His camel could not see him either, and for that camel the world was a desolate and mournful waste. He groaned and grunted most lugubriously during the whole time of his bereavement. I did not know that a camel was capable of so much affection, nor did any of us realize that the general theme of grief and loss could be treated with so many variations.

Camping at night was great fun. After a day in a camel saddle, any sort of vertical or horizontal position was pure comfort. Also a piece of cheese and a little dry bread, together with some milkless tea, made a meal such as the Ritz knows nothing about. Our tiny tent served as retiring quarters for Mrs. Harrison and Husseinah. Husseinah came down at this inopportune time with a severe attack of asthma, and threatened to queer the whole pitch. It took an alarming amount of adrenalin to bring her to, and our total supply was only one ounce. However, the third injection made a new woman out of her, so that hurdle was topped.

The nights were astonishingly cold. It was this which had brought on the asthma. None of us had bedding enough to be really comfortable. During the day the sun was hot, but we shivered through the night. Nearly everyone had a camp cot, and the first night we seemed a very civilized group. After that the cots were turned on edge to keep off the cutting wind, and behind this barricade a fire was kept up through the night. That is to say, such was the intention. It always went out before morning, and the last state of the boys was worse than the first.

The sun by day made more trouble. Our complexions blackened till the boys looked like a company of stokers. The sun did things to Mrs. Harrison's face which rouge cannot approach. Her soul was much grieved by this extraordinary coloring. Being a well-vulcanized brunette, it was not my face which suffered, but my somewhat less toughened feet. I have traveled through the deserts of Nejd in midsummer, and the resulting sunburn was only a trifle, giving a most fashionable tan to my skin. I watched with superior disdain as my feet turned a bright red on their upper surfaces. By the end of the third day, I realized that the sun has a higher voltage in Oman. I draped a curtain over my brilliant feet. It was too late. The mischief was done, and my left foot blistered upon arrival, the skin underneath looking like nothing I have ever seen outside of a pathological laboratory. I was very much afraid that a full square inch would go on to necrosis. It could scarcely have looked worse if it had been boiled. Not over a square quarter inch of the skin did actually die, but it took me three weeks to get the foot healed up.

Four days of travel and the fleet arrived in port. We came up the long *wadi* which is the home of Sifala, and, rounding a tall mountain with a watch tower on its summit, we saw the oasis stretch out before us. The gardens extended for a mile and more along each side of the *wadi*. We learned that afternoon how beautiful a *wadi* can be. We agreed with the Arabs. Heaven is simply a perfect oasis.

Every hill was crowned with a watch tower. Sifala's next-door neighbor has a collection of sixteen of these monuments to military preparedness. Indeed every large garden has a small tower. Some are in ruins, and all are unoccupied, which informs the visitor that an era of peace has begun. That means that Sheikh Eesa has been able to suppress the incorrigible urge to steal each others' property which is the curse of Arabs. Half a mile up the *wadi* was a large square castle, which was to be our home for a month. It walls were two and a half feet thick, and the great upstairs room where we first rested was provided with some sixty holes through which muskets could be pointed at enemies on the opposite side of the *wadi*.

The castle was full of dirt, and swarming with flies, but it was large and had a good upstairs *mejlis*[1] which we could use for an operating room. There was space for in-patients, and for the clinic. We cleaned out the dirt, and bought local mats for the floors. Screening was tacked into place over the operating-room windows. A tiny date-stick hut was put up for Mrs. Harrison and me, and we were ready for work. We all voted it a

[1] *Mejlis*, a term used for an official reception and for the room where it is held.

first-class branch hospital, worthy of the traditions of its parent in Muttreh.

We found ourselves in a large center of population. Sifala itself is an oasis of only moderate size, but the *wadis* that extend in various directions must contain a dozen more. We estimated at ten thousand the people who live in those parts. All of the oases are full of mosquitoes, and therefore full of malaria. The mosquito is an astonishingly ubiquitous beast. One of the worst nights on the entire trip was spent next to a solitary well, a dozen miles from its nearest neighbor, and surrounded by long stretches of utterly arid desert. The "poisonous little birds" sang in our ears all night long, and they terminated their solos by taking breakfast. I was soaking myself in atebrin during those five days, and I hope that it gave them a bad stomach-ache.

Wherever we go there is plenty of malaria. In Sifala such patients numbered a hundred and fifty out of seven hundred and fifty individuals who came for treatment. We take a hundred-ounce tin of quinine with us on tours of this sort, and we expect to leave both the quinine and the tin behind. We can do a good deal for malaria. We teach the people to use quinine, and we give a good many dozens a period of freedom from the disease.

The malaria of Sifala needs study. There are two very distinct types, one of which runs only a slight fever, but develops a very marked enlargement of the spleen, and a second which runs a high fever with chills, but which causes little or no splenic enlargement. We left our methyl alcohol behind, through an oversight, and to our very great regret were not able to study the type of parasite in the blood.

We take Neosalvarsan with us too, but this does not represent a very great contribution to the people, for three to four weeks is the longest possible period of treatment, and for most of the patients the period of treatment is less than that. How much good two or three doses of salvarsan does to a syphilis patient is certainly a problem. However, it is to be noted that the prevailing type is a mild one, and in Sifala the numbers suffering from this disease are small. We met with scarcely two dozen cases in our entire stay. Rheumatism we did not see, and only a few cases of enlarged tonsils. We saw no deficiency diseases, and no goiter.

The treatment of malaria is the one medical achievement which stands to the credit of trips of this sort. Surgery makes more of an impression, and does more good. A baby of seven months came in with a lipoma on its back about the same size as its head. He was a frail citizen, but we scored a distinct success with him and turned him back to his mother better than new. A good time was had by all. The crop of hernias was pretty good, but our harvest very meager, for most of them came in just a few days before we left. However, the six cases that we did were all of them successful, and that represented a real contribution to the efficiency of the community. Our reputation grew nicely as a result of these satisfactory results, and that always seems a very desirable outcome.

An old man with a sliding hernia had more hernia to operate on than all the rest put together. He was not only old, but completely blind, and his hernia was making him no trouble so far as I know. However, he reckoned it incompatible with his manly dignity to carry such a deformity around. He could feel it even if he could not see it, for it was the size of a child's head. Sheikh Eesa sent him in as a special case, for he is a court favorite. He has the satisfaction now, of knowing that he has been restored to normal; and, unless some stroke of apoplexy or other catastrophe carries him to an untimely grave, we are going to have some reputation in those parts, from now on. He is a very strong believer in medical missions.

One hundred and two trichiasis operations were the major contribution that we made to Sifala. Shergieh is full of bad eyes, and the number of blind is appalling. For most of them we can do nothing. There is a very large group of sufferers from trichiasis, many of whom will eventually be blind unless they are treated. This group of eye cripples can be given very complete relief. They are the victims of chronic conjunctivitis, most of it due to trachoma. When this is continued long enough, the lids contract on their inner surfaces, because of the deposit of scar tissue which chronic inflammation always causes. This contraction curls the lids inward, and the lashes rake back and forth over the cornea, and such an eye is ruined unless something is done to straighten the lid.

The Arabs get to be very expert in pulling the troublesome hairs out, and such an eye can be kept going for a long time, if this is faithfully done. It is a delicate and painful job though, and is not attended to with sufficient care in most cases, so the results are generally very poor. The doctor who can repair such a lid once for all, is a much appreciated individual, and there are a great many eyes saved by this simple operation.

The Omanees have developed an operation of their own for the relief of this condition, two or three operations in fact. The simplest thing that can be done is to brand the lids with a hot iron. The resulting ulcer lasts for ten days to two weeks, and leaves behind a distinct deposit of scar tissue on the external surface of the lid. Scar tissue contracts wherever it is and in extremely mild cases this may be sufficient to uncurl the lid and cure the trouble. There must be some successful cases, or no one would resort to this measure. The successes however are rare. I have never seen one, and of the failures I have seen many dozens.

A far greater deposit of scar tissue is obtainable by making a simple incision in the lid, and tying into the open sore a bit of twig, the caliber of a lead pencil. Healing can be delayed in this way for about six weeks, and the contraction of the resulting mass of scar tissue amounts to something. I have seen a number of very good results, on cases which obviously had been of very considerable severity. The lid uncurls, and the resulting scar is not nearly so noticeable as might be expected. I have seen two eyes ruined by this operation. An infection spread from the dirty and tedious sore, and destroyed the lid completely.

There is a simpler operation which simply excises a bit of the skin of the affected lid. A generous piece of the skin of the affected lid is caught between two bits of properly shaped wood, whose ends are then tied very firmly together. The imprisoned skin dies, and within ten days the wooden pincers drop off leaving a nicely healed and almost invisible scar. For a perfect cosmetic result on the external surface of the lid, this is the world's best, but I have never seen a case which was benefited by it. It would have to be an extremely mild case of trichiasis which could be cured by a simple excision of the lid skin.

On our way to Sifala we met a man and his wife who were traveling to Muttreh for treatment. She returned and stayed with us in Sifala the whole time we were there. She was suffering, she was anxious everyone should know, from a snake which swam about in her stomach. A careful examination showed no basis for this belief, and it was Mrs. Harrison's special job to convince her that this was an imaginary disease. Lots of hard work was put into this piece of educational work, but the results were not complete nor satisfactory. Her husband, it appeared, was suffering from hemorrhoids. These were more real, and after an operation were well and thoroughly cured.

There were a number of other patients who required operation for piles, and this is very interesting, for inland Nejd appears to be more or less free from such troubles. An old Bedouin, so thin that his skin seemed dried down against his bones, came in with a hopeless Madura foot. Amputation sent him home happy. The women did not contribute many patients to our surgical work. One girl came in for a tonsillectomy. I had explained to her that if she would promise to hold her mouth wide open, I would promise not to hurt her. I kept my promise and so did she. I think I have never seen that particular part of the operation better performed.

These trips would be very enjoyable affairs if we did not see so many hopeless cases, begging for treatment.

Medical relief is entirely lacking in these out-of-the-way corners and every pathological condition has an opportunity for unlimited development. A woman came to the clinic in Sifala with one of the largest ovarian cysts which I have ever seen. She has watched it grow larger and larger for fifteen years. Now she walks with the curious exaggerated erectness of someone carrying a great weight in front of her. This case did not come to the operating table. She wanted some medicine to cure it. I recommended operation, for her condition was good and the removal of such a cyst is not difficult, but she would have none of it. Her husband urged the operation, but it was evident that she was accustomed to having her own way, and she had it this time.

This woman I reckoned as a very good operative risk, but there are always those who are not. The specter of operative deaths hangs over a tour always, because some such case has been accepted for operation. It seems to be the fate of tours such as this one to have at least one patient die no matter what care is taken to prevent it.

We have developed a fairly watertight technique, and on these trips we use all the technique we know. On the trip to Sifala, in twenty major operations we had one stitch abscess. We should not have had that, but our silk ran short, and we used catgut for one hernia. Catgut is practically as good as silk as far as asepsis is concerned, but our technique in its use is distinctly below par, and we paid the penalty, or rather I suppose I ought to say that the patient paid it. His convalescence was prolonged a month.

In spite of our best efforts, the specter caught us. It was a case of prolonged intestinal obstruction, due to a cause which we could not determine. His condition seemed good, and he certainly was not suffering from cancer. The ten-year history excluded that. Operation disclosed a series of bands, tying his large intestine snugly up against his spleen. Freeing these bands was a simple matter, and before the operation was over, his bowels moved in such quantity as I have never seen equaled. This continued for twenty-four hours, and he was more comfortable than he had been for years. All his friends were delighted. That was real surgery, they thought.

After his auspicious convalescence was three days along, he developed a most alarming heart attack. His special nurse was full of information. He had suffered for years attacks of this sort, and many times had been given up for dead. This time he succeeded and did die, in spite of all we could do to prevent it. I wasted very little time explaining that it would help if we were told such things beforehand. After all he was dead, and his friends seemed very untroubled about it. It would be fine, though, to have a big trip some day, on which nobody died.

Sometimes the very fates seem set against us. Years ago on such a trip, our record had remained unblemished in spite of a large amount of work. But one of our favorite hernia cases, on his thirteenth day, when he was ready to go home, developed an embolus which snuffed him out like a candle.

That time nothing happened, but on a trip to Sur a catastrophe of that sort had repercussions that were serious. I was surprised to have six goiters on that trip, and on a second there were some others. Evidently there is a small goiter center there. I have not seen that many goiters in as many years. We did them all under local anesthesia, to which we added half a grain of morphia for the very large ones. It is asking a good deal of a woman to go through such an operation without some reinforcement of that sort.

The combination worked extremely well, on all but the last case. Her goiter was large, and it extended down behind the sternum. The operation however went unusually well, and the loss of blood was negligible. Unfortunately, she had an idiosyncrasy to morphia, and of course there is no denying that half a grain is a large dose. She went into a profound coma, and died a few hours after the operation was concluded.

We had plenty of repercussions that time. Her husband, it appeared, was away on a business trip. I had supposed that it was her "man" who brought her, but it appeared that someone else had given her away that time. After a week, the husband returned. He was beside himself. It is a distinctly disturbing experience to sit tête à tête only two feet away from a well-armed and enormous individual, and have him assert with great emphasis, "If you do not get out of this city within two days, I will myself come over and shoot you." Explanations helped not at all.

He felt perfectly safe as he sat there making his vociferous threats, but I had more comeback than he supposed. The city was divided into factions much like the Arab tribes of the desert in their organization and spirit. Several members of his own clan were at that moment in the hospital recovering from operations. They did not want the doctor driven out of town for ten or fifteen days. At least they must get well first. So they sent out a very effective S.O.S., indeed several of them.

And they got action. The tribe held an official meeting which thoroughly and officially sat on the truculent troublemaker, and sent me an official delegation to reassure my presumably troubled mind. I might stay as long as I wished.

We stayed on for about three weeks. The patients which constituted my first line of defense went home cured. From more distant parts the dead woman's brother arrived, and the storm became worse than ever. He was full of threats. What was worse he did not come to me in person to blow it off in wordy steam. The boys could scarcely pass through the bazaar. This looked more serious, for now I had no effective defense. The owner of our rented house, who in such a case is the visitor's official host and responsible for him, begged me to leave. He disclaimed all responsibility if I stayed. That seemed an ominous sign, for the one ethical anchor that holds in Arabia when all the rest are gone is the obligation of hospitality.

We had planned to leave in about another week, and we allowed this affectionate brother to speed the parting guest by that much. I hope that he got lots of satisfaction out of it. That was the only time in all my experience that one of these trips ended in that way. It is dangerous business being a surgeon. If only we could guess right always, what a soft life it would be! However, we have been most cordially invited to return to that truculent city, and it is this woman's husband who wants us to come. As soon as possible we are going to go.

These trips are our only way of reaching the inland oases. It is an expensive way of working. The trip to Sifala cost us about thirteen hundred rupees. An absolutely accurate figure cannot be fixed, for the depletion of the hospital medicines has to be estimated. We took in about seven hundred, which was better than most trips. There have been trips, as for instance one to Sur, where we received in fees a sum greater than our expenses. Unfortunately it is far more common to have the receipts practically nothing.

Fees are small on such a trip, even smaller than in Muttreh. The only thing that makes possible any considerable sum in the way of receipts, is the volume of the work. Patients run up to a hundred and fifty a day, which is far too many. However, some of them require very little of the doctor's time. In Sifala we did over a hundred trichiasis operations and fifty to seventy-five of the day's attendances were these patients coming back for daily treatment. We do trichiasis operations for twenty-five cents apiece, which is below cost, no matter how we figure it. But when the numbers run over a hundred, the sum is a help. The rich pay up to a dollar and a quarter per eye, but there were only two aristocratic eyes in Sifala as judged by this standard. There were several at a dollar apiece, and quite a group at fifty cents, real bargain-counter rates, we thought.

Hernias paid up to six dollars, and we were much surprised to see how readily they paid this fabulous sum. The one difficult case, with his sliding hernia which very nearly established a record for anatomical complexity, paid a dollar and a half. He was below cost, too. We only had six hernias to do, which was a great grief to my hernia-inclined soul. I have become much interested in the problems of the hernia, and always want some more. There were almost a dozen who applied during our last week, and it was simply a matter for tears to turn them away. One came with us to Muttreh. If only the ruling sheikh had not been so worried about the matter of uncompleted cases, we might have accepted every one of them. Mobarrek would have stayed behind, then, to watch over their convalescence.

"The love of money is the root of all evil." We had a new variation this time. One of the Bedouins arrived utterly penniless. At least that was his assertion. He felt that life would not be worth continuing unless he could have his hemorrhoids operated on. He offered his donkey in payment. Mobarrek, who is our credit man, decided that he could sell the animal for two dollars at least, maybe more if we took him to Muttreh. There is a good demand for donkeys. So we took this unusual fee, and inasmuch as the donkey had evidently not suffered from overeating for a long time, we bought some alfalfa and gave him a good time. One of the boys was planning to ride him back to Muttreh, and thus we could get along with one less camel. Under this treatment he fattened up, and it was evident that he was a pretty good little beast. Perhaps the eventual fee would be larger than we expected. We came to be really fond of the cheerful little animal.

But after ten days the Bedouin left the hospital, with a very good result, and a little vaseline for use at home. He returned quietly at night two days later, and took the donkey with him, too, riding him back, I have no doubt, nicely fattened as he was.

I feel that this Bedouin should have a great future. He would do well in Wall Street. Trading in a donkey for your operation, and then, after the doctor has fattened him up well, taking him back without embarrassment or risk to ride home on, seemed to us to indicate real financial genius.

The medical contribution which these trips make is considerable, but their principal function is educational. Before we meet and get acquainted, our medicines are reported as incredibly effective in curing children's eyes. I only wish it were true. This extraordinary virtue only demonstrates that the eyes of little children have been ground up to make the medicine. This hideous homeopathic notion runs through a good many of their medical ideas. Surgery is a modern form of the black art.

The trip makes us acquainted. They know afterward what we can and what we cannot do. I think that perhaps nothing goes so far toward convincing them that we are simply purveyors of trained service, as our refusal to tinker with hopeless cases, even when tempted by a large fee. "Surely," said a hopeless eye case to me, "you have some medicine which might benefit me a little." But when the patient is a hopeless case of glaucoma, as this man was, there is nothing that will by any possibility do him any good at all, and that is what the patient is told.

We insist that every operation be watched by at least one friend of the patient. That doubles the number of flies that are brought into the operating room, but it is worth it. Nothing could be further removed from the black art than a surgical operation. It is safe to say that not one of these Arabs has ever seen anyone wash his hands for ten minutes or even for one. He watches the surgeon and his assistant get ready for the operation, and comparison of notes with his friends shows him that this extraordinary ritual is always gone through with, in spite of the cost in soap and time. Anesthesia, and particularly spinal anesthesia, is a precise and careful bit of service. In it is skill which the wayfaring man though a fool can appreciate, but no black magic is there. The patient can converse, and he is evidently in his right mind. Moreover, he is suffering no pain, even if his hemorrhoids are being operated on, or a large hernia is being mended.

This education is important. There is lots of illumination from such a trip. The Arabs travel a great deal. Not once in a hundred cases do we deal with a patient who cannot come to Muttreh. After such a trip many of them do. One of the hernia cases, who arrived too late to have his operation done in Sifala, traveled with us all the way to Muttreh. When he got to Muttreh he knew what to expect. He expected us to give him the best service we were capable of giving. We did give him just that. He did not expect us to perform some magical miracle, when once we had been bribed enough to exert our powers.

These trips are valuable, too, as missionary enterprises. No one preaches on the street, even in the coast cities. Their own religious services are not held in such an undignified way. But we preach. It is Christian preaching, and we do lots of it. There is a difference between truth and error. The doctor does not say that. He has no time to argue such a question. His stethoscope and his scalpel preach that. The contrast between the twenty-two hernias without a stitch abscess, and the twenty-third, which fell into septic sin and disgraced the whole company, is too evident to be missed. It is a bad thing to fall into sin when you are operating. Your sin finds you out.

The microscope is a great preacher too. The bright red tubercle bacillus shining evilly there among his blue compatriots, is a very definite and objective thing, and shows what a precise diagnosis can be. And a louse under the microscope, that is a real lesson. Even the evil eye is not half so dangerous.

And redemption for those who repent and have faith. Medicine preaches that too. There are an appalling number to whom no path of redemption is open; the hopeless blind eyes, what a list of causes they have: glaucoma, smallpox, ophthalmia, red-hot nails as the antidote for political intransigence; cancer cases which are far beyond any possible relief. But there are far more to whom we can offer real help. The hernias, the hemorrhoids, and the trichiasis cases; the old gunshot wounds, which need only to be properly cleaned up; the malaria cases, which must be taught the use of quinine; the ulcer cases, which need cleanliness and care and patience. Even the syphilis cases are most of them in this list. With them it takes lots of faith and a good deal of repentance, but there is a path.

After a medical trip of this sort, an inland oasis has a pretty good idea of what the Christian message is. But the demands on the doctor are severe. To lose one's temper is almost the unpardonable sin. The Arabs are gentlemen of dignity and pride, Bedouins the most of all. To meet them with dignity and graciousness is our very first duty. But a hundred and fifty come at once, which is bad enough, and fifty of them are women, which is worse. Everybody is sure that he should be treated first, and if a fee is charged they must argue about that. Such a debate is a very interesting fencing display. Often the doctor in his stupidity has given the patient medicine different from what he wants. That topic, too, has in it great possibilities for spirited conversation. I am afraid that we all lose our tempers occasionally, and the message of Christ gets labeled as an ill-tempered, impatient, and undignified affair. Then we must weep some tears of repentance and plan to do better next time.

The staff has just as hard a time as the doctor. On a recent trip, one of our temporary helpers, who is not at all a Christian, though a very helpful spirit and a good worker, gave us a bad time. We were in a very untamed locality, and we watched our step. One of the loose-tongued youngsters of the city called this inoffensive, white-bearded old man a eunuch. The slimy word he used would be bad enough as it stands, but in the local vernacular it means rather one who practices sodomy, and is literally the worst insult that was available. The reaction was immediate and furious. The boy ran lightly away, and the insulted man swore that he would pursue the youngster, and kill him with his big dagger. This, he felt, must be attended to at once, without counting ten. It made no difference if the ruler of the city executed him the following day. How could anything short of the dagger atone for an insult like that?

My first assistant is one of the best Christians I ever worked with; he caught this perilous situation on the fly, and fielded it very neatly. He interviewed the boy's father without a moment's delay. The boy was summoned and officially punished, though the two or three light strokes were pure fiction so far as pain was concerned. However, they stood as an official atonement, and the insulted old man accepted the boy's father and the boy himself as friends again. I was informed of all this only later, for Mobarrek knew that he could manage it better without any help from me. However, that particular man will not come with us again on a trip of this sort. With a little less skillful fielding of that particular ball, the whole impression of the trip might have been very badly marred, to say nothing of putting the whole company in real personal danger. Running around avenging insults with a dagger is an extremely dangerous form of outdoor sport in backwoods Arabia.

Missionary work on these trips is not limited to indirect educational effects. We have services every Sunday, and everybody is invited. Sometimes ten listen. Sometimes a hundred. The services are held in the hospital courtyard or some other equally convenient place. They are looked on as an interesting contribution to the city's life. We sing at these services, which is a shocking thing to do, for music is forbidden in those places. People sing in theaters. People come and look on much as they did in Abu Dhubbi, when the visitors from Ras el Kheima amused them. But they listen to the message with great interest, and such a service is a great opportunity. The doctor, when he is responsible for a service in such a place, tries to tell with much care just what it is which the Christian mission wishes to give these people, and to tell it so it can be understood.

Twice at least we have found men whose minds are

so ready for the Christian message, that they were able to follow Christ at their first exposure to it. I met such a man once in Um el Gowein. From his father he had inherited some Christian book—perhaps a gospel, perhaps a prayer book. The book had been read to pieces and lost. He had lived for years hoping to meet someone who could tell him more about this teaching which he revered highly. He read the four Gospels which I had with me, and found in them a foundation for a faith which was beautiful and dominating from the very start.

He promised to follow us to Bahrain as soon as he could get his affairs settled. I am afraid that some disease carried him off, for he never came, and I have not heard from him since. However, Dr. Dame made a similar trip into the same district and discovered such an undeveloped but genuine Christian. With education and training, he has become one of the brightest and best Christians that we have.

Trips are strenuous things. They are well filled with things that are the reverse of beautiful. The camel men may get into a noisy quarrel, but that happened only once on the whole Sifala trip. The camels may wander away and delay us, and that happened three times. The flies may bother us, and that happened all the time. They bothered the camels even more than they did us, and one afternoon was made extremely fatiguing because my camel was continually trying to kick off some of her innumerable flies. To kick, a camel has to readjust the levels of his whole upstairs plateau, in the crevices of which I had carefully fitted my various supportive bones.

A camel has a fast delivery, like a baseball pitcher. Repeatedly she nearly dislodged me. I hope she dislodged at least a few of the offending flies. Riding a camel is supposed to be a sort of bromidic job, and it is quite in order to go to sleep, if you can. That afternoon my pleasantest dream would have terminated with me sitting on the hard and stony road.

But there are beautiful things to be seen on those trips. We came back through Shergieh under a hot sun. A month before, rain had fallen, the first in two years, and the vegetable world was making up for lost time. The *ithl* trees were in blossom. Their blossoms are tiny things, not more than a soft fuzz on the dark red lines which support them. But the erect and gracefully curved central stalk remains the most delicate shade of light green; and for feathery beauty I have never seen such a bouquet equaled, even when New York florists put forth their best efforts.

The thorn bushes were in bloom too. Their offering was tiny bright yellow fluffs, about a centimeter in diameter and perfect spheres. Their scent filled the air, and they spread their beauty over the whole landscape. There are few perfumes to compare with the delicate aromatic fragrance of these soft fluffy globes. Kumbar rode his free camel up to one of the fragrant bushes and brought to the Khatoon, as Mrs. Harrison is affectionately called, some of the tiny fluffs with their feathery fragrance.

But I think that the most beautiful thing I ever saw on one of these trips, was the mountains through the rain. It had been a hard day, and the afternoon was half gone. We were on the camels eight hours that day. To make matters worse it began to rain. It was a slow and tantalizing rain, that soaked through our clothes and made us thoroughly wet.

Night was coming on, and the consequences of being soaked to the skin seemed pretty serious. I usually succeed in taking a heavy cold after even a small wetting, but I was much more concerned about Mrs. Harrison for she was being soaked along with the rest of us, and her past record has been far from perfect.

So it seemed to me unusually desirable that the rain stop. I explained this to God and prayed very earnestly, and I am afraid a little foolishly that it might soon stop, and it did not soon stop. It soaked us first. Moreover, it kept up till we were almost ready to make camp and the night was upon us.

However, I somewhat shamefacedly rebuked myself for my fears, and decided that I should be able to trust this situation to the same God who had taken care of me so many times before. Once I got my faith back to a more or less normal working voltage, I suddenly realized that I had before me such a vision of beauty as I have seen only once or twice in my whole life. The rain had become worse. In the distance it evidently had given way to mist. We were riding through a wide valley. The sun was hidden by the clouds.

There before us the mountains rose silver gray in the mist, tier upon tier like great waves of some eternal sea, fixed and changeless in their beauty. The eye rose from one tier to another of frosted silver battlements; there were seven in one place, each lovelier than the one before, till the last faintly visible range was reached, and it seemed to us that when we passed beyond that we should find ourselves in the presence of the Eternal God.

With the glory of that vision hanging over our souls, we reached camp and found there the answer to our prayers waiting for us. We made huge fires, and all got dry. I found the largest piece of fuel of all. It was a tree about ten feet tall, long since dead and rotted at the base. A strong pull broke it off, and two of us hauled it into camp. That was a real piece of wood. Its trunk was three inches thick, and the fire assumed proportions that shocked the Bedouins. Such a waste of good firewood they had never seen, but it was going to waste all around us, and could not do anyone any good, so we let it do us a great deal of good.

We had a roaring fire. Indeed, before the evening was over we had four. I meditated on the extraordinary blindness of my timid soul. Prayer is the soul's sincere desire, and this desire was answered by God, even though He completely disregarded the noise of my lips, or rather the thoughts of my mind. Not one of us suffered the slightest inconvenience from our wetting, and the process of getting the fires going and drying out in front of them afforded us the most enjoyable night of the entire trip.

XII
ECONOMIC AND SOCIAL CONDITIONS

I HAVE LIVED in a good many primitive places, but Sifala was unique. We did not expect to find a competitor for Delmonico's there, but we were not quite prepared for the leanness that we found. The gardens are beautiful, which makes the obvious poverty of the place the more remarkable. I doubt if any finer gardens can be found in Oman anywhere. The finest dry dates which go to the Bombay market come from this district. Many of the gardens are only eight to ten years old, and the older trees show the scars of the drought years, but they are beautiful; and, with the green fields of alfalfa, barley, and wheat, we expected to find an opulent type of living among the people.

That was a long way from the truth. I think that salt fish must be about the cheapest and least desirable form of protein in the world, and we did not suppose that in such an oasis as this the people knew what salt fish looked like. The normal commerce between the Bedouin tribes of the open desert and the oasis dwellers is an exchange of the products of the goat for the products of the palm tree. The Bedouins bring in goats first of all. Fresh mutton, i.e. goat mutton, is never absent from the markets of Hassa or Riadh. The Bedouin brings in clarified butter, which is made from goat's milk and is the only cooking fat which the oasis knows. There are some hides and some coarse goat's-hair cloth.

In exchange for these, the Bedouin carries home dates, with which he supplements his diet of goat's milk. The two communities live together in a symbiotic relationship. The Bedouin has freedom, and lots of it. He does not have very much else. Most important of all, he does not have to work. The oasis dweller has a much more varied and adequate diet, but mixed with lots of malaria and plenty of hard work.

But we found the economics of Shergieh badly out of joint. The Bedouins bring for sale in the Sifala bazaar only a very little clarified butter. Fresh meat was almost never seen. For days on end the only thing to be had was salt fish from Muttreh. That is an indicator of poverty in the first place, but it is also an indicator of something else. There are plenty of places where the people are poor. Indeed, in Arabia they are nowhere anything except poor. Moreover, there have been instances when the money paid for the meat and cooking fat of the Bedouins was less than that paid in Sifala for a much poorer food material.

It was not difficult to discover the reason. It is a result in an indirect way of the great drought of twenty years ago. The people moved away then, the richer ones to Zanzibar. They moved away from the little oasis, but they held on to the gardens, and now when the rains have returned, they still own them. They have remained in Zanzibar, and the gardens that we were looking at are nearly all worked by tenants for owners who are thousands of miles away. The produce of the gardens is not traded with the Bedouins. It is taken to Muttreh and sold there, so that the profits can be sent to Africa. A fraction of the price goes to buy salt fish for the Sifala tenants.

And as the complement to this unnatural situation, we see the curious sight of the Shergieh Bedouins buying their dates in Muttreh, and carrying them home from there. Both the oasis dwellers and the Bedouins exchange their produce for what the Muttreh bazaar can give them, and at a bad financial disadvantage. Indian merchants deposit a large fraction of the Bedouin produce as profits in the banks of Bombay. Foreign ownership of the date gardens has made both the oasis and the Bedouins dependent on Muttreh, whereas they should be dependent on each other.

Gardens such as those we saw in Sifala ought to support a good bazaar, but the most casual visitor can see at once that this is the bazaar of the poor. The permanent shops are only one or two, and their stock of goods very poor. Everything is brought to the market and sold by auction. A large dried fish, having had sold from his central back bone every significant bit of meat, was auctioned as a rather gruesome mummified head, with a long naked vertebral column attached, the few crumbs of dried flesh still on it making it, I suppose, a usable soup bone or perhaps flavoring extract for some gardener's otherwise tasteless kettleful of rice. We had our money with us in *rials*, and these are worth about a hundred and eighty *baizas*.* But this market knows nothing but *baizas*, and to change this *rial* it had to be

* A copper coin, worth a seventh of a cent.

The city gate of Muscat.

Date-stick huts, typical of the residences in which most of the people of Ōman live.

auctioned like any other commodity, to our considerable loss.

In every other place I have camped in, we could rescue ourselves from starvation by falling back on chickens. In this desert community, too, chickens exist, for we could hear the crowing of the cocks in the morning. They were scattered and lonely birds. Eventually we found places where a few eggs could be bought. Chickens themselves, it was almost impossible to get. Our best efforts netted us only four chickens in as many weeks. No chicken under any circumstances is seen in the bazaar.

This was so surprising that we investigated, and we found that here we were dealing, not with economics, but religion, a remnant without doubt of the animism which prevailed before the religion of Mohammed swept everything else out. A chicken is dreadfully unclean. No self-respecting Sifalaite would think of touching one. There is nothing in Mohammedanism to lead to any such belief. As a matter of fact the people of Sifala will eat them when cooked. At least they said they would, when we asked. They do so only rarely however, for no one, not even a slave, is willing to handle the repulsive things.

Yielding to the temptation of a good price, a woman wrapped up one of these offensive birds in a cloth, and brought it to us. Women have the dirty and disagreeable things to do in Arabia anyhow. She was so embarrassed and hesitant in explaining what it was that she wanted us to take custody of, that the rooster seized his opportunity and got away. A quarter of a *rial* was swiftly disappearing, and no one would lift a finger to catch or even to touch the bird. One of the young men standing near took pity on the woman. He put a cartridge in his rifle and shot the fleeing rooster. That evidently brought the creature within the category of handleability. He was brought back and his throat cut with the official Mohammedan formula.

It would be interesting to know more about this pre-Mohammedan relic. There is a trace of the same sentiment among the Baloochees in Muscat, but they are too practical a people to let it make any difference in the day's commerce. Such a custom is a real handicap to the community, for the chicken makes a valuable contribution to the food resources of a primitive community. They forage on the general landscape much as the goats do. Without costing their owners any money, they bring in a very respectable amount of food.

On our tours, ancient superstitions and customs of this sort are quite frequently encountered. Many years ago when visiting Abu Thubbi, I met a group of visitors from the mountains behind Ras el Kheima. They talk perfect Arabic to the outside world, but among themselves they have a second language which seems entirely different. Their women at home, I was assured, do not know Arabic at all. They were orthodox Mohammedans. too, so far as prayers in the mosque were concerned.

They maintained their conventional behavior after breakfast, which in those opulent days was a fairly substantial meal. However, after their midday lunch, and after their evening dinner, they treated the scandalized natives to a thrilling exhibition. The fifty guests gathered in two circles, of approximately twenty-five each. Each circle had a cheer leader who led them in a remarkable guttural chant, Ha–ha–ha. The leader beat the time. It was done in perfect unison, for they had evidently practiced it all their lives, and could be heard for half a mile. After perhaps thirty seconds of this, the leader waved one arm over his head and emitted a tremendous shrill scream. The rhythmic chanting then continued under his direction for another thirty seconds.

The two groups kept this up for perhaps five minutes, and their appreciative audience included half the town. The graybeards, in whose hands rest the spiritual destinies of the place, shook their heads. "It is not permissible," they said. I think the sheikh enjoyed it. Like many rulers, he was interested in new and strange things.

Once, while visiting Sohar, medical work stopped for several days. The great feast had arrived, and everybody reckoned it his main job to celebrate. It was immediately evident that, perhaps from their historical background, or more likely from outside altogether, unusual elements had been added, in this case, unfortunately, unusually evil elements. The different trades of the city were for the moment organized into guilds, and out into the public square each guild sent a large group which spent the entire afternoon in sword dancing. There were perhaps two dozen such groups. The blacksmiths were there, the tinners, the carpenters, the weavers, and the dyers. One group was more flamboyantly dressed than the others. These, we learned to our surprise, were the male prostitutes of the city. I have visited no city outside of Oman where that sort of pathological depravity is accorded public recognition and acceptance.

This may or may not be a direct importation from Africa. The Arabs blame lots of things on the dark continent. Its existence in Oman without any question is the result of slavery. Slaves can be imposed on for anything and everything. No children are used in this form of dissipation. And whatsoever a society soweth, that shall it also reap. In Muttreh it is no longer the Africans who make up this unfortunate class. It is young Arabs and Baloochees.

We made a tour to Muttreh ten years ago before the hospital had been established. While we were there I had an opportunity to watch an eclipse of the moon, as seen through Baloochee eyes. An eclipse of the moon is not a very terrifying thing to us, but there are places where it is. Orthodox Mohammedanism has no place for terror over an eclipse either, but evidently in the days of ignorance, as the Arabs term the days before Mohammed came, an eclipse was a dreadful occurrence.

That night in Muttreh the atmosphere was charged with dread apprehension. Word had been passed around that the moon would be completely eclipsed. Mobarrek is really a Baloochee himself, and I got the local atmosphere through him. We watched together, and suddenly, as the first faint edge of the earth's shadow became visible on the moon's surface, the night's activities began. Apparently every coffee mortar in the city was being busily pounded, which gave an effect like that of a great chaotic brass band composed of nothing but kettledrums. I learned something that night. There are no end of medicines whose potency depends on their being compounded in the shadow of an eclipse. That must be the reason why my American medicines fail me sometimes. And the amount of medicine manufactured is greater than I supposed. Muttreh was being provided against many diseases for many days.

While we listened, the shrill treble of children's voices was added to the deep brass orchestra. Groups of boys were marching up and down the long crooked streets chanting, "I repent, Oh Lord, I repent." There was real music in their chant, and several groups could be distinguished in the still night. One group approached and another receded faintly in the distance. "*Toe–bah, Yah Rubee, Toe–oh–bah.*" Each house as the singers passed responded in like spirit, "*Toe–bah, Yah Rubee, Toe–oh–bah.*"

Another note was added. The great orchestra with its penetrating childish vocalist had been filling the air with apprehension and contrition and dread for half an hour, when from the great mosque, where the worship of the city centered, there broke on the still air, the magnificent baritone of its leading mullah, in the call to prayer. "*Ullahu Akbar.*" "God is Omnipotent, Come to Prayer." That splendid voice was the embodiment of confident faith. It dominated the streets and lanes of the city with a note of command. The men of Muttreh gathered to pray.

There was something very dramatic and moving in the splendid wrestling match which went on for three or four hours between that superb voice, with its confident, almost haughty faith, and the timorous fear that the great brass band with its childish singers had been pouring into men's and even more into women's minds. Every fifteen minutes, till long past midnight, the call to prayer rang out over the city. It must have been a very small number of the men who were not in the mosque praying for part of that time. And the voice did not fail nor become discouraged. Its timbre was just as resonant, and its spirit just as confident and dominating, at the end as at the beginning.

But the great orchestra with its superstitious fears gradually faded, and after an hour and a half or two hours only a scattered few of the medicine pounders were heard. The children outlasted the rhythmical pounding, but they grew weary eventually, and doubtless they went to bed. Victory was to the voice of faith. Long after the others were silent, the tremendous message still rang out every fifteen minutes. "*Ullahu Akbar.*" "God is omnipotent...." Even a stranger could feel the terror and apprehension fade from the atmosphere, as the night wore away, and feel the triumph of the mosque.

That night I learned as I had not before the strength of the faith of Mohammed. Men become jittery from pure fear when a huge scorpion devours the moon before their eyes. Evidently there is a corner of our psychology which likes that sort of scared religious faith. There is another corner which prefers the mullah's message, *Ullahu Akbar*. The outcome of that night's wrestling match was an epitome of Mohammedan history. It may go to show us that in the long run the second corner in men's souls is larger than the first. After all, truth does make a deeper appeal to men than error. On that, every good and acceptable and perfect hope for humanity's future will have to rest.

We all went to bed then. I suppose that the mullah in the mosque did eventually. The frightened apprehension with which the night started was still fresh in our minds as I asked Mobarrek:

"Do the people actually believe that a scorpion is devouring the moon?"

"Not many of them any more," said my instructor. "But we all know that on an eclipse night, unless our repentance is very intense, dreadful things will happen to us."

"Well," I said, "there seemed to be lots of repentance in Muttreh tonight. Will any of it last into tomorrow?"

Mobarrek looked at me with a good deal of surprise. "None of it will last till tomorrow. This kind of repentance is for tonight only."

It is only fair to add that on medical tours we also see the best side of Mohammedanism. Coast cities are a poor place to study any religion. There are always colonies of unattached men who are birds of passage of one sort or another. Wickedness flourishes. Money is relatively plentiful in these emporiums of trade, and where money is plentiful, religion is not. A very interesting Punjabi Indian visited us in Muttreh a few years ago. He was traveling through the different port cities of Arabia under the patronage of Bin Saoud. He planned to write a book extolling the virtues of Islam in its far-flung territories. What he found so disheartened him that I am afraid his book never appeared. He went to the wrong places. The small inland villages would have furnished him with much better material.

"I do not know," said Sheikh Eesa to me, when I proposed an injection, to build up his strength a little. "Will it interfere with my prayers?" I am not sure that I could find in any coast city a ruler who would ask such a question. Religion means a great deal to the men and women in these outlying districts. We used to visit a woman in Birka. She had an inoperable cancer of the breast, and she knew just what lay before her. She faced death with open eyes and a heart full of peace. She did not come from the sophisticated city.

I have seen beautiful services on these trips. One which remains particularly in mind, was in Ajman. Along that coast each community begins the great feast with a sunrise prayer meeting, to which even strangers like myself are invited. It was held perhaps a mile from the city on the edge of the desert. Palm trees were scattered thinly through the great sand dunes, with a resulting park effect, that was very beautiful. Practically every man in the city was there, and all in bright holiday clothes. Prayers were in unison, all facing Mecca. The blue sky above, and the cream-colored sand dunes below, the graceful palm trees scattered about us, constituted a cathedral made impressive by God's own beauty and power. The musical prayers were intoned by the leader, and followed by a rolling *A---meen* from the whole body of assembled worshipers. An air of feast-day joy pervaded the service.

The conclusion of the service was signalized by the ear-splitting discharge of an enormous cannon, the largest in the place. Almost on the moment came the answering boom from the distant west, to tell us that Um el Gowein had also finished its service, and only a few seconds later from the east a low, thunderous roll told us that in Sharga too, the sunrise prayer meeting was finished. I have never seen a service anywhere which succeeded in bringing so vividly to mind the fact that a world-wide fraternity was praying together. The sun rose a few minutes later.

Oman is not an orthodox province. The religious services and spirit are those of the Sunnis rather than the Shiahs, but the Omanee are members of a small puritanical sect, called after its founder the Abadhis. In the days of the decadent caliphs of Damascus and Baghdad, they seceded from the main body of Mohammedanism, and came to live in Oman as dissenting protestants. Their distinguishing religious peculiarities seem trifles to us, relating principally to the position of the hands in prayer, and the substitution of a permanent hell for a temporary purgatory in the future history of Moslem sinners. Such differences look important in Oman. When I visited Sheikh Eesa, the greatest chief of the Abadhees, his reception room was filled with Arab visitors from Sur. They had come to refer a dispute to the benevolent old sheikh for adjudication, and their personal regard for him was evidently high; but they would not go and pray with him in the mosque, nor do I suppose that they were invited to do so.

Women have to carry the heavy burdens in inland Oman just as they do in Muttreh, but they have a better time of it than elsewhere in Arabia. In Sifala the veil has almost disappeared, and women simply cover their mouth and chin. It is a pleasure to see them walking openly through the streets, without embarrassment or hesitation.

Many of the girls learn to read. The little boys and girls study together in the same school. The boys outnumber the girls in the schools that I have seen, but the claim is made that in some areas the literacy of the women runs along fairly well with the men. A still more unusual feature of Oman life is mosques for the women to pray in by themselves. So far as I know such mosques are absolutely unknown elsewhere.

We see a good deal of the women on trips of this sort. They come in large numbers to the clinic, and their manners there could stand improvement. The men are impatient enough, but they will sit in a row and wait their turn, if they are taught with sufficient patience. The women seem incapable of regimentation, and when, their time arrives, confusion reigns. They insist on coming in groups, and everybody wants to be attended to first. Fifty women each pressing for immediate attention produces a dusty situation.

They delay the clinic most dreadfully, too, because of the appearance of extreme modesty which they must maintain. "How can I sit there and let a man see me?" "Certainly you can. It is permitted. Without question he will immediately cure you," and so on ad infinitum, until the insistence of the friends who have accompanied this shrinking flower of a hundred and eighty pounds is yielded to and the patient seats herself before the doctor. She answers questions very creditably when once we get under way, but sometimes it takes quite a time even after she has seated herself in the dangerous presence.

However, Mrs. Harrison assures me that they are often most charming women. They have never seen a doctor most probably, to say nothing of having seen an American doctor, and it is not surprising that, driven by great need into a situation they genuinely dread, they do not show up well en masse. It is not altogether easy to love whole masses of people anyway. The outside surface of human beings which is presented in crowds is essentially unattractive. When we know them intimately and individually, every human being is a beautiful individual.

The ordinary women in Shergieh have lots of freedom, but the wives of the sheikhs and the nobility are an imprisoned company. I was asked by the son of the ruling sheikh to come and see a sick toe. It appeared that it was a female toe. All that was wanted was a diagnosis, and such suggestions as I could make for home treatment. I was taken to where a door stood ajar, perhaps three inches. Through it protruded a large and substantial foot, together with a most immodest six inches of uncovered ankle and leg. This latter surprised me in such an atmosphere of extreme seclusion. The diagnosis, however, was very easy. The big toe of this substantial individual was suffering from a very bad and very typical in-growing toenail.

I must admit that this surprised me, more probably than it did her. Parisian styles in footwear certainly have not invaded Sifala. But I guess that in-growing toenails may occasionally develop from just the pure cussedness of the human body. It is well endowed in that direction.

XIII
THE DOCTOR AS MISSIONARY

As I have said earlier, the medical missionary is supposed to be an extra-legible edition of the Gospel. That is a heavy assignment in itself. But he is supposed to do more. He hopes to change some of the people around him and leave them genuine Christians. That is one of the most difficult things in the world to attempt, but it is not greatly different from what such a doctor would be doing at home. We have two jobs. We earn our share of the world's food and clothes and shelter by doing an honest piece of work as a doctor, and we are missionaries as far as we are able. The best medical missionary I ever knew is J. M. T. Finney, of Baltimore.

These services are needed in America, but they are needed more in Arabia, where the doctor's nearest colleague may be five hundred miles away. In such a place the doctor starts from nothing flat and at first he is looked on with great suspicion.

> The English, the English, with hats of height,
> We hope they die this very night.

We heard that for a year or two as we opened work in Kuwait. But eventually such a spirit fades. The little girls do not chant these choice classical bits in our ears as we walk through those streets now. The doctor there is looked on with respect and even with affection.

The supposition is that with such a reputation behind him, the medical missionary will have a great influence in changing those around him. There is a real basis for the idea, but it is like asking a man to cut down trees with a fifty-pound ax. So much strength is needed to handle the ax that not much is left for the trees.

The danger that hangs over this part of the doctor's work is the same that hangs over his medical work, i.e. that it will be an imported alien thing. Much of the opposition to missionary work in Arabia is due to the fact that becoming a Christian is supposed to make a Westerner out of the Arab.

In Dubai, one of the most exclusive towns of the Persian Gulf, I found to my surprise that a Hindu temple was permitted with no opposition. It was looked on as casting much discredit on the intelligence of its devotees, but being free from all Westernizing influence, no one objected.

The resentment which the Arab shows when one of his colleagues becomes a Christian is largely due to the fear of political results. I found this to be the principal reason for the keen uncompromising opposition to the establishment of a Mission hospital in Dubai. "If we let you in, next week the British will come and put up a consulate, and after that we will be slaves." I replied that this was ridiculous. There never has been the slightest connection between our work and the British government. I was an American, not an Englishman. However, my friend insisted that it would certainly have that result. He was mistaken, I think, but not so completely mistaken as I supposed at that time. A year or two later I thought that I saw an opportunity for another visit, and I asked the Gulf resident if such a trip would be acceptable. The cordiality of his response gave me food for thought. They would be extremely glad, he assured me, to see me succeed in getting an invitation, and make another visit. In taming the untameable, medical missionaries are sometimes useful instruments.

Muttreh is finally getting away from the deadly notion that in becoming a Christian an Arab leaves his nationality behind. The little Christian group there are better nationals and better patriots than they were before. They are not less opposed to alien influence in the city, but more. The Sultan has no more loyal group of subjects than this tiny church.

Their loyalty to the Sultan has been strengthened by their Christian faith. More important is the fact that their membership in the community has remained unbroken. They have been actively engaged in selling our medical services to their neighbors. No shopkeeper has worked harder to keep his bills collected than these boys. One of the members of this little church, not connected with the hospital, has to sell his own unskilled services in the open market, and he has been able to do it very successfully. The result of all this is that while there have been a certain number of hard words to digest, they have not lost their community membership, in any sense, and they have not been drawn away and made into aliens.

But the fundamental question remains, of course. "Is it worth while to persuade a man to change his religion?"

He was a Mohammedan in the first place. Presumably that religion suits him pretty well. At least many million people have been devoted to it, and thousands have died for it. I yield to very few people indeed in my admiration for Mohammedanism. There is in it a wonderful philosophical symmetry and geometrical beauty. The Taj Mahal is its best embodiment, though the Taj is too much embroidered to be a perfect representation. The difference between the Mohammedan and the Hindu religions can be seen better, I think, by comparing the Taj with the great Hindu temple in Madura, than by reading hundreds of pages of philosophical exposition. I will even break a lance for the assertion that theoretical Mohammedanism can stand comparison with the inheritance from the Greek philosophers, which constitutes such a large part of our own mental furniture.

Nobody in Arabia needs to be saved from his Mohammedanism any more than men in New York need to be saved from their Greek Stoicism. They need to be saved from their fears and their hates and their pride and their sin. Oman is a land of division and strife. When we were on a recent visit to Sur, a delegation came from a little town less than a mile away to ask us to come and make a visit there, too. I explained with some surprise that our time was limited and we expected people to come for a mile or two to get treatment. They knew that, but a sharp and active enmity prevailed between the two towns, and their lives would not be safe, they told me, if they came. The city of Sur itself is divided into four factions, and riots and murders are common. While we were there, a quarrel between two gardeners over the placing of a wall had hundreds lined up with daggers and guns ready, and an extremely serious internal war was averted only by a hair's breadth.

The very air is full of cruelty. That was not so true in the days of comfortable plantation life, but in these days of financial struggle, of debts and increasing poverty, the stock of neighborly altruism has run low. Divers in debt are thrown into prison, mortgages are foreclosed without pity. Women are divorced in spite of their tears. I once sent Mohammed to Sur to get the place ready for a medical visit. A tiny slave boy was a fellow passenger. He belonged to the captain, and like small boys the world over he violated the proprieties and polluted the atmosphere with a bad smell. His irritated owner hunted up a hammer and a nail and then made the little offender lie down flat on the bare unprotected deck, where he nailed his ear to the floor, and left him exposed in the sun for the whole day. The passengers protested, but it did no good. Finally, as the day wore away toward sunset, Mohammed utterly refused to drink the captain's coffee, which would make him a partner in his cruelty. This stirred some chord in that hard soul, and so, as night came on, the nail was pulled out and the boy released.

And perhaps more than anything else, Oman is a land of hate. Zaharah, one of our neighbors, after years of conventional family life, found herself forced to share her husband with a partner wife. The world does not often produce a more vivid and intense type of hate than her attitude toward Safeeah through the following years. Hate is a poisonous thing.

The divisions and the cruelties and the hates that fill life with poison are most of them due to simple fear.

There are a good many things to be afraid of in Oman, poverty holding first place. Who is going to blame people for being afraid of hunger and starvation when they look them both straight in the face every day of their lives? Who will remain unafraid when every pestilence spreads unchecked, and when to all the real dangers of life are added the Jinn and the evil eye, none the less dreadful for being fictitious?

But I do not believe that fear, even with her dreadful children, revenge and cruelty and hate, is the major trouble in Oman. Men want to rank above their fellows. We get some strange results from that. Our cook is very much of an urbane gentleman. Also he is an excellent cook, and it is a pleasure to have him as an associate and a friend. But Abdullah thirsts for a position of distinction among his companions, and to secure this prize he borrows money, apparently whenever and wherever the opportunity offers. Common honesty would seem to require a passing thought as to payment of these loans, but the closest approach to a twinge of conscience about the matter seems to be a lurking fear that some time he will go to prison for debt. That is undesirable for it militates against his desired position of local pre-eminence.

The money lender pursues the same goal from the opposite side. He hunts high and low for men who will walk into his web. Interest rates run to fifty per cent. He also wishes to be a person of distinction, and to this end mortgages are foreclosed and markets are cornered. We have recently watched the current wage for labor forced down from fifteen to ten cents a day because an influx of new workers from Makran made it possible for the rich employers to get men at the lower figure. The idea of paying men more than an utterly broken and disorganized labor market required seemed not to enter anyone's mind.

In the Orient we see a good deal of sex irregularity. Polygamy and free divorce are legal, and in Oman male prostitution is a recognized and accepted profession. It is, of course, an extremely powerful instinct that this gratifies, but it is a mistake, I think, to feel that the fundamental explanation of its pathological manifestations lies along the line of unusual animal instincts. On the contrary, we have here the world's supreme means of stimulating and gratifying the feeling of superiority over our neighbors.

On a recent visit to Riadh, which certainly comes close to being the world's capital city of religious and racial pride, we found to our surprise that interest in genuinely religious problems was very slight. Only once in the entire three weeks of our stay were we, as visiting missionaries, called on to discuss such questions. But polygamy was up for discussion constantly. Our evil monogamous teachings were attacked in the king's court and the servants' quarters. To question the right of a man to dominate over four women evidently jeopardized the whole structure of Mohammedan superiority.

I talked with an earnest student from Arabia who was taking an agricultural course in Cornell. We discussed polygamy. "Yes," he said, "it will have to go. A law is to be proposed in the Baghdad parliament which will abolish it." That boy's hope has not come true yet, but it will eventually for the reason that light is stronger than darkness. When the beauty of the Christian family is exhibited, the competing system of polygamy is doomed.

No doubt the time will come when a strong Christian majority of the community will result in a real Christian government. That time has not arrived yet, even in America. In Muscat and Muttreh, where the tiny church may perhaps number ten individuals, it is obvious that the government will not be turned over to the church for a long time, nor will the advice of the church be asked on any legislative nor any financial nor any educational question. The social gospel in Muttreh will have to consist in the people's being good neighbors, paying taxes without protest, observing the laws, and being loyal subjects of the Sultan.

The taxes which that small group pays will not be much of a sum, and the service they can render to the Sultan will not be great. Nevertheless, they will make a very great contribution, a contribution depending simply on their being first-class Christians. No laws will be passed because Christian ethics demand them, still less because the Church suggests them; but because of the extraordinary power of example, a great many laws will be passed.

My friend, the leading Persian merchant of Muttreh, declares that his home country has gone to the dogs. His sister walks the street with an uncovered face, just like a man. Persian law forbids the wearing of the veil, and the women have their hair bobbed by official order. Whole shiploads of wild Baloochees have come over to Muscat from Persia to escape such an appalling reign of sin. The Christian group in Persia numbers only a few hundred, but already there are a whole lot of laws at least partly due to their example.

Slavery is going the same way. In Sifala we used to go over Sunday afternoons to visit the local judge, a Zanzibarite, who mourned the loneliness of his post and was glad to entertain some visitors. I asked about slavery in those parts. "Slaves?" he said. "They are all free now, and will not even say 'How do you do' when they see me on the street." Twenty-five years ago Oman was full of slaves. Now the visitor sees scarcely one.

The notion of the equality before God of all sorts and conditions of men is a Christian idea, and its essential kernel is the conviction of the equality of men and women. Polygamy and free divorce are really symptoms of a deeper disease, the evil notion that a woman is essentially inferior to a man and created to minister to his wants and whims and demands.

The destruction of the home is the gravest sociological blemish of practical Mohammedanism. Nothing is easier to show than that this attitude toward women is completely out of harmony with the underlying philosophy of Islam, but in practical life that does not help matters much. Such lessons in co-operation as we have learned in the West, we learned in the home, and it is our capacity to co-operate instead of cutting each others' throats competitively which is the measure of our possible future progress. The Arabs are a great race of individualists, but as co-operators, they are a total loss. Partnerships are almost unknown in the business world, and co-operative social enterprises impossible.

Oman shows the same exaggerated individualism as the rest of Arabia. When we were first invited to Sohar, it was governed by the Sultan's uncle, who was a most gracious host. He was recalled shortly afterward for his enemies feared that he was setting up an independent kingdom in that corner. On our last visit to Sur we met one of the leading sheikhs of the far inland country, and he delighted our souls with an invitation to visit his inaccessible country. We set a time, but when the suitable day arrived, we learned that this rugged individualist was out on a fresh war with his neighbors. Oman's entire history has been one long record of wars and raids and fights, a sort of *opéra-bouffe* imitation of Balkan politics. Twenty-five years ago, when I arrived, the country had a single ruler; but this lasted only a short time, and for twenty years past it has had at least a half-dozen.

Iraq is the supreme illustration of Mohammedanism's destruction of all capacity to co-operate. The archeologists have pushed back the horizon of the country's history many centuries, and now they can read the record with some certainty as far back as five or even six thousand years ago. As far back as they have been able to penetrate, they find Mesopotamia covered with a network of irrigation canals. By means of those canals, the Tigris and Euphrates rivers made of Mesopotamia the garden spot of the earth.

It was a tremendous thing, that irrigation system. Modern engineers scratch their heads and indulge in tall speculations when asked how much it will cost to reproduce it. It must surely have been the development of a thousand years in the first instance. A step at a time, the rivers were set to work, and finally the great network of canals was completed. It will take hundreds of millions of dollars to re-establish the system.

This system lasted through scores of centuries. Doubtless it was improved and perfected as time passed. But with the introduction of Mohammedanism, there was an immediate change. The deputies who governed Mesopotamia from Medina and from Damascus had increasing difficulties in keeping the canals in order, for to live under such a system men must know how to work together. The outstanding governors of the period, like El Hajjaj, were able to restore order and efficiency, but when their harsh rule relaxed, confusion crept back over the land like a recurring plague. The great complicated system was less and less well maintained till in 1257 the Mongols took Baghdad. They tried to destroy it.

But as a matter of fact they did no such thing. In the nature of the case all that was possible was cutting the dykes at a few critical places and inflicting more or less serious damage. An irrigation system cannot be carried away as loot, nor can it be burned down like a house. The real trouble was that the capacity for co-operation had been reduced to so low a level by six hundred years of Mohammedanism that, far from being able to develop such a system, they were not even able to repair a comparatively trifling damage to it. From that day to this, Mesopotamia has been little more than an empty desert. Wherever the visitor goes, the remains of the old canals are seen. Desolate heaps of ruins stand as monuments to Arab individualism. Into these heaps the archeologists dig and recover reminders of great civilizations, wonderful gardens, and dense populations who enjoyed comfort and prosperity because men could live and work together.

It is here that the Christian Church will make its greatest community contribution. The time is going to come, and probably sooner than we suppose, when polygamy will be abolished and divorce curbed by an enlightened public sentiment which condemns such things. Christians in Arabia will doubtless be a very small number for many years to come, but, however small, the creation of an indigenous Christian community will be the salvation of Arabia. The missionary is working to save individual men and women, and he knows that through them he will save the race.

But how are individual men and women in Arabia changed? I have been asked that question a great many times. "What do you do there?" It was a puzzled and somewhat irritated political agent asking the question. I had just come back from a visit to Riadh, then even more inaccessible than now. I think that he had the picture of a political agitator in his mind. He was much troubled over the possibilities of riots and bloodshed.

All that the missionary can do is to give to those who care for it a picture of the Christian life and an opportunity to follow. The daily behavior of the missionary is the outline, and the details are inevitably fitted into that. I remember an eccentric, but still sincere, visitor in Muttreh whose request for a ride in a missionary's car was somewhat brusquely refused. Through all the years following it seemed impossible for that initial outline to be rubbed out.

As opportunity offers, we can tell those who are interested different things about Christ and explain different points in His teaching. That fills in certain parts of the picture, and for men of the investigative type of mind, it is extremely important. A North Indian scholar passed through Muttreh during his wanderings and stayed for a number of weeks. It was a very great pleasure indeed to talk over with him our vision and understanding of Christ. That man is now, some years later, an outstanding Christian. Certainly, if Christ was a teacher from God, His teachings ought to show it, and they do. The trouble is that for many men there is a great gulf between admiring those teachings and following them.

There is another way of telling men something about Christianity. For many of us it is a comparatively recent discovery. Instead of explaining to our friends the philosophical conclusions to which we have come, we can tell them our own experiences in the way of reinforcement and guidance.

Mobarrek is the best assistant that I have ever had the pleasure of working with. He began life with a very attractive personality. His ability is far above the average. His efficiency has increased steadily through the thirteen years that he has been with us. He does our minor surgery. He has charge of the intravenous injections. He stains the blood smears. We could scarcely run the hospital without him.

But his soul was well vulcanized. How many hundreds of times he listened to the Christian message, I would not dare to guess. The more earnestly he heard that way of life presented, the more carefully he wrapped himself in his mantle of Mohammedan observances. He had a good time in the hospital, but his matrimonial history was stormy and disappointing. The wife of his boyhood died. He never got over that. His next wife he quarreled with and beat her so that she was confined to her bed for days. Some meaningless rumor had come to his immaculate ears. He finally divorced her and tried another one.

There seemed a long distance between him and the love of God.

One evening it seemed that I might do well to share with him some of the deep things in my own life. I do not think that the deepest corners of Mobarrek's life ever were his sins. It was the dreadful black darkness that he went through after his first wife died, the only real wife he had ever known. I knew something of the darkness that we go through when ties are broken and the world left empty. So we shared our experiences. It was not an easy thing to do, though not so hard as hauling a half-forgotten sin up for inspection. In those two hours Mobarrek, with all of his vulcanized exterior, and with his dark and stormy matrimonial past, caught a glimpse of what the Christian faith could do for him. He left behind his own broken and disreputable plans, and took God's plan in their place.

There was much surprise in the group of young men with whom Mobarrek was so popular when he became a Christian. It is not a popular thing to do in Oman, and he heard many hard words during the next few weeks. He was kept on in the exclusive hockey club where he was a member, but he went through a good deal. When he was serving as the resident medical officer in Dhufar for a few weeks the Sultan at first kept him waiting on the beach without a house, and then housed him and his assistants in an old stable. He was ostracized from all contact with the leading people of the city. But his efficiency and courtesy gained him great popularity before the trip was over, and the Sultan decorated him officially, to show his special favor.

Mobarrek's Christian faith has been deep enough to

show. He has to collect the hospital bills, and in Muttreh that is a very difficult piece of work. One day Mobarrek lost his patience with a particularly delinquent individual who kept putting off and putting off again the payment of his bill. He lost his temper, and his words were hot. He knew what a Christian ought to do under such circumstances, for I had been compelled to show him the way more than once. It is a thorny way and it hurts the feet. Mobarrek sat down in a coffee shop and turned the matter over in his mind. Then he went back and begged the man's pardon for his words and his temper.

Because his faith is deep enough to show, it is radiant enough to be contagious. He is the center of a little group that numbers half a dozen already, while there is a fringe of outsiders who are being drawn in, and the group grows constantly larger.

Zaharah came by a different path. God gave her a good mind and at least two first-class tempers. She is a born leader. At home I feel sure that she would have been president of the federated women's clubs of half a dozen states. As a girl she did not live a monotonous life, and after she married Mohammed, neither did he. Through her husband, she led the whole clan.

She came to be feared more and more because of her temper. Her wild quarrels brought neighbors in scores, and sometimes in hundreds, to look on and see her disgrace. She had no children, so after some years Mohammed, her husband, took another wife. He wanted a son to carry on his name and line. Soon the new wife did have a baby boy, and that made matters worse. Some women do not seem to mind it very much if their husband takes a second wife, but Zaharah resented it fiercely. Her mind boiled with hatred and the desire for revenge.

Perhaps twice a year there would be a terrible explosion. The course of the episode could be charted like an attack of fever. First she quarreled with her husband, over anything or nothing. She would curse him and sometimes even strike him. He is a man of considerable patience, and it took a good deal to get him started, but she kept industriously at it till he was touched off. Then, to quote my own small boy, he would "beat the very juice out of her." So far as eye juice was concerned, that was very literally just what happened. Zaharah always felt better after this katharsis had occurred, and again matters would rest for some months.

But she was extremely ashamed of these outbursts, for in Oman such public quarrels are a great disgrace. One day, after a particularly bad session, I found her sitting in the path which leads to our house, utterly dejected and broken.

"Sahib," she said, "I have done it again."

I sat down next to her. "Zaharah," I said, "Christ can conquer your temper for you if you will give yourself completely into His hands." Zaharah wanted that. There was no doubt of it. Her own plans for her life had not worked out well. "And," I continued, "you will have to take Safeeah as your sister."

Safeeah was the partner wife, the focus for all the hate and resentment that was poisoning Zaharah's life.

It is not easy to give up hate and resentment of that intensity, but Zaharah finally nodded, and we prayed a word at a time, my voice leading hers. After a few sentences we came to the hard one, "And, God, I take Safeeah to be my sister." There was a pause and then she repeated the difficult words. Now Safeeah and Zaharah sit together in genuine sisterhood. She has not lived an altogether monotonous life since that experience, but her control over her high-tension temper is more and more complete, and she is one of the strongest members of the little Christian community which is growing up in Muttreh.

Noobie is another type, and, as an Indian once said, "the difference is very different." He was stolen as a mere baby and sold as a slave to the Bedouins of Oman. It was as a freed slave that Noobie came to us, and with that background he listened to the Christian message. He did not understand a great deal, and it hardly occurred to him that any of this teaching was for him. In his work he was faithfulness itself, with a dreadful pathetic eagerness to do all that he was supposed to do, and more. We watched him grow out of the psychology of slavery into the independence of a free man.

Of necessity he did much of his work under Mobarrek's supervision. It was Mobarrek who had suggested taking Noobie on in the first place. Suddenly Mobarrek became a Christian. That opened a new world. Evidently it was possible for others than white men to be Christians. That much Christian teaching, I rise to remark, he had heard literally thousands of times, but it does no good at all to say a thing, even to say it very many times, if it runs counter to the mental attitude of the listener. But Mobarrek's stand as a Christian was a demonstration that could not be missed. Noobie wasted no time. He became a Christian too.

There were at least two remarkable things about Noobie's conversion. Rarely is an initial surrender so complete, and rarely is the content of Christian knowledge so slender. Noobie follows Christ with a literalness that worries his friends. Every waif and stray in the vicinity comes to him to be fed, and, when food runs short, Noobie goes hungry himself so that the waifs and strays will not need to. None of us knows half as much as Noobie about human suffering and privation. It has left his heart soft. His business and financial head is a little soft too, I am afraid. He worries by night over his debts, and feeds the beggars by day, while he goes hungry himself. He trusts God to take care of him, and I feel pretty sure of it myself, though the job would be less taxing if Noobie were a better business man. Even now, two years after his baptism, his stock of theology is meager. Asked by one of the missionaries what books we have from God, he replied that we have the Old and New Testaments, and the Koran, this being a conventional Mohammedan statement. But Noobie is a good Christian. The factory does not turn out any better grade than this particular model, and I do not believe that the joy in the presence of the angels of God was greatly disturbed by Noobie's high estimate of the Koran.

The little church is a tiny group, but it is a radiant one. Mobarrek has brought his wife, and that little family shines like a bright light in the darkness of Muttreh. Noobie has brought Door Melek, which gives us another family group. Zaharah has brought Mohammed. The radiance of the group is bringing others into it. Khair Nissa is one of those remarkable women who in the Orient find self-expression and financial support by selling themselves to one man after another. Her last temporary husband she found to be insane, and she repudiated part of the contract. The radiance of the group drew her, and its loyalty held on to her through the period when she desired the good, but could not let go of the bad. Now she is one of the brightest Christians of them all. And there are Kumbar and Meerook and Khamees, who are not so far along but are on the way.

The Sultan has made a visit to America and England, and he has returned filled with ambition to make something better of his country. Already the government offices show much improvement, and there is a fine school building going up. The Iraq Petroleum Company has begun to suspect our barren rocks of hiding the liquid gold which is inundating Bahrain, and soon will be inundating Kuwait. With airplanes and curious instruments their canny engineers are going over us with a fine-toothed comb.

But the hope of Oman lies in none of these things. It lies in that tiny group with not a dozen in it, of whom one or two can barely read and write. To them the youngsters of Muttreh already look for an example of how men and women can live together.

XIV

THE FUTURE

THE HOSPITAL OF the future, what will it be? Twice as large as the one we have now. Accommodation for a hundred patients at least, we will need, if we are to minister to a community of three hundred thousand. There must be an X-ray machine, and with it a laboratory of pathology. We will have to train a competent technician. There will be a study of basal metabolism, blood chemistry, and many other things that progressive hospitals have to do.

But in more important ways the hospital of the future will be simply the continuation of the hospital of the present. In it convalescent patients will be nursed back to health surrounded by the same living conditions which they left to come to the hospital, and to which they return immediately after they are discharged. Patients sleep on the floor now, and fifty years from now, when we have arrived at the utopia of our dreams, they will still be sleeping on the floor. They will cook in their own rooms, play with their own babies, be nursed by their own wives, and live in their own homes while they are with us.

A hospital of this sort has possibilities as an educational institution. Some day a nurse will catch the vision. She will train the wives of our hospital patients for three weeks, and they will be apt pupils. Every one of their Arab homes can imitate our cement floors, and with such a floor and a little guidance, they can imitate our cleanliness. Lessons in infant feeding, child care, and many other things will not be out of reach in the three weeks which are available.

And reaching out from that as a beginning, there is no end to the projects that a visiting nurse can foster among the graduates of her three weeks' course. We might even get something done for the eyes of Muttreh, those eyes that are going to open up on the day of judgment and condemn us. In a country like Oman, health, eyes and all, is much more an educational problem than a therapeutic one. Some day a nurse will be sent out, one of those whose touch quiets pain, and the still music of whose voice brings peace to women's hearts, and at the same time a born teacher who leads other minds with the ease and surefootedness of a mountain guide. She will be the queen of two kingdoms, women's ignorance and women's suffering, and she will transform them both. The Muttreh hospital will be an instrument in her hands.

The hospital will have a larger personnel. Our present reversed *E Pluribus Unum* policy will be outgrown eventually. A first-class technician will preside over an impressive array of diagnostic machines. There will be trained ward help. These must not be imported, but must be local boys trained for the work. No danger point must be guarded more carefully than this one. It is much easier to get competent aliens for all these jobs, but the hospital of our dreams had far better grow slowly and remain Arab, than sprout over night to its full stature like a mushroom and be an alien thing.

A hundred in-patients, with double that number attending the out-patient department every day, visiting nurses carrying the message of cleanliness and health to the widest limits of the community—for these such a hospital will need not one doctor but half a dozen. Two, we will say, as directing spirits, with years of experience and great competence. Missionaries from America for the next twenty years, thereafter Arabs of capacity and training, if all goes well. Under them will work three internes, perhaps four. Those internes will come from the medical schools in Beirut and Baghdad, and it will not be difficult to organize a residency of four or five years for men of unusual ability. At the end of such a period of service, they will be physicians of first-rate competence. Training of this sort is one of the most important functions that such a hospital will perform.

That is a shining vision. Who pays the bill? "On that point," says the Arab, "hangs a long discussion." In any case, not millionaires in America. Oman must pay its own way in medicine as it does in economics. But can it? The question is not well put. Can modern medicine come down to the level of Oman, in point of costs? Neither now nor in the future can Oman pay for the American brand of medical relief.

Can she pay for her own indigenous brand? She pays for the beginnings of it now. Not the whole bill of course. No doctor's fee is included in the bills that Mobarrek carries to the hospital's clients, and the doctor's fee is the most important item of all. To care for that, the amounts would have to be doubled, and such a heavy load would be fatal.

Insurance could do it, and the only form of group insurance that Oman knows anything about is free government service, paid for by taxation. The resources of Oman are small enough, but it would not be difficult to organize a health service for the whole country, if the government would make this the first call on its resources. Such a health service will be faced by a task of great difficulty. The date gardeners must be freed from malaria, the wandering nomads from Madura foot, the town dwellers from trachoma, syphilis, and gonorrhea. The lepers must be segregated and that dreadful disease eliminated. None of these objectives are out of reach if our medical staff can be kept indigenous, and if the developing missionary hospital can eventually transform itself into a department of the government, with wholehearted community support behind it.

But the missionary is not satisfied with the development of a hospital, even if its service reaches the entire province. We are in Arabia to make men and women Christians. The hope of Oman lies in a sincere and active church, however small, which will be the beginning of better things in that empire of blackened rocks and deep poverty. What will the church of the future be in Muttreh and Oman?

Part of the answer we can give with confidence. It will be a church characterized by great loyalty to Christ. Without deep loyalty, felt as personal devotion to a personal Master, a Christian can hardly stand in Oman. The currents run too strongly against him. Noobie is going to have many imitators, men with the true Christian attitude, who will go hungry so that beggars may not, yet who get badly into debt, because they have not found any guidance from Christ on that point. We have no word from Him urging thrift or abstinence from debt. In a country of great poverty like Oman, a real Christian must see as Christ would have seen. Our duty to help the poor, to give to every man that asketh, to distribute any extra coat we possess to someone who has none—the church in Arabia will understand that.

Also the church in Arabia will be characterized by great loyalty to the brotherhood of man. At least we hope it will be, for the whole future depends on it. Contrary to some impressions, this will be a very difficult lesson to learn. In some ways the Arab is an extremely democratic individual. The sheikh is likely to be an ordinary man, raised by circumstances to leadership. In the mosque the slave stands next to his master as they both stand before God. In our coast cities, the blood of the royal families is mixed with blood from Africa, brought over originally in slaves.

But on the other hand, every major Arab tribe has a top layer of as unbending a type of aristocrat as this world knows anywhere. Only two or three years ago, a cabinet minister in Iraq was shot in cold blood. The minister was a man of the ordinary stratum of Arab life. He had married a girl from among the Mesopotamian aristocrats. She had been sent to Syria for advanced education, and there she met this extremely attractive and able young Arab. They fell in love and were married quite after the age-old fashion, and the girl's father wiped out the stain by murder.

It will be a long time, most likely, before the church

includes any of these aristocrats in its number, but smaller degrees of the sentiment are common enough. The Arab looks down on the Persian, and the Persian on the Baloochee, and the Indian on them all. But in the little church in Muttreh, we have overcome that feeling very completely, and the larger church of the future will do equally well, we hope, with more difficult problems when they are presented.

A more difficult question is that of community relationships. Doubtless our grandchildren's grandchildren will see a thoroughly Christian Arab community. In the meantime what is to be the relationship of a Christian to his surrounding non-Christian neighbors? The Christian has separated himself from his neighbors religiously. It is extremely important for him to realize that economically, socially, and patriotically he is still a member of that community. In its enterprises he must carry his share and a little more.

The great feasts of the Mohammedan calendar have social as well as religious aspects. Indeed, their social aspects far outweigh everything else. The barbecued meat from these feasts is often sent to us, and in this way we celebrate their feast with them. During these feast days, food is sent to the poor, and it is reckoned as a great disgrace if anyone goes hungry on such a day. The beggars gather in great companies around the doors of the rich. Neighbors gather in groups of good fellowship, and hospital helpers are excused from such duties as are postponable, so they can sit with their friends and drink tea and coffee. Little girls have new red dresses, and the little boys new caps, and we will do well to see that little Christian boys and girls share that sort of childish joy with the other children of the town.

We have in Muttreh one community of Shiahs imported from India who do not care to mix with anyone else at any time. Nothing is gained by an effort to force ourselves upon such people. They are complete aliens, and consciously avoid every sort of community responsibility. They afford an excellent example of what we must not do. But the vast majority in Muttreh look on these feasts as opportunities for community comradeship, and so far as we can "rejoice with them that do rejoice" we must be quick to do so.

And finally, the church of the future in Muttreh will be a church free from all contaminating support from alien powers. Persecution of Christians who have recently been Mohammedans is sure to come. We must rely on the Sultan and the local powers-that-be, even if we distrust them exceedingly. Probably nothing that we can do will go as far to remove from the minds of our Mohammedan brethren that fear which lies at the bottom of all persecution, as trusting our political and social interests to the community that we live in.

The church in South America is a strong church and one of the reasons for its strength is the fact that it caught this vision early. There were villages where Protestants fought for years for the privilege of sending children to the public schools and having their dead buried in the public cemetery. To the government's earnest request that they accept a special school of their own, they sent back a courteous refusal. Eventually they won the privilege of being reckoned citizens of the state, along with all others, and the church was an indigenous and accepted institution from that hour.

The largest and strongest church will be in Muttreh, but there will be many branches. A Christian community will rise among the palm trees of the Bottina. Certainly if Christ came to reach the poor, and if it is the captives that He wants to free, then of all the areas in Arabia the Bottina is His special field. We will have to study that field and its problems more deeply than we have done in the past. The most difficult part of all will probably be getting started, and the church of the Bottina will be a church of great poverty, its members tied down by extreme drudgery, but it will be a radiant church. It need not be quite as poor as the people are now, if we can make freedom from debt one of its characteristics. We will do well to go further than that, at least in our attempts, and make another of its characteristics the ownership of each garden by its cultivator. For that much social vision there is abundant basis in the Old Testament and in the New as well. No man is kept out of the Kingdom of God by drinking moderately, but it is true nevertheless that a drinking church will be a weak church, and just as we expect the church in Arabia to take a strong stand against alcoholics, so it will do well to stand for freedom from absentee ownership, and as far as possible for freedom from debt.

So much is true in any country and at any time, but in a country like Oman, where the emerging church has to live and make its way in the midst of a very hostile environment, the argument is reinforced. A tenant is half a slave in any part of the world. In Oman he is two-thirds of a slave, and it is very difficult for a slave to live as a Christian if his master does not approve. If the individual Christians own their own gardens and keep out of debt, they may be poor. Indeed, it is certain that they will be very poor indeed, but they will be independent and make their way in spite of their poverty.

The members of such a church will have to work desperately hard. They will be partners with the bullocks just as the Bottina cultivators are now. Such a church will be Baloochee for the most part, and it is not difficult for a Baloochee to work hard if he can see some chance for a fair living as a result.

But the strength of the future church in Arabia will not depend on economic arrangements. It will depend on the depth of her experience of God. That will depend on individual reactions, and very little on the group. The Arab is above all things an individualist. We can learn something from the Abadhi, who occupy Oman now. They came as a persecuted and feeble sect, but they grew to dominate absolutely the faith of Oman. The lesson here would seem to be the absolute necessity for a large degree of loose-jointed individualism within the brotherhood. "For freedom did Christ set you free, be not entangled again in a yoke of bondage." The essence of bondage is the domination of one man by another, and the essence of freedom is the absence of that domination. Within the limits of sincere Christian faith, every man must be left free to do what is right in his own eyes, in belief and ritual and practical life. The only things in this world that are uniform and symmetrical and true to type are dead things, and the only religious beliefs that are uniform and classifiable and orthodox are dead beliefs.

And what of the community as a whole? Where will the next fifty years find her? The prospect is not alluring. Ceylon will probably continue to eat our fish, and prices will remain low. Perhaps America will decide to eat Oman dates again, and then the price of them will rise, but probably not. The moneylenders will hold the entire community in economic bondage, and the Baloochees will continue to be a heedless and unthrifty race, and walk as they do now, into Shylock's office, begging him to tie them hand and foot.

One thing without doubt will be new. Arabia appears to rest on a lake of oil, Bahrain and Nejd are already sending out thousands of barrels every day. That oil increases the wealth of Arabia a little. It increases the wealth of Wall Street a great deal. Thousands of men find work, and it is paid for at a figure a little above the market rate, so the economic situation in Arabia has been lifted a little. Large subsidies are paid to the rulers of the different territories where the wells are located, while law courts, customs houses, roads, and palaces are being built. Bahrain's business street has been changed until it is almost unrecognizable.

Some changes come from this. The center of life is no longer the mosque but the oil derrick. All the desirable jobs, and there are hundreds of them, are found with the oil company. The individual commercial successes of this generation come from some connection with the same omnipotent power. The income of the local government is from the same source.

There are some good results. We are building a good school in Muscat. We have more roads than we used to have. Muscat's modern epoch was introduced by Captain

Walker and Major Murphy, who between them cut a motor road for two miles through the mountains from Muscat to Muttreh. That brought taxis to Oman, and progress has ridden in automobiles ever since. Henry Ford is the chief civilizer of Oman. The old state of static placidity is maintained with great difficulty by a man who has to dodge motors as his major amusement.

In Muscat and Muttreh we listen to between fifty and a hundred radios, and that completes the process. Every week the news comes to Arabia. This intellectual diet is served from carefully prepared menu cards, by the propaganda offices of Rome, London, Berlin, Baghdad, and Cairo. The different points of view are very stimulating to thought.

This exposure to the views and news of the world has certain valuable results. The Sultan of Muscat, the Sheikh of Bahrain, and the Sultan of Nejd find themselves exposed to the conscience of the world in their treatment of their subjects. These rulers have had their incomes enormously increased because of the oil which flows from their wells. It is no longer possible for such money to be pocketed by rulers for their own personal indulgences. In three of the Persian gulf cities bloody riots have taken place, with the demand underneath that this money be spent for the public good.

The school system in Bahrain is a very notable thing already, and Kuwait is only a little way behind. Even Muscat is to have a fine school, and these schools will teach thousands of the rising generation useful things like arithmetic and geography. They are going to teach them lots of dangerous things too, even if such subjects are not mentioned in the curriculum. Pupils will learn the duties of the rulers toward their subjects, and that the rights of a governing body spring from the people and from nowhere else. In schools that are reinforced by radios and newspapers and Ford cars, lots of dangerous thoughts are generated.

The hope is that from this ferment of ideas we may expect honest and efficient administration of public affairs, and a growing emancipation of the common people from exploitation of all sorts. Thus far that hope has been very completely disappointed. The creation of a large educated class simply increases the number of those who are anxious to exploit the public. In Iraq at present the number of educated individuals has greatly increased, but during a recent visit when I bought melons from wayside vendors, they appeared to be even more ragged and forlorn than they were under the Turks. The same thing is certainly true of the coast cities of Iran.

It is legitimate to hope that this is an interim situation, and that the future will see better things. There is some basis for such a hope. Western civilization for better or for worse is conquering the world, and Western civilization has various elements in it. German anti-Semitism is a Western thing, and so is Japan's present campaign in China. But Western civilization also has in it good things. The belief in the essential equality of every individual is a Western idea, as also the belief in the equality of men and women. If the better elements of Westernism can prevail, we will go on to a new and splendid epoch in all the sections of Arabia.

The church will have a great role to play in Oman and in Arabia as a whole. She worked under much the same circumstances in her early days. Periods of persecution alternated with periods of toleration, and the church grew better and better as the surrounding environment grew worse and worse.

The struggles of one chieftain against another are going to furnish a ludicrously shifting definition of treason and patriotism, the two meaning the same thing but carrying a different dating. The church will have to learn how to be loyal to the government, without any indissoluble attachment to a single ruler. It will be a long time before any of these countries will develop a really representative government. It takes a very large number of honest men in public office to make a representative government function even tolerably. In a dictatorship, even one honest man can extend his influence over an entire country.

The church will be loyal but she will be persecuted. Factional interests are often furthered by the persecution of minority groups, as Germany is illustrating for us today. Demagogues usually require scapegoats, and Christians serve this purpose very well, just as Jews do.

But if the church is faithful, she will eventually change the character of the state, and she is the principal factor in ensuring that the final development of Oman will be along the better possibilities of civilization, rather than the worse. Oman will be conquered by the church which she is persecuting, just as was true in Rome so many years ago. It took hundreds of years then, and the cost in suffering was high. Perhaps the cost will be no less this time, but the Church of Christ has been set up in Oman, and the future belongs to her because the power of God is with her.

SOUTHERN
JUN 1964
BOUND